SI

The author thanks K Mark Stevens, Ingrid Morejohn, William Hurst, How Man Wong, Bill Newlin, Zou Xi and Chen Bo for their advice, research material and other help during the writing of this book.

A Note on Transliteration
Addresses in this book are given in *Pinyin*. *Dajie* is a main thoroughfare (sometimes translated as 'Avenue'); *lu* is a road and *jie* is a street; *xiang* and *long* both denote an alley or lane. Chinese characters for names and addresses of hotels, restaurants and shops are provided in the listings under 'Practical Information'. Names of all sights and other places described in the book are also given in Chinese characters in the Index.

SICHUAN

May Holdsworth
Photography by How Man Wong

Hong Kong

Distribution in the United Kingdom, Ireland, Europe and certain Commonwealth countries by
Hodder & Stoughton, Mill Road, Dunton Green, Sevenoaks, Kent TW13 2YA

British Library Cataloguing-in-Publication Data.
A catalogue record for this book is available from the British Library

Grateful acknowledgement is made to the following authors and publishers
for permissions granted:

Alfred A Knopf Inc for
Video Night in Kathmandu by Pico Iyer © 1988 Pico Iyer

Penguin UK and Random House Inc (permission requested) for
Riding the Iron Rooster by Paul Theroux © 1988 Cape Cod Scriveners Company

Wylie, Aitken & Stone for
China to Me by Emily Hahn © 1944 Emily Hahn

Jonathan Cape Publishers and Bantam Books Inc for
Birdless Summer by Han Suyin © 1968 Han Suyin

Alfred A Knopf Inc for
A Single Pebble by John Hersey © 1956, 1984 John Hersey

Penguin Books Ltd for
Poems of the Late T'ang translated by A C Graham © 1965 A C Graham

John Murray (Publishers) Ltd for
Forgotten Kingdom by Peter Goullart © 1957 Peter Goullart

Han-Shan Tang Ltd (permission requested) for
The Junkman Smiles by C R G Worcester © 1959 G R G Worcester

Series Editor: Anna Claridge
Illustrations Editor: Caroline Robertson
Map Design: Bai Yiliang

Photography by How Man Wong
Back cover photograph by Ingrid Morejohn
Additional photography courtesy of the Cecil Beaton Collection, Imperial War Museum 180, 221;
the Joseph Rock Collection, Harvard-Yenching Library, Harvard University 112; Joseph F Rock, ©
National Geographic Society 141; Rare Birds of China, represented by Kennedy Fine Arts of London
and the Altfield Gallery of Hong Kong 22, 142; Ingrid Morejohn 48, 61, 67, 84, 93, 98, 114, 139,
151, 162-163, 186, 191, 209, 227; Martin Williams 122, 127

Production House: Twin Age Limited, Hong Kong
Printed in Hong Kong by Sing Cheong Printing Co Ltd

Horse-race Hill with its stupa, Kangding

Contents

MAPS

*Chengdu food stall with a gimmick—the contraption shown tosses up
dumplings for sale to passers-by*

Sichuan Province: 'Heaven on Earth'

In a half-forgotten local history a Chinese writer once set down these lines in praise of the richness of his homeland:

> Both rain and drought follow the will of the people,
> Famine is unknown.
> Time has never seen a lean year;
> Everyone knows it as Heaven on Earth.

'Heaven on Earth' (*Tian fu zhi guo*)—a description dating from the third century—referred to Sichuan (Szechwan), that unique province sprawled across a bit of central and much of southwestern China. From the yak-grazed slopes and scattered alpine meadows of its western plateau to the limestone gorges through which the Yangzi River tumbles eastwards into neighbouring Hubei Province, Sichuan covers a huge area. Slightly larger than France though only one-seventeenth of China's total territory, it is a populous province of more than 109 million people.

A glance at a relief map will show Sichuan divided naturally into two distinct parts, western and eastern. In the west, the rim of the Qinghai-Tibetan plateau projects into the province, giving way in its southern part to parallel mountain ranges enfolding deep chasms. One of these, the Great Snowy Mountains (Daxue Shan), soars to an average elevation of 4,420 metres (14,500 feet). The snow-tipped Gongga Shan (see page 136), to the south, is a thrilling sight for those who manage to see it. From here, westwards and northwards, spreads the immense and empty land that early travellers called the Tibetan Marches. Between 1928 and 1955 it was a separate province, Xikang (Sikang), a buffer zone which retained its Tibetan chieftains and all but defied Chinese control until it was incorporated into Sichuan.

Eastwards, the land slopes gently down to the softer contours of low hills and rolling plains. Here is the 'rice bowl of China', first named as the Red Basin by German geographer Baron Richtofen. And here, strictly speaking, is the ancient writer's Heaven on Earth. His hyperbole is readily explained. Aeons ago, the basin was covered with a crust of soft sandstone and shale, rich in minerals and brittle enough to crumble into a purplish red soil. Coaxed by ample rainfall and subtropical warmth, rice, wheat, maize and other food grains burgeon irrepressively out of this fertile soil. This is the very heart of Sichuan. And within it, swarming with life and industry, is its largest expanse of level land—the alluvial Chengdu Plain. Intensively cultivated and supporting an enormous population, the plain is crisscrossed by one of the oldest irrigation systems in the world, so that, here and there, the landscape flashes vivid green and silvery grey, a mosaic of paddy fields and water channels. Poorer provinces traditionally looked to Sichuan for a share in Heaven's largesse. To Sichuan's discredit, this largesse used to include the opium poppy, whose crop was so valuable that its widespread cultivation displaced grain in the last century (see page 152).

Violent tectonic upheavals in China's geological past created Sichuan's phenomenal landforms. Uplifting, faulting and subsidence on a massive scale caused the tilting of the terrain in a series of steps from the towering Tibetan tableland in the west to the soft valley floors of the east. Large tributaries of the Yangzi—the Minjiang, Tuojiang, Fujiang and Jialing Jiang—dissect the eastern part in parallel swathes roughly from north to south. These tributaries, it is said, gave Sichuan (meaning 'Four Streams') its name, although the province has so many rivers that there are several other contenders to this claim.

On this wild and fecund land prehistoric man lived 30,000 to 50,000 years ago, as evidenced by a skull fossil unearthed in Ziyang, southeast of Chengdu, in 1951. Little else is known of the area's early history; painted pottery discovered at Daxi in Wushan (see page 197), similar to the Yangshao ware of the Yellow River basin, suggests that in around 2500 BC the civilization of north China penetrated down to the upper Yangzi valley. Nevertheless the region remained peripheral to the rest of China, no more than a barbarous fringe inhabited by aboriginal tribes. Of these, peoples known as the Ba and the Shu are thought to have established kingdoms between the 16th to the third century BC. In 1985 this period dramatically emerged out of archaeological obscurity when workers digging near a brickworks in Guanghan, north of Chengdu, broke through to a pit filled with thousands of bronze, gold, jade and ceramic artifacts. There were stylized masks cast in the image of a grotesque face, with butterfly-wing ears, a scrolled nose, goggling cylindrical eyeballs and an ear-to-ear grin; life-size figures; wine vessels and other decorated ritual objects. These finds point to a sophisticated Shu culture distinct from that of north China. Little information about the excavations has so far been released, although two or three of those spectacular masks have now been put on display at the Museum of Chinese History in Beijing.

The Ba and the Shu were in time subjugated; when the First Emperor of Qin, Shihuangdi, unified the empire in 221 BC, the territory which is present-day Sichuan was incorporated into the Chinese polity. Subsequent Han Chinese immigration and settlement reinforced its integration with China proper. But the region's geographical isolation, cut off as it was from the rest of China by mountain chains, as well as its economic self-sufficiency, encouraged separatist tendencies throughout its history. Sichuan was to demonstrate, time and again, that it was very much a world of its own. During the period of war and disunity known as the Three Kingdoms (AD 220–265), it became the independent Kingdom of Shu Han under the general Liu Bei (see page 190).

While remoteness and inaccessibility bred resistance to control by a central political authority, the province's size and primitive communications made internal unity also elusive. 'When the Empire is at peace, Sichuan is the first to have disorders; after peace is restored, Sichuan is the last to be stabilized' is often said of the province's volatile political record. At no time did this saying seem more apposite than when, hot on the heels of the Republican Revolution of 1911, Sichuan became a battleground for local strongmen and their private armies. In the scramble for power, military leaders fought each other for domination of the province, until it simply fell apart and fragmented into warlord fiefdoms.

Sichuan's history during the first three decades of the Republican era was a dark period of military strife, unbridled power-grabbing and economic disruption. Any semblance of an orderly provincial administration was swept aside by the ambitions of army commanders who rose and fell in a confusion of shifting alliances and internecine squabbling. Once secured of a power base, a commander would control the territory held by his forces as its *de facto* ruler; he would become, in other words, a warlord. Independent of the national government, warlords arrogated to themselves such functions as defence and revenue collection; and so insatiable were their growing armies that taxes had to be levied in advance of the incomes earned. By 1934, for example, Guanxian County (see page 57) was paying taxes that would fall due in 1991. Beset with crushing debts, small landowners saw their meagre acres forfeited, and tenant farmers, unable to meet spiralling rents, drifted into crime and vagrancy.

Some of the warlords in Sichuan hung on to power into the 1930s; others threw in their lot with the Kuomintang (Nationalist Party), led by Chiang Kai-shek, to fight the communists, who were proving more of a thorn in Chiang's side than the Japanese and their incursions in Manchuria. Determined to achieve 'Unity before resistance', a policy aimed at eliminating communist ascendancy in the rural areas, Chiang pressed on with his campaign to squeeze the Red armies out of their soviet base in Jiangxi, southeast China. Thus began the Long March (see page 143), an epic trek which started as a retreat from Chiang's pursuing troops and ended as a triumph of endurance and survival. About a third of the route cut through Sichuan from south to north. Countless marchers died ascending the icy precipices of the Great Snowy Mountains and crossing the treacherous marshes of its undulating grasslands.

The Sino-Japanese War, which was finally declared in 1937 despite Chiang's foot dragging, thrust Sichuan into unforeseen prominence, for when Nanjing fell to the enemy, the inland port of Chongqing was adopted as the Nationalist capital (see page 148). Entire factories and colleges were moved up from the coastal area to be out of the reach of Japanese depradations. Hundreds of thousands of refugees flooded in. Such wholesale immigration gave Sichuan's infant industries a new impetus.

Present-day Sichuan is engulfed, like the rest of China, in a modernization spree. Some of the visual aspects of this seem harsh and ugly—the pollution of the cities,

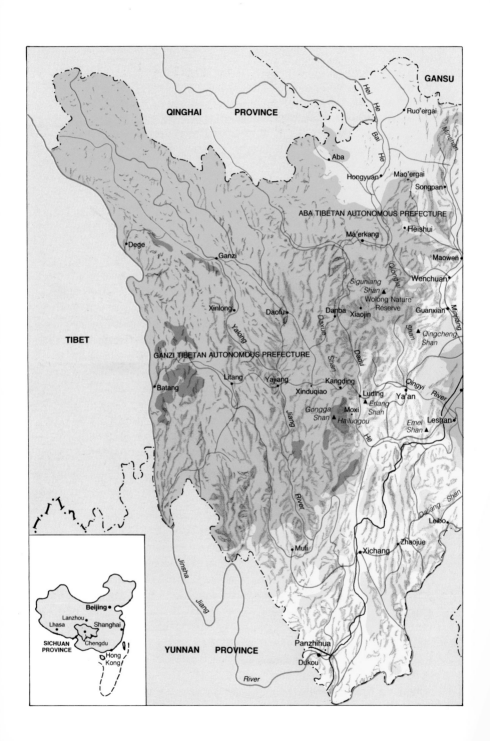

GANSU

QINGHAI   PROVINCE

Hei He

Bai He

•Ruo'ergai

•Aba

Minshan

Hongyuan•   Mao'ergai•

Songpan•

ABA TIBETAN AUTONOMOUS PREFECTURE

Ma'erkang•   •Heishui

•Dege

Maowen

Ganzi•

Qionglai

Wenchuan•

Siguniang
Shan
Wolong Nature ▲
Reserve

Xinlong•

Danba• Xiaojin•

Shan

Guanxian•

Minjiang

Daofu•

Daofu•

Daxue

•Qingcheng
Shan

TIBET

Yalong

GANZI TIBETAN AUTONOMOUS PREFECTURE

Shan

Dadu

Litang•   Yajiang•

Kangding•

Qingyi

Ya'an•

River

•Batang

Xinduqiao•

Luding•
▲Erlang
Shan

Jiang

Gongga Moxi•
Shan Hailuogou
▲

He

Emei
Shan ▲

•Leshan

Daliang   Shan

River

•Leibo

•Muli

•Zhaojue

Jinsha

Jiang

Xichang•

YUNNAN   PROVINCE

•Panzhihua

Dukou•

River

SICHUAN
PROVINCE

Lanzhou•
Lhasa•
•Shanghai

Beijing •

Chengdu•

Hong
Kong

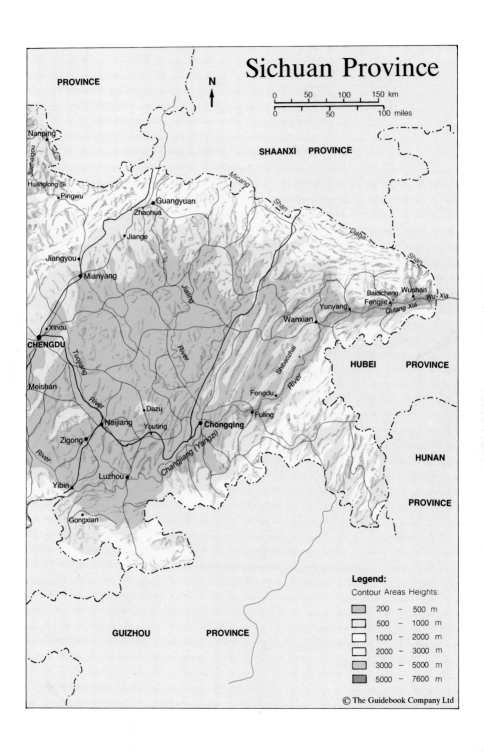

Sichuan Province

PROVINCE

N

| 0 | 50 | 100 | 150 km |

| 0 | 50 | 100 miles |

SHAANXI PROVINCE

Nanping

Jiuzhaigou

Huanglong Si

Pingwu

Guangyuan

Zhaohua

Jiange

Jiangyou

Mianyang

Micang

Shan

Daba

Shan

Jialing

Baidicheng

Wushan

Fengjie

Wu Xia

Yunyang

Qutang Xia

River

Wanxian

Xindu

CHENGDU

Tuojiang

Shibaozhai

HUBEI   PROVINCE

Meishan

River

Fengdu

River

Dazu

Youting

Fuling

Neijiang

Chongqing

Zigong

Changjiang (Yangzi)

HUNAN

River

Luzhou

PROVINCE

Yibin

Gongxian

GUIZHOU   PROVINCE

Legend:

Contour Areas Heights:

	200 – 500 m
	500 – 1000 m
	1000 – 2000 m
	2000 – 3000 m
	3000 – 5000 m
	5000 – 7600 m

© The Guidebook Company Ltd

the lorries lurching on tracks too narrow for them, the stained concrete of the newer buildings—yet the countryside remains immemorially agricultural. Prosperous Sichuan is, after all, clear vindication of the economic reforms of Deng Xiaoping (who hails from the province). It was from here that Zhao Ziyang, local Party chief from 1975 to 1980, directed experiments in the privatization of agriculture. Peasants, you hear everywhere in China, are the new rich. They are the ones who proudly display Japanese colour televisions in their newly built homes, for all that frequent power cuts render the sets almost useless at peak viewing times.

For the traveller in Sichuan, such anomalies are part of the adventure of observing Chinese society in flux. But in more than one sense is the province a microcosm of China. For, unlike many other provinces, whether they boast Buddhist mountains, open grasslands, neat chessboard fields, venerable monuments or minority communities, Sichuan possesses all of these spectacles plus the bonus of the best cuisine in China. Much of the province remains unexplored by the Western traveller—much of it is out of bounds to foreigners in any case—but, having visited the more accessible sights, strike off into the fringes of those wilder areas, and the province reveals itself to you in all its glorious diversity.

Getting There and Getting Around

Until railroad construction began at the turn of the 19th century, the Yangzi River provided almost the sole access to mountain-enclosed Sichuan. The journey was time-consuming and tedious, not to mention perilous, especially during high-water seasons. In 1887, the Rev Virgil C Hart, charged with reviving the American Methodist Episcopal Mission at Chongqing, took nearly a month to sail up to his destination from Yichang, 650 kilometres (400 miles) downriver. He noted ruefully that in getting over the notorious rapid at Xintan, his boat made five miles in 13 hours. To reach Chengdu from Chongqing involved another 20 days by boat or 12 days by sedan chair or pony.

By Boat

The Yangzi is an indispensable waterway still. Indeed there is no better way for hopping from one riverine town to another than by taking the scheduled steamers which ply the 2,480 kilometres (1,540 miles) between Shanghai and Chongqing. These are supplemented by a network of ferries that connect shorter distances. Its abundance of rivers provides Sichuan with some 8,000 kilometres (nearly 5,000 miles) of navigable channels. One of them is the Minjiang, whose lower course, from Leshan to Yibin, is navigable year-round. A useful service from the tourist point of view is the **passenger boat from Leshan to Chongqing**.

For most visitors, though, the most attractive trip by water is the one on the Yangzi between Wanxian and Yichang, along the stretch in which the Three Gorges lie. The information given below assumes that passengers start or end their journeys in Yichang or Hankou (Wuhan).

Passenger shipping on the Yangzi consists of scheduled services (*ban chuan*) and cruise boats.

■ SCHEDULED SERVICES: WUHAN–CHONGQING

Going upstream from Wuhan, not only are there more ports of call, but the journey takes about 100 hours (four nights on board), compared with 57 hours (two nights on board) going downstream. Moreover, the service makes no concessions to sightseers, since the Xiling Gorge is passed at night. Not every sailing makes the same stops, but the timetable below shows the main daily service on this run.

Conditions on different steamers also vary; the East is Red Shipping Company may have updated its name to Golden Line, but it has scarcely modernized the rustier vessels in its fleet. Most of them, though, have four classes of accommodation starting with second class (there is no first class). Second class consists of twin-berth

cabins with attached shower and lavatory. Bedding is provided. In third class, you may share a cabin of up to a dozen berths. In fourth class, passengers are stacked in 12 to 24 double bunks. Fifth class is below deck and unspeakable. From third class down washing facilities are communal.

At mealtimes an insistent loudspeaker system announces sittings in the steamer's huge and chaotic dining room. You need to buy a meal ticket in advance. Bottled soft drinks and snacks (biscuits, nuts, etc) are sold in the vicinity of the dining room. On some ships a separate dining room for second-class passengers makes feeding less of a fight, but it is always a good idea to bring some of your own food (see page 27). There is an unceasing supply of hot boiled water, trickling in a mud-laden stream, from a tap somewhere on board.

MAIN PASSENGER SHIPPING TIMETABLE:
WUHAN (HANKOU TERMINAL)–CHONGQING

Upstream				Downstream	
Arrival	Departure	Port		Arrival	Departure
	9.00 ↓	Hankou	↑	16.00	
21.00	21.30	Chenglingji		7.30	8.00
(second day)				(third day)	
12.00	12.30	Shashi		23.00	23.30
18.00	18.30	Zhicheng		19.30	20.00
22.00	23.00	Yichang		17.00	17.30
(third day)					
10.30	11.00	Badong		11.45	12.15
				(second day)	
15.00	15.30	Wushan			
18.10	18.40	Fengjie			
23.10	23.40	Yunyang			
(fourth day)					
9.00	11.30	Wanxian		18.00	4.35
17.50	18.20	Zhongxian			
21.20	21.40	Gaojiazhen			
23.15	23.40	Fengdu			
(fifth day)					
3.30	4.00	Fuling	↑	11.30	12.00
12.20	↓	Chongqing			7.00

Tickets may be bought through branches of China International Travel Service and China Travel Service (see page 32), or direct from Chaotianmen docks (opposite

Crossing the Dadu River by rope

A Tibetan woman near Songpan

Wharf 2) in Chongqing and the Yangzi Passenger Terminal (80 Yanjiang Dadao) in
Hankou, Wuhan; they are sold up to four days in advance of the sailing.

■ CRUISE SHIPS

A more luxurious way (with prices to match) of seeing the Three Gorges is to book
yourself on one of the 11 cruise ships catering predominantly to foreign tour groups
and high-level Chinese cadres on state-sponsored holidays. Reservations should be
made in advance. The season is from the beginning of April to the end of October,
depending on bookings. Fitted out with air-conditioning, observation decks, bars
and—on the larger vessels—swimming pools, these ships offer arranged excursions
on shore and other entertainments during the three- to four-day cruise. One of them
is chartered by the international travel company, Abercrombie & Kent, whose relax-
ing cruise itinerary includes shore visits, lectures and film shows on board. Bookings
should be made at Abercrombie & Kent (their office address in Hong Kong is listed
on page 236).

By Air

Direct international flights to Chengdu and Chongqing are available only from Hong
Kong. Chengdu-bound passengers have a choice of two airlines. **Dragonair**, the
Hong Kong-based airline, offers flights on Tuesday and Sunday, returning on the
same days. Services to Sichuan by the Chinese airline—**China Southwest Airlines**
(CSWA), an offshoot of Civil Aviation Administration of China (CAAC)—are operated on a scheduled chartered basis. There are four flights a week to Chengdu (Monday, Wednesday, Thursday, Saturday) and three flights a week to Chongqing (Monday, Thursday, Saturday), all returning on the same days. A host of Hong Kong
travel agents, including China International Travel Service (CITS) and China Travel
Service (CTS), will take reservations (which the airline will hold for a maximum of
three weeks before the day of departure). The flight to Chengdu takes about two
hours and ten minutes; it is a little less to Chongqing.

Otherwise foreign visitors enter China via Beijing, Shanghai or Guangzhou (Can-
ton) and fly onwards to Chengdu or Chongqing. There is a local airline with its
headquarters in Chengdu, the **Sichuan Provincial Airline**. The daily flight between
Chengdu and Chongqing takes an hour. Other domestic flights connect Chengdu
with the following provincial cities: Changsha, Guilin, Guiyang, Hangzhou, Hefei,
Kunming, Lanzhou, Lhasa, Nanjing, Shenyang, Taiyuan, Urumqi, Wuhan, Xiamen,
Xi'an and Xichang. From Chongqing there are air services also to Changsha, Guilin,
Kunming, Nanjing, Taiyuan, Wuhan and Xi'an.

BY RAIL

It would be a pity to leave China without experiencing a rail journey. Trains remain the most common mode of long-distance transport for Chinese travellers. This does mean that you are sometimes competing for tickets with a population that is increasingly on the move, so it is worth paying a handling charge and buying them through a travel agent or your hotel; they are likely to have allocations on the most popular routes. 'Hard seat, soft seat, hard sleeper and soft sleeper' describe the four classes of compartments precisely. It is difficult to reserve a hard sleeper for a long journey, as this class is most in demand.

Most provincial centres are linked to Chengdu by rail. Below is a list of only the fastest and most direct services between the destinations that are likely to interest Sichuan-bound travellers. Short-distance rides within the province are dealt with under the relevant city or town.

BEIJING–CHENGDU SPECIAL EXPRESS

Twice daily service (leaving 6.56 am or 5.07 pm) delivers you to Chengdu in about 35 hours or 39 hours respectively, depending on the train you take.

BEIJING–CHONGQING SPECIAL EXPRESS

Daily to Chongqing, with a stop in Chengdu before Chongqing, taking about 43 hours. This Special Express leaves Beijing at 12.09 pm.

GUANGZHOU (CANTON)–CHENGDU EXPRESS

Going more sedately than special expresses, this daily train covers the distance in approximately 39 hours. Departs Guangzhou at 5.05 pm.

KUNMING–CHENGDU SPECIAL EXPRESS

Leaving Kunming at 11.30 am, this train, after burrowing through hundreds of tunnels and rumbling across as many bridges, deposits passengers in Chengdu at 9.15 am the following morning. En route it calls at Jinjiang, Xichang and Emei. An interesting approach to Sichuan.

CHENGDU–CHONGQING SPECIAL EXPRESS

Departing at 8.57 pm (best to eat dinner beforehand), you are roused from your sleep prior to the train's arrival at 6.15 am the following morning. This service runs daily. In the return direction departure is 6.56 pm and arrival in Chengdu is 5.30 am the next day.

By Road

Long-distance scheduled public buses run between towns, for example Chongqing to Dazu, Chengdu to Ya'an, Emei to Chengdu and so on. You need to find the long-distance bus station and, more often than not, fight your way on to the vehicles. In Chengdu, scheduled long-distance buses leave from either the Xinnanmen Bus Station (for Leshan, Emei, Zigong, Kangding and towns en route), or the Ximen Bus Station (for Nanping, Songpan, Ma'erkang etc). During the tourist season **tour buses** are available to the popular sites, including Emei Shan, Jiuzhaigou and Dazu. The best places in Chengdu to find out if tours are available include the Jinjiang Hotel (most travel agents are located on the second floor), Beizhan (North Railway Station), where various travel agents operate from a row of kiosks to the left of the station building, and the Jiaotong Hotel. Remember that the cheaper tours—other than those offered by CITS—are geared towards domestic tourists, and will not necessarily come with an English-speaking guide. They will also be around 15–20% more expensive for foreigners, for whom a higher travel insurance premium has to be paid by the tour operator.

Chongqing's main long-distance bus station is the Jianxin Bei Lu one. From here buses go to Dazu, Nanchong and Neijiang, among other towns.

To Yunnan by Road The jumping-off point for the overland trip to Lijiang, Dali and other places in northern Yunnan is **Jinjiang**, near the large industrial Dukou in the southern part of Sichuan. It can be reached by rail from Chengdu. Buses from Jinjiang to Lijiang cover the distance, 305 kilometres (190 miles), in two days.

To Lhasa by Road Travelling all the way on the Chuan-Zang (Sichuan–Tibet) route is not allowed for foreigners, although a few intrepid backpackers have done it. Travel organizations in Chengdu report that a special permit from the military authorities is required. Parts of the road are, in any case, in very poor condition and the journey can be hazardous (see page 120).

A number of travel agencies in Chengdu can arrange for you to be driven around the northern or western parts of the province, where the roads are bad, in a **jeep** or **land cruiser** (known as *yueye*, an ingenious recent addition to China's vocabulary, conveying as it does the idea of 'traversing the wild'). Obviously the ideal way to travel to the mountainous destinations such as Jiuzhaigou and Hailuogou, this method need not impoverish you if the expense can be shared between three passengers. Count on spending Rmb 600–700 a day for transport, a driver and a guide. Accommodation on the way is basic and therefore cheap. You should try to arrange to pay for food and lodgings separately.

Facts for the Traveller

Climate

With a subtropical monsoon climate, the Sichuan basin has hot, humid summers and short mild winters. It receives a lot of rain, particularly from June to September. So abundant are the clouds that, when it is not actually raining, skies are often overcast. In winter it is frequently foggy. The moisture that hangs in the air, together with the long period of frost-free days in the agricultural year, helps the land to bring forth three crops annually—spring maize, paddy rice and winter wheat.

Of the two principal cities, Chongqing is hotter than Chengdu in summer. Indeed, the 'Mountain City' has recorded an absolute highest temperature of a staggering 44°C (111°F). To avoid the heat, spring and late autumn are the best times to visit the region. By April the temperature around the Golden Summit on Emei Shan, some 3,000 metres (9,840 feet) above sea level, will have risen above freezing, and in September it is a bracing 8° Centigrade (46° Fahrenheit).

CHENGDU

AVERAGE TEMPERATURES

	JAN	FEB	MAR	APR	MAY	JUN	JUL	AUG	SEPT	OCT	NOV	DEC
Max °C	10	12	17	22	26	28	30	30	25	21	16	11
Min °C	2	4	9	13	17	20	22	22	19	14	9	5
Max °F	49	53	62	72	78	82	86	86	78	70	60	52
Min °F	36	40	48	56	63	69	72	71	65	58	49	10

AVERAGE RAINFALL

	JAN	FEB	MAR	APR	MAY	JUN	JUL	AUG	SEPT	OCT	NOV	DEC
mm	5.9	10.9	21.4	50.7	88.6	111.3	235.5	234.1	118.0	46.4	18.4	5.8
in	0.2	0.4	0.8	2.0	3.5	4.4	9.3	9.2	4.6	1.8	0.7	0.2

Impeyan pheasants, taken from a set of original paintings of rare and endangered species of Chinese birds by J Fenwick Lansdowne. The 32 paintings were completed with the cooperation of ornithologists in Beijing after the artist made field trips to Chengdu and the Wolong Nature Reserve, among other places in China.

CHONGQING

AVERAGE TEMPERATURES

	JAN	FEB	MAR	APR	MAY	JUN	JUL	AUG	SEPT	OCT	NOV	DEC
Max °C	10	13	18	24	27	30	34	34	28	22	17	12
Min °C	5	7	11	15	19	22	25	25	21	16	12	8
Max °F	51	55	65	74	80	86	93	93	83	72	62	54
Min °F	42	45	52	60	66	71	77	76	69	61	53	46

AVERAGE RAINFALL

	JAN	FEB	MAR	APR	MAY	JUN	JUL	AUG	SEPT	OCT	NOV	DEC
mm	19.7	19.5	39.3	89.7	157.8	166.4	142.4	138.4	136.3	97.3	47.8	25.0
in	0.8	0.8	1.5	3.5	6.2	6.6	5.6	5.5	5.4	3.8	1.9	1.0

EMEI SHAN

Arriving at Emei Shan on a clear day is a matter of luck. For a large part of the year the weather is rather fickle, and frequent drizzle and fog can blot out the fine views and make the climb a damp drudgery. You will probably be told that May to September is the best season to visit. Yet most rain falls in July and August, when walking on slippery mud-encrusted trails can be somewhat nerve-wracking. It is not for nothing that local hikers sometimes carry umbrellas, which, apart from their intended purpose, can also double as walking sticks—a very useful piece of equipment. During the winter months (November–March), when the cloud cover tends to be low, Emei Shan's topmost peaks (Wanfo Ding and Jinding) can be utterly clear and bathed in crisp sunshine. The temperature, though, stays well below freezing. Snows begin around November and may lie around until March.

AVERAGE TEMPERATURES

Height in metres (feet)		Jan	Mar	May	Jul	Sept	Nov
500 (1,640)	°C	7	14	22	26	22	13
Emei Town, Baoguo Si,	°F	45	56	71	79	72	56
Qingyin Ge							

Height in metres (feet)		Jan	Mar	May	Jul	Sept	Nov
2,000 (6,560)	°C	-1	5	14	18	14	5
Xixiang Chi,	°F	31	41	57	65	57	41
Huayan Ding							
3,000 (9,840)	°C	-6	0	6	12	8	-0.3
Wanfo Ding, Jinding	°F	21	32	43	54	46	32

JIUZHAIGOU AND HUANGLONG SI

Cooler and drier conditions prevail in northwestern Sichuan. Rainfall is moderate (about 800 millimetres or 32 inches a year), and the temperatures in the valleys rarely exceed 18°C (65°F) in the summer months. The weather varies further with the elevation. At the edge of the Qinghai-Tibetan Plateau, the atmosphere is cold and thin on the high mountain passes. It is the rarefied air and strong sunlight which cause the great daily temperature swings at these altitudes. Jiuzhaigou and Huanglong may be snowbound between November and February and closed to visitors. The tourist season gets going in June, when the lakes begin to fill with snowmelt and the colours of the azaleas return to the hillsides. July and August are rainy. Some travellers say the best time to visit is late summer and early autumn; October is distinguished by the foliage turning a golden-red.

AVERAGE TEMPERATURES

	JAN	FEB	MAR	APR	MAY	JUN	JUL	AUG	SEPT	OCT	NOV	DEC
°C	-4	-1	4	9	12	14	17	16	12	8	2	-3
°F	25	31	39	48	53	58	63	62	54	46	36	27

HAILUOGOU

The flowers on the slopes of Hailuogou start blooming in late April or early May. It may rain at that time. The weather is fairly mild except for the winter, although there are great swings of temperatures between daytime and night-time.

AVERAGE TEMPERATURES

Height (metres)	Jan		July		June–Sept	
	Max	Min	Max	Min	Max	Min
1,600-2,000						
°C	6	2	21	19	19	17
°F	43	36	70	66	36	33

Height (metres)	Jan		July		June–Sept	
	Max	Min	Max	Min	Max	Min
2,000–2,400						
°C	2	0	19	16	17	14
°F	36	32	66	61	63	57
2,400–2,800						
°C	0	-3	16	14	14	11
°F	32	27	61	57	57	52

Small waterfall in the highlands of Sichuan

Clothing

The dress code in China tends to be casual, practical and modest. Unless your programme includes a Yangzi cruise there is every chance that you need never put on anything dressy while in Sichuan. On the other hand, skimpy clothes will draw stares; even young Chinese, for all their enthusiastic embracing of Western fashions, tend to roll up their trousers to just below the knees to cool off rather than don shorts or mini-skirts.

To combat the mugginess of the hot season travellers should wear cotton rather than synthetic fibres. By the same token, umbrellas may be preferable to nylon raincoats. Winter, though short, can throw up some surprisingly chilly days, when thick woollens or anoraks are necessary. A raincoat with a hood, except when it is too hot to wear one, will come in handy and should not take up too much space. While travelling at high altitudes wear layers of clothing which you can discard or put on as the temperature fluctuates.

Above all make sure that your feet are shod in sturdy, comfortable shoes. You are unlikely to need hiking boots (unless you are planning to climb Emei Shan or Hailuogou in winter) but the tougher sort of trainers with a good grip on the soles are ideal. For indoors, canvas or cloth slip-on shoes made in China are both easily available in the cities and light to carry.

Packing

Keep it simple, especially if you are travelling outside the main cities, where a backpack to carry your things makes sense. Apart from clothes, here is a checklist of things to take if you plan on penetrating the more remote areas: a Chinese phrasebook, a flashlight, toilet paper (which you can buy everywhere, even in the smallest towns and villages), a small bar of soap, a towel, a sheet bag if you mind sleeping in used bedclothes, a spoon for meals on the hop, a metal water bottle to fill up with boiled water from hostel thermoses, a Swiss army knife or similar, an enamel mug with lid (widely available in Chinese department stores), tampons for women, razor blades for men, sunscreen, lip salve, plastic bags for a variety of uses, basic first aid—an analgesic such as aspirin in case you are struck by altitude sickness, mosquito repellent, Elastoplasts, something for an upset stomach and antiseptic cream.

Gone are the days when toiletries which are taken for granted in the West are unavailable in China. If you start your Sichuan travels in Chengdu, you can equip yourself with Western brands of shampoo, Tampax, sanitary towels, cosmetics, shaving cream and lip salve quite easily. It is simplest to drop into the Garden Arcade, a shopping centre next to the Jinjiang Hotel, or the People's Market. Kodak and Fuji slide and print film is also on sale at these places.

Before leaving a city for, say, Jiuzhaigou, Huanglong Si and western Sichuan, stock up on biscuits, instant noodles, tinned and dried fruit, bread (the Jinjiang Hotel in Chengdu has a bakery on the ground floor, among the shops left of Reception), nuts, instant coffee and creamer if Chinese tea is not your favourite beverage. There will be occasions when it is simply not possible to drop into the nearest snackbar and you have to make do with something from your personal larder.

Visas

Everyone must get a visa to go to China, but this is usually a trouble-free process. Tourists travelling in a group are listed on a single group visa issued in advance to the travel agent involved. Their passports will not be individually stamped with the visa or on arrival in and departure from China unless specifically requested.

Tourist visas for individual travellers can be obtained directly through Chinese embassies and consulates. Certain travel agents around the world can arrange individual visas for their clients. It is simplest in Hong Kong, where a large number of travel agents handle visa applications. The application procedure is quite routine; all you need to do is fill in a form, supply a photograph and hand in a fee with your passport.

Visa fees vary, depending on the source of the visa and the time taken to get it. In Hong Kong, for instance, you can get a single-entry three-month tourist visa either through a travel agent or through several branches of China International Travel Service and China Travel Service within a working day (application handed in at 9 am and collected at 4.30 pm) for around US$40, while a visa processed in 72 hours might cost half that. A three- to six-month multiple-entry business visa costs US$50–60 in Hong Kong.

A China tourist visa's period of validity—90 days—begins on the date of issue. Once in China, visa extensions can be obtained at Public Security Bureaux (Gong'an Ju) in most major cities, but only within a couple of days of the original visa's expiration.

Aliens' Travel Permits The visa gives automatic entry to all of China's cities and areas that are open to foreign tourists. There were 747 such places in late 1991, and the list is being expanded as local facilities such as lodgings and transportation improve. An alien's travel permit has to be obtained for anywhere not on the open list, and this involves a formal application through the Public Security Bureau. The officials may require a written request or invitation from a sponsoring organization in China, including CITS on occasions.

The 39 open cities and areas in Sichuan encompass most of the places a foreign traveller is likely to visit, although all of the province west of Ya'an and some of the areas north of Songpan and Ma'erkang remain officially closed. Nevertheless some foreigners have travelled freely in those areas in recent years. As places are being added to the open list at a fairly brisk rate, up-to-date information on specific cities and towns is not always easy to obtain (do not expect travel agents or airline ticket sales employees to enlighten you: they are quite likely to sell you tickets to destinations that are closed). Moreover, a greater flexibility in interpreting the open-areas rule by Public Security officials has been evident for some time; more often than not, they take no action on infringements as long as the foreigner without the necessary permit leaves a closed area within a day or two of arrival.

Customs

A customs declaration form must be filled out by each visitor upon entry. The carbon copy of this form is returned to you after customs inspection, and it must be produced on departure from China. Failure to do so may result in a fine. You are asked to list on this form the amount of foreign currency you are bringing into China, as well as personal possessions such as tape recorders, cameras, watches and jewellery (all of which must be taken out with you when you leave). If you have purchased antiques in China you may be required to show the official receipts to the customs officials.

Four bottles of alcohol, three cartons of cigarettes and unlimited amounts of film and medicines for personal use may be taken in. Firearms and dangerous drugs are strictly forbidden. There is no limit to the amount of foreign currency you can bring into China; it is advisable to keep exchange receipts for possible inspection upon departure.

Money

Chinese Currency, called Renminbi (meaning 'People's Currency') and abbreviated to Rmb, is denominated in *yuan* (colloquially called *kuai*), which are each divided into 10 *jiao* (colloquially called *mao*). Each *jiao* is, in turn, divided into 10 *fen*. There are large notes for 100, 50, 10, 5, 2 and 1 *yuan*, small notes for 5, 2 and 1 *jiao*, and coins for 5, 2 and 1 *fen*.

Foreign Exchange Certificates (FEC), introduced in 1980, are the form of cash given to visitors in exchange for foreign currency. They were designed to be used instead of Renminbi by foreigners and overseas Chinese for payment at hotels, Friendship Stores and trade fairs, and for guided tours, airline and train tickets, taxis, international phone calls, parcel post etc. FEC came to be highly sought after within China because they gave access to imported consumer goods and services catering mainly to foreigners, and furthermore they may be reconverted into foreign currency. This led to a black market exchange between FEC and Renminbi. Since then, there has been a series of devaluations of the Rmb, and the spread between black-market and official rates has narrowed. At the time of writing, hard currencies (particularly US dollars) were in greater demand than FEC on the black market.

It is ironic that law-abiding travellers who do not acquire any Renminbi may actually find themselves quite disadvantaged in the rural areas, where the unfamiliar FEC may be refused as payment.

All the major freely negotiable currencies can be exchanged at branches of the Bank of China, hotels and Friendship Stores. It is vital to carry enough cash in Rmb when travelling out of the main cities, since domestic banks do not handle exchange transactions. Bank counters are located at China's several international airports for departing travellers who wish to reconvert FEC into hard currencies (but remember to keep enough for the airport departure tax—Rmb 60 in 1992, payable in FEC). You may be required to produce your exchange receipts when reconverting FEC. FEC may also be taken out when you leave China, but it is impossible to change them abroad.

The internationally recognized American, European, Japanese and Hong Kong **traveller's cheques** are accepted. **Credit cards** may be used in a limited number of hotels, banks and Friendship Stores, and you should check with your credit card company or bank before you rely on this form of payment for purchases.

Tipping is officially forbidden in China. However, in the larger cities—Beijing, Shanghai, Guangzhou, for example—the practice is becoming acceptable, and service staff in the joint-venture hotels, guides and drivers will generally welcome tips, if not always expect them.

Prices in China

Unless you are backpacking and going 'hard class', do not expect China to be a bargain for individual travellers, although the cost of living in Sichuan is obviously somewhat behind that of the more developed eastern and southern provinces or the main cities. China's present official policy is to charge rates for tourist services simi-

Stone watchtowers looming above a Qiang village in northwest Sichuan

lar to those prevailing elsewhere in the world. Those who knew China 'in the old days', when nothing seemed to cost more than a few *jiao*, may feel rather resentful of this. It is an inescapable fact that with greater prosperity, inflation has reared its head in China and prices for some things have risen steeply. Some travellers also dislike the two-tier pricing system that prevails—one for the population as a whole, and another, higher, level for visitors. It is as well to recognize, though, that food items, transport, housing and other necessities of daily life are heavily subsidized by the Chinese government, and there is no reason to allow foreigners to benefit from the artificially low prices. This will change. Already, as the Chinese economy is slowly freed from total central control, domestic prices are moving closer to market rates.

Nevertheless, for the moment, the double standard remains and continues to apply to fares, hotel and restaurant services, and entrance fees to parks, museums and historical sites—at least to those institutions that are run by the government. Some foreigners have pointed out that there is a hidden extra charge, since they are required to pay in FEC, which fetch a premium on the black market (though this premium is narrowing and is barely significant).

Actually there is a further price variation—the tourists whom China classifies as 'compatriots' from Hong Kong, Macau and Taiwan are charged at rates lower than those for other foreigners.

Travel Agencies

A number of state-owned corporations handle foreign visitors to China. The largest is **China International Travel Service** (CITS), whose offices are located in all Chinese cities and which also has representative offices or branches abroad. Other large nationwide organizations providing similar services are **China Travel Service** (CTS) and **China Youth Travel Service** (CYTS). Formerly CITS handled only foreign travellers, while overseas Chinese were looked after by CTS. With recent policy changes this distinction no longer exists. In the small county towns these separate organizations are usually rolled into one, with the same members of staff wearing several different hats, sometimes including that of foreign affairs liaison within the local government set-up.

CITS offers a comprehensive service covering accommodation, transport, food, sightseeing, interpreters and special visits to schools, hospitals, factories and so on. It also provides services such as ticket sales for walk-in customers, for which a handling fee is charged. Many individual travellers have found the service provided at some branch offices wanting; this apparent unhelpfulness can often be put down to a lack of resources which are generally expended on tour groups. Lately competition has been introduced into China's tourism industry, with non-state organizations setting up a travel sideline ranging from running hotels to offering guided tours. The Jinjiang Hotel in Chengdu bristles with travel agents, but most of them have few facilities beyond selling tickets for guided tours, and the confused traveller should shop around, compare prices and check out itineraries before making a choice.

Private enterprise has also entered the scene. In Chengdu, budget travellers have been catered for by individual tour operators who neatly bridge the gap between the ponderous national organizations like CITS, and the local agencies which have little or no practice at dealing with Westerners. Information on **Tray Lee's New Experience Tours** may be obtained at the Jiaotong Hotel (a favourite with backpackers), and in the Flower Garden Snackbar on the south bank of the Jinjiang River, where Mr Tray Lee—who speaks fluent English—has his 'office'.

Communications

China's post office system is rather slow but reliable. The larger hotels in Chengdu and Chongqing have service counters for stamps. Most travellers in Chengdu who have used the **post office at the Jinjiang Hotel** (a little way down the corridor off the lobby to the right) have found the staff there helpful and efficient. You can post packages of up to 20 kilos (44 pounds) and travellers have reported that the post office even provided tape and wrapping paper. Jinjiang Hotel is also the best place in Sichuan to receive poste restante mail (more reliable than the General Post Office); the Jiaotong Hotel will also keep mail (in a box at Reception).

Modern communication facilities are becoming more widespread, with hotels offering business centres where telexes and faxes can be sent, and collect or reverse-charge calls can be made. If you are in a city, the best place to make an international telephone call is invariably one of the top hotels, where International Direct Dialling is available. Otherwise you have to go through the telephone exchange operator and, generally speaking, the lines are frequently busy and you have to wait for the call to be put through. The waiting time can vary from a few minutes to several hours. Long-distance telephone calls within China take longer to connect than international ones. Out of Chengdu, Chongqing and Leshan, making any sort of telephone call can be fraught with difficulty.

Time Zone

All of China is on Beijing time, which is seven or eight hours ahead of GMT, and 12 or 13 hours ahead of Eastern Standard Time, depending on the season. Daylight saving time is in use during the summer months, when clocks are set forward by one hour.

Health and Altitude Sickness

No inoculations are required before entering China. In recent years, the US Consulate in Hong Kong has advised intending travellers to China to be inoculated against hepatitis A and B, Japanese encephalitis, tetanus, polio, cholera and malaria. This is a daunting list, but it should be considered alongside the specifics of your itinerary. The most common ailments contracted by tourists in China are upper respiratory infections and chest colds. Precautions against more serious disorders are sensible if you plan to spend more than a week or so, during the summer months, in very out-of-the-way places. Drink only boiled water or bottled drinks at all times. Hotels and *zhaodaisuo* always supply thermoses of boiled water, and mineral water (Emei or Gongga brands can be found in Sichuan) is fairly widely sold. If eating at street stalls, make sure the food is freshly cooked. Because Chinese standards of sanitation lag behind those in the West—as will be quickly evident when you see people spitting in the street—it makes good sense to wash your hands carefully before eating anything. Peel all fruit and avoid raw leafy vegetables unless you are in an up-market restaurant. It is always sensible to bring a simple first-aid kit (see Packing above). Your doctor may agree to equipping you with a course of general antibiotics if you plan on a relatively long stay.

Altitude or mountain sickness can affect anyone whatever their age and fitness level; some people have experienced it on the Golden Summit (Jinding) at Emei Shan (3,077 metres or 10,092 feet above sea level), others have been unaffected crossing passes at higher altitudes. Obviously, those with an existing heart or respiratory problem should first consult a doctor before visiting certain places in Sichuan.

The condition occurs because at higher altitudes the body has to adjust to a diminished supply of oxygen, which induces such symptoms as a headache, nausea and shortness of breath. If stricken, take it easy, drink plenty of fluids (avoid alcohol) and, if you smoke, stop. Painkillers like Panadol may help to tide over the discomfort. In normal circumstances, the body will acclimatize to the rarefied air in a day or so. Prolonged symptoms should be taken seriously, the best cure being to descend to a lower altitude at once. There is no need, however, to be an alarmist, since in Sichuan you are unlikely to be staying at high altitudes for more than two or three days.

Zhaodaisuo

Zhaodaisuo are best described as hostels. Once out of the main cities and larger towns, the visitor has no alternative to putting up at these spartan quarters. The term *zhaodai* means to 'look after', 'entertain' and generally 'serve' a guest or customer; *suo* is a 'place' or a 'centre'. Not the slightest whiff of service in its most rudimentary sense can be discerned in the *zhaodaisuo*, however. They are strictly utilitarian shelters for a night or two where only the most basic amenities are available.

Be warned that what a Westerner understands as 'basic amenities' is not by any means taken for granted by the Chinese. To the majority, city-dwellers included, flush lavatories and running hot water are undreamt-of luxuries. *Zhaodaisuo* plumbing amounts to one central washroom with a few cold-water taps and one hot-water tap. Along one side, below the taps, there may be a sink or concrete runnel halfway up the wall. This is where you can place your washbowl, usually provided in each guestroom. There may or may not be showers. If showers are available, they will have hot water only at a set time, usually a few hours in the evening, but always be prepared for that to give up on you in the middle of your ablutions. Somewhere about, there is a tank from which boiling water, as opposed to merely hot water, is dispensed. This is drinking water. Thermos flasks for storing drinking water are another standard issue. Often the tank is jealously guarded by a *fuwuyuan*, the member of staff on duty. If you get on the right side of her, she—it is usually a she—has the power to make your stay a restful one, by conjuring up an extra blanket, or giving the floor a sweep, or helping you to master the temperamental workings of the hot water system.

Lavatories are invariably the squat type: holes in the ground with a sort of footplate on either side. A little privacy is ensured by the holes being separated by low walls, but there are no doors. While the more sophisticated lavatories will have some mechanical device of drainage, generally water is a missing element in lavatories and the resulting stench is something one just has to endure. (Public conveniences on the road are simply fly-ridden cesspits. For some reason the ones in towns often have entryways cut out in the shape of a vase. Pay lavatories, where a *fuwuyuan* collects 10 or 20 *fen* per visitor, are beginning to make an appearance in some towns.) Remember to have your own supply of toilet paper.

Guestrooms range from doubles to dormitories. Foreigners are not expected to share with locals and so are automatically checked into the most expensive category. As this comprises double or triple rooms priced at between Rmb 8 to Rmb 18 per bed, the tariff is hardly worth quibbling over unless you are really down and out or belong to that band of travellers whose greatest thrill is in ferreting out the cheapest deals. In most cases, foreigners are charged as much as double the domestic rate.

Two or three beds with not very clean sheets and a quilt, a washbowl, a table, a chair and a thermos flask complete the bare furnishings. The floor is usually concrete. Chinese travellers are never without their own mug or a screw-top jar for their tea. Foreigners are advised to do likewise. The enamel mugs with lids widely sold in towns are ideal for drinks and for ladling water out of a washbowl if the shower fails.

The absence of service can hardly be blamed on the po-faced *fuwuyuan*. The concept of conciliating customers by small attentions to their comfort is alien to her. *Zhaodaisuo* were never meant to be run on commercial lines, for they are halts set up originally to accommodate officials from out of town. Thus you have, for instance, the Xiaojin County People's Government Zhaodaisuo, whose *raison d'être* is to put up cadres gathered for a meeting. But *zhaodaisuo* are not all municipal institutions. In one town you may stay at the the Posts and Communications Zhaodaisuo, in another the Electricity Generator Factory Workers Zhaodaisuo. Occupation- and commodity-related hostelries have existed in China since before the communist takeover in 1949. Some were established in large cities by trade associations or guilds from neighbouring provinces, rather like clubs where salt merchants, say, from Shaanxi, or seamen from northern ports could find a ready welcome in Chongqing and Shanghai. Nowadays *zhaodaisuo* are usually accountable to *Guojia*—the State. But with independent tourists getting off the beaten track to destinations ill-equipped to cope with them, these hostels occasionally find themselves catering to foreigners, which leaves some of them a little confused. It is not unusual to be turned away in the more obscure places because, rather than risk committing a bureaucractic blunder, the *fuwuyuan* extricates herself by denying that there are vacancies.

For those moments when a yearning for clean sheets and modern sanitation becomes overpowering, Isabella Bird (see page 192) provides a salutory example of stiff-upper-lip stoicism. Her room at an inn within a day's march west of Wanxian (see page 188) was screened off by partitions 'with remarkably open chinks'. The air must have been heavy with unpleasant odours, given the proximity of a pig-sty and a cesspool. Inside were two rough bedsteads covered with old straw and mats, on which four or more coolies would lie down to sleep under wadded quilts. 'It is needless to say,' she added, 'that these beds are literally swarming with vermin of the worst sort.' Tattered strips of paper, which once covered the rafters, hung down between black and slimy walls, '. . .and when the candle was lit beetles, "slaters", cockroaches, and other abominable things crawled on the walls and dropped from the rafters, one pink, fleshy thing dropping upon, and putting out, the candle!' All the same she had a good night's sleep on a camp bed squeezed between the verminous bedsteads, with her luggage stowed on an oiled sheet laid on the damp mud floor, and her clothes and boots hung from her camera tripod, out of the way of rats.

Close-up of River Viewing Pavilion in Chengdu

Food in Sichuan

Sichuan cooking enjoys immense popularity in the West—deservedly so, yet some people still consider its most salient characteristic to be its ability to sear the mouth and bring a sweat to the brow. But if that were all, Sichuan restaurants could not survive a week in London, Paris or New York. Sichuan food is undeniably hot and spicy, but those gourmets who have developed a taste for it also like it for its earthiness and robustness—insipid it is not.

Probably the most distinctive feature of the Sichuan cooking style is its leaning towards strong and even extreme flavours. Local people attribute the development of their cuisine to the weather in Sichuan. They say that chilli- and pepper-flavoured food stimulates sweating, which cools them down in the hot summer, while in the damp cold winter, it produces the opposite effect of warmth and comfort. But the chef is undoubtedly also helped by the prevalence of many local ingredients to salt, pickle and spice the food. For example, the Sichuan peppercorn, known as *huajiao*, thrives in the Minjiang valley. Unlike the black peppercorn, this reddish brown berry from a shrub (*Zanthoxylum Bungei*) imparts an anise flavour and aroma and a mild spiciness when roasted and ground. From this one humble spice alone, the Sichuanese chef can conjure some half a dozen different flavours by blending it with other ingredients. A classic one is *mala*, obtained when Sichuan pepper, chilli and soya sauce are added to a nutty base such as ground sesame or sesame oil (*mayou*). Its effect on the lip and tongue is a tingling sensation, which has given rise to a play on the word *ma*, meaning to be numb or to have pins and needles. Another is *chenpi*, a blend of seasonings dominated by the fruitiness of tangerine peel. *Chenpi niurou*, a preparation of matchstick-shaped beef slivers deep fried to a dark brown crispiness and finally glazed with seasoning and tangerine peel, is chewy and delicious and makes an excellent *hors d'oeuvre*.

Perhaps at a loss for words—for how does one describe a flavour that is at once peppery, salty, vinegary and sweet?—Sichuan chefs call a third classic relish 'peculiar taste' (*guaiwei*), as in *guaiwei ji*, a cold dish of shredded chicken tossed in a thick sesame-based sauce.

This method of combining different flavours also yields *suanla*—sour and hot—and *yuxiang*—fishy fragrant, which owes nothing to fish but much to fermented soyabeans, garlic and wine.

In Sichuan, as elsewhere in China, Western visitors often find it difficult to avoid eating in hotel dining rooms and established city restaurants which have at least an English-language menu if not English-speaking staff. Yet it is possible to try the streetside eateries now that private-enterprise and family-owned restaurants have burgeoned everywhere, run by proprietors eager to be helpful. In many of these places raw ingredients are laid out in full view, so that, having made your selection, you can leave the cook to make up his own combinations. There will be a preponderance of vegetables, for meat, sliced or chopped up into bite-sized pieces, is frequently treated as an adjunct for flavouring rather than as the basis of a dish. Some of the vegetables will be familiar, such as cabbage, spinach, broad beans, potatoes, aubergines, cucumbers, kale and carrots. Others are more exotic to the Western palate, like *qingsun*, Chinese mushrooms, white radish and bamboo shoots.

Garlic, chives and spring onions are liberally employed. There is nothing so appetizing as a plain dish of blanched chives with slices of pork, or mustard greens sautéed with minced garlic. A classic Sichuanese dish is *Mapo doufu*—cubes of beancurd strewn with minced pork and chopped red capsicums and glistening with chilli oil. The inventor of this dish is said to be Pockmarked Grandma Chen, who ran a famous inn in Boji Jie, off Xi Yulong Jie, in Chengdu, some 400 years ago. (Today there are several branches in the city, the main one being located on Jiefang Bei Lu.) Another classic dish is *guoba xiaren*, whose distinctive ingredient—golden crispy rice crackling scraped from the bottom of the pot—is softened with a sizzling broth of shrimps poured over it in front of the guest at the table. There are several variations on this theme, such as combining the rice crackling with a broth of chicken, pork or eel. But the Sichuanese dish that is most widely eaten and loved for its classic simplicity and depth of taste is Viceroy's chicken (*Gongbao jiding*), a quick-fried ensemble of diced chicken, crunchy peanuts and green capsicums said to be named after a late-19th-century provincial governor by his obsequious host at a banquet in Chengdu.

At a more sophisticated level, returned-to-the-pot pork (*huiguo rou*), camphor and tea smoked duck (*zhangcha kaoya*), and beef steamed in ground rice (*fenzheng niurou*) usually feature on restaurant menus. As its name suggests, *huiguo rou* is twice-cooked. The pork (always of a cut with both lean and fat meat) is first boiled, left to cool before being thinly sliced, and then stir-fried in a piquant sauce in which soyabean paste, sugar, chilli, ginger and garlic predominate. Finally stems of spring onions are scattered at the end both for extra flavouring and to add colour. Smoked duck is a banquet dish in which the oily taste of the bird is subtly palliated by smoking it over camphor-wood and tea. In *fenzheng niurou*, the ground-rice coating over previously marinated beef, subjected to hot blasts of steam in a bamboo container, becomes soaked by the meat juices, with the result that the concoction is at once aromatic and succulent.

The people of Chengdu are proud of their 'fast food', which has a long tradition of being sold by vendors on the streets. As those vendors dispensed their snacks from mobile kitchens carried on shoulder poles (known as *dan*), the noodles (*mian*) they

Chillies, the one ingredient universally associated with Sichuan cuisine

popularized came to be called *dandan mian*. Into a bowl the vendor would put a spoonful or two of a seasoning of Sichuan pepper, soya sauce, chopped spring onions, vinegar and hot oil rendered a bright red by chillies, pour steaming stock on this, fill up the bowl with separately cooked noodles and top the whole concoction with a sprinkling of crisply fried minced pork. Nowadays this dish is more widely available in restaurants, where it is either eaten on its own as a snack, or served to round off a meal as a last course. Of dumplings and ravioli, there is a great variety, the most distinctive of which may well be the sort first sold off a Chengdu stall by a man named Lai Ruanxin. A helping of Lai *tangyuan* consists of four dumplings each stuffed with a different scented sweet filling, osmanthus blossom being a favourite. The dumpling itself is made of glutinous rice flour. It is customary, besides, to dunk the dumplings into sugar and sweet sesame paste before consumption.

Sichuan has its own version of the *fondue*. The original source being attributed to Chongqing, it is known as the Chongqing hotpot (*huoguo*), and the stock in which the ingredients are simmered is uniquely Sichuanese, for it is a powerful consommé turned dark by *huajiao*, fermented soyabean and hot bean paste, and laced with rice wine. Into the communal chafing dish set over a spirit flame are thrown thinly sliced raw meats, fish, vermicelli and cut-up portions of vegetables, although the favourite ingredients by far, certainly among those who hail from Chongqing, are tripe and other offal. Some restaurants have taken to providing individual hotpots, a boon for vegetarians and those who prefer milder flavours and wish to dilute their own stock. Either way a hotpot dinner is invariably a jolly and entertaining occasion, particularly on a cold winter evening.

Chengdu: Provincial Capital

Sooner or later, the visitor to Chengdu comes upon the wide boulevard (**Renmin Nan Lu**) which slices through the city centre and ends in a colossal **statue of Chairman Mao**. Local residents were wont to compare Chengdu with Beijing, but the only point of resemblance to have survived is that straight north–south drag, divided into six lanes by lines of trees, including two side lanes for bicycles. There is no core either, in the way of an imperial palace, but the statue of Mao Zedong, backed by an **Exhibition Hall** in the socialist-realist vernacular, now provides a focus. Once a Governor's residence, set behind several courtyards, stood here—at one time it was occupied by Zhao Erfeng, the Butcher of Monks (see page 136)—but it was demolished along with other relics of the imperial era. The city walls with their four gates at the compass points, enclosing a Chinese as well as a Manchu district, were pulled down in the 1960s, though by then they were very damaged, and consisted merely of broken embankments of masonry. (A gate of the old wall is left in the north of the city, down a rutted road—Xiti Lu—but it is enclosed within a military area and cannot be inspected at close quarters.)

There Mao stands on his high platform, one arm raised in greeting. Red flags flutter on either side. Beneath the statue, a slogan urges passers-by to 'Realize the Four Modernizations; Unify the Fatherland; Vigorously Develop China!' To his left, one block from the square in the angle made by Dongyu Jie and Yanshikou, is the **People's Market** (Renmin Shangchang), which was burnt down in the aftermath of student demonstrations in June 1989, but has now risen from the ashes as one of the largest and most modern department stores in China.

Roads radiate outwards from this central square, spanning the rivers that formed three sides of the original city. Of course Chengdu is no longer confined within these watery boundaries. Since becoming provincial capital in 1938, it has developed rapidly into the cultural, transportation and industrial centre of China's southwest region, and its population has grown to two and a half million.

The city is believed to have been founded more than 2,300 years ago, emerging from obscurity when the Qin Dynasty (221–206 BC) established the County of Chengdu after China was unified under one empire. It became the capital of Shu Han, the independent kingdom of Liu Bei (see page 190), in AD 221. By the tenth century its commercial importance was something to be reckoned with, so much so that the earliest form of paper money was introduced by its merchants to oil the wheels of trade. Commodities centred on the products of Chengdu's surrounding farmland and the more distant frontier regions, but a touch of luxury was provided by *jin* (brocade), woven in the area since the third century. An earlier name for the city, Jincheng (Brocade City), was derived from this.

To some people Chengdu still seems like an overgrown town; others boast that it is a cosmopolitan metropolis. It might sound patronizing, though it would be true, to say that it is very much a provincial city. It lacks the character of, say, lowering grey Chongqing, with its hilly location, its proximity to a bustling waterway and its winter fog. Chengdu seems more intimate by comparison, and also blander. It has some high-rise buildings, but not many, and those that have been plonked down here and there are still surrounded by warrens of residential alleyways with their neighbourhood markets and stores. In appearance and feel it is similar to many other regional centres in China.

Not all of them, though, have as interesting a street life. Dashing Khampas from western Sichuan, knives glinting from the folds of their *chubas*, sweep through the streets; suddenly a group of Yi, distinguishable by their fringed woollen capes over workaday clothes, materialize at the entrance of a hotel or restaurant. In **Binjiang Park**, by the banks of the river which wends across the southern half of the city, the Jinjiang (on some maps called the Nanhe), vendors stir their 'Chongqing hotpots' in winter and sell ice-cream in summer, while elderly citizens huddle over cards or mahjong tiles in pools of shade under dusty trees. Early in the morning, these retired folk from the neighbourhood gyrate to the scratchy strains of modern dance music—an alternative form of gentle exercise to *taiji*, perhaps? On Tuesday and Friday evenings, around 7.30 pm, a bit of the park turns into **English-speaking corner**, where people gather to practise and meet any native speakers who pitch up. In the first few years after China's opening to the West, such groups tended to be rather tedious, but today's mix of students and workers can be very forthcoming and astoundingly well informed—visitors who have participated in the discussions have found the experience fascinating.

Young Western travellers are often found south of the river, at some of the restaurants which line the bank, along a lane (Nanhong Lu) leading to the Jiaotong Hotel and Xinnanmen Bus Station. This is where the backpacker scene is to be found. There are several lively restaurants (including the **Flower Garden Snackbar**, whose French toast, porridge, omelettes, potato chips and yoghurt drinks are a life-saver to many a Western traveller pining for home cooking, although it is perfectly happy to supply Sichuanese fare—without the chillies—as well). Tourist guides hang out here and at one or two other restaurants along the lane. These enterprising English-speaking individuals have resourcefully cornered the market for taking budget travellers to a performance of **Sichuan opera** (at which you are led backstage before curtain-up to see the actors putting on their make-up), a **Chinese Traditional Medicine Hospital** or villages and sites farther afield—as one advertising flyer promises, 'Anything you wish . . . just ask!' Past the swimming pool is a teahouse where chess enthusiasts meet, though lately the game of Go has become more popular.

A walk along the north bank of the river will take you past several **teahouses**, where guests seated in curve-backed rattan chairs linger over newspapers, chess or gossip, while their pet birds twitter from the rafters in shiny bamboo cages. Teahouses abound in Chengdu, some of them occasionally livened by a storyteller or musicians. They can also be found in People's Park (Renmin Gongyuan) and in the grounds of Du Fu's Thatched Cottage (see pages 51 and 56). A few *jiao* secures a lidded bowl with tea-leaves and an endless supply of hot water, poured with expert aim from a steaming kettle as the attendant makes her rounds.

Going westwards along Binjiang Lu, one soon comes upon the red painted façade of Binjiang Hotpot Restaurant and the adjacent 'Top Glory' Karaoke bar, its door emblazoned with the promise 'Everyday is Spring'. Nearby is the **Black Coffee** (Hei Kafei) and the White Hibiscus Hotel, a subterranean maze of dimly-lit bar, nightclub and cheap beds for hire in what used to be an air-raid shelter.

The **Jinjiang Hotel** is one of the most prominent landmarks in Chengdu, not just on account of its size, but also because it has represented an oasis of comparative comfort and services to foreign visitors for longer than all the other hostelries in the city. Constructed in 1962, it is an angular building which must have derived its inspiration from no-nonsense municipal architecture. On the pavement left of its gate, an open-air **gallery** of works by local artists has become an institution most fine evenings. It caters to tourists, of course, but it nevertheless makes a pleasant promenade, and there is plenty to look at. Certainly, for souvenir-hunters, a worthwhile memento might be found among paintings such as those featuring a single tiger, or the beautifully graphic calligraphy scrolls, on which one Chinese character standing for 'Longevity', 'Tranquillity' or 'Good Fortune', for example, is inscribed in thick, bold brush-strokes. Painted fans are both decorative and practical, and a bright 'One-hundred Butterflies' picture is a piece of gaudy fun. Often to be seen hanging around the entrance of the hotel are illegal money-changers, middlemen who buy Foreign Exchange Certificates and hard currencies (see page 30) off tourists in broad daylight.

Opposite the Jinjiang, the **Minshan Hotel** is a glossier edifice, but turn right out of its entrance into **Nanfu Jie** (the street sign is not in English), past two schools, and the alleys yield a glimpse of old Chengdu. Along Nanfu Jie there are courtyard teahouses, a doctor's surgery and ramshackle dwellings with strips of radish hung out to dry, probably for pickling and eating in winter. The **Greenstone Bridge Market** (Qingshi Qiao Shichang), found along **Xinkai Jie** to the right, offers bulbs, cut flowers, shrubs, potted plants, fertilizer, glazed planters, rocks and dwarf trees with their roots packed in soil and wrapped in straw. (In summer, cut flowers are widely sold by florists-on-wheels, a mobile display of blooms attached to bicycle handlebars and pillions.) Further on, Xinkai Jie becomes a goldfish, vegetable and dried food-

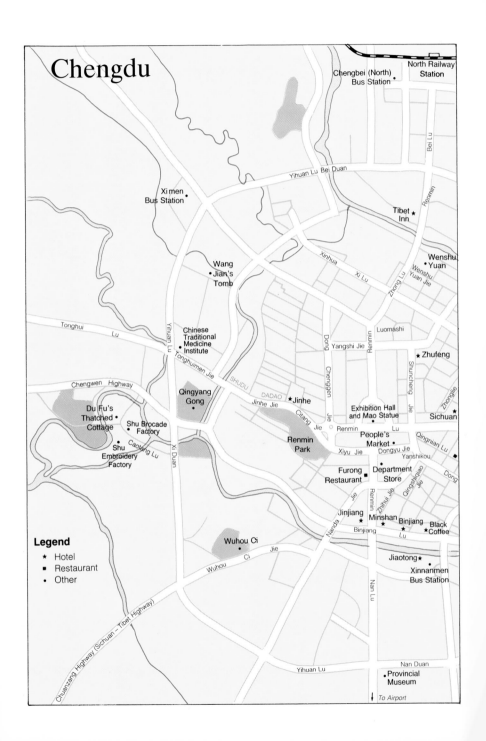

Chengdu

North Railway Station

Chengbei (North) Bus Station

Bei Lu

Renmin

Yihuan Lu Bei Duan

Ximen Bus Station

Tibet Inn ★

Xinhua

Xi Lu

Wenshu Yuan

Zhong Lu

Wenshu Yuan Jie

Wang Jian's Tomb

Luomashi

Tonghui Lu

Chinese Traditional Medicine Institute

Dong

Yangshi Jie

Renmin

Shuncheng Jie

★ Zhufeng

Zhongjie

Yihuan Lu

Tonghuimen Jie

SHUDU

DADAO

Chenggen Jie

★ Jinhe

Sichuan

Qingnian Lu

Qingyang Gong

Jinhe Jie

Citang Jie

Exhibition Hall and Mao Statue

Lu

Dong

Chengwen Highway

Du Fu's Thatched Cottage

Shu Brocade Factory

Renmin Park

Renmin

People's Market

Yanshikou

Caotang Lu

Xiyu Jie

Dongyu Jie

Shu Embroidery Factory

Xi Duan

Furong Restaurant

Department Store

Qingshiqiao Jie

Jinjiang

Nanda Jie

Renmin

Minshan ★

Binjiang ★

Black Coffee ★

Zhuhui Jie

Binjiang

Lu

Wuhou Ci

Ci Jie

Jiaotong ★

Wuhou

Xinnanmen Bus Station

Nan Lu

Chuanzang Highway (Sichuan – Tibet Highway)

Yihuan Lu

Nan Duan

Provincial Museum

↓ To Airport

Legend

★ Hotel
■ Restaurant
• Other

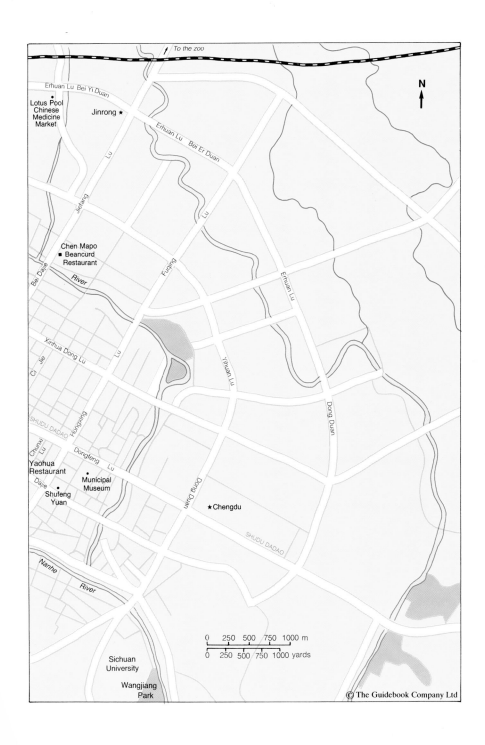

To the zoo

N

Erhuan Lu Bei Yi Duan

Lotus Pool
Chinese
Medicine
Market

Jinrong ★

Erhuan Lu Bei Er Duan

Jiefang
Lu

Erhuan Lu Bei Er Duan

Lu

Chen Mapo
■ Beancurd
Restaurant

Be Dajie

Fuqing

River

Erhuan Lu

Xinhua Dong Lu

Lu

Yihuan Lu

Ci
Jie

SHUDU DADAO

Hongxing

Dong Duan

Chunxi
Lu

Dongfeng   Lu

Yaohua
Restaurant

Dajie

Municipal
Museum

Shufeng
Yuan

★Chengdu

Dong Duan

SHUDU DADAO

Nanhe

River

0   250   500   750   1000 m

0   250   500   750   1000 yards

Sichuan
University

Wangjiang
Park

© The Guidebook Company Ltd

stuffs market. Back at the Minshan, walk past the Tibetans selling bits of long-dead animals and other fortifying 'medicines'. If you are there in the evening, have a look at the junk stalls offering 'antiques' as well as communist paraphernalia such as badges, posters and, lately, 'protective' portraits of Mao Zedong and Zhou Enlai. Follow the crowd to one of the *getihu* (private enterprise) restaurants nearby. The surroundings are rather dismal, but the food is hot (in both senses of the word), filling and delicious.

Residents do their shopping in the department store (Baihuo Dalou) on Renmin Nan Lu, at the People's Market, and in an underground mall with its entrance near Mao's statue. The tunnel used to be a bomb shelter. Down an entrance at no. 8 Renmin Xi Lu, near the junction with Dongchenggen Jie, the underground passage contains the **Chengdu Folkways Artistic Hall**, a sort of Madame Tussaud's with 25 tableaux of life-size statues representing familiar figures from 'Old Chengdu'—teahouse patrons, the pawnbroker, the prostitute, the pavement dentist, the fortune teller, the beggar, the rickshaw puller and so on. The whole exhibit is quite evocative of street life in pre-Liberation days.

Young Chengdu consumers like to patronize the shops along **Chunxi Lu** and **Qingnian Lu**, where they find their jeans, T-shirts, leather jackets, cassette tapes of Cantonese and Taiwanese pop songs and Japanese products from colour film to Walkmans. **Derentang Pharmaceutical Shop** is here, a great draw for overseas Chinese in search of bargain ginseng and other traditional tonics. One of the more esoteric branches of Chinese cuisine, in which Chengdu has an established reputation, is *yaoshan*, a meal with a variety of restorative medicinal ingredients as its base; if you stand in need of nourishment, *yaoshan* dinners can be had at **Tongrentang Yaoshan Zibu Canting** in Dong Dajie and at the **Baicao Yuan Restaurant** on the Minshan Hotel's 21st floor.

Possibly less conducive to balancing the *yin* and the *yang*, but an experience to be savoured nevertheless, is a visit to **Long Chaoshou**, an eatery which ranks as one of Chengdu's most famous snack joints. The restaurant makes no concession to atmosphere, being housed in premises somewhat akin to a public hospital ward, but the specialities are highly popular and worth every *fen* of the few *yuan* they cost. Many people get no further than the ground floor, where a selection of snacks (*xiaochi*), either variations on the theme of the stuffed dumpling or pastries or noodles, can be had for a set price from 2 *yuan* to 10 *yuan*. Travellers have recommended eating upstairs, which has booths and table settings and a large number of desultory waiters. Set menus of all kinds of Sichuan specialities in three or four price ranges are offered. Long Chaoshou is at 8 Chunxi Lu Nan Duan (Southern Section).

Getting Around in Chengdu

If you arrive by air, make for the car park where you can hire a taxi or catch an **airport bus** downtown. In the last couple of years, Chengdu's Shuangliu Airport has been expanded with a new terminal building. The bus will take you to the street running alongside the **China Southwest Airlines Ticket Office** (referred to on some maps as the Civil Aviation Ticket Office) near the Minshan Hotel, and this is where you can pick up taxis and other transport to your final destination in the city. The **Sichuan Provincial Tourism Administration** building is also here, housing branches of travel agents (CITS for instance) and a sales outlet for plane, boat and train tickets—a useful place to get information. The taxis will tout for fares; it would be sensible to agree on a price beforehand or insist that the meter is used. There is an additional toll charge if you take a taxi from the airport to the city centre. Again, hire one whose meter works.

In contrast to the situation of only a few years ago, there are now frequent **minibuses** that ply the main city roads. One of the most useful routes is from the stop outside the Minshan Hotel to Beizhan (North Railway Station), which takes you along Renmin Lu through its south, central and northern sections. The minibuses display their routes on the windscreen, but in Chinese characters only. However, the conductor or conductress will usually shout out the destination at each stop.

Regular **buses** and **trolley buses** are available as well. Visitors may find bus no. 16 useful, as it runs between the North and South railway stations (Beizhan and Nanzhan). Trolley bus no. 1 plies the route from Beizhan to Xinnanmen Bus Station.

Nowadays, there are many more **taxis**, so that it is occasionally possible to hail one in the street. Fares are regulated, based on a set rate for the first 3,000 metres (variously advertised on notices pasted in the cabs as Rmb 9.80 and Rmb 12.60 at the time of writing). Between 10 pm and 6 am, an additional Rmb 0.30 per kilometre is charged. Most Chengdu Municipal Taxi Company vehicles display a telephone number for complaints (26640).

Chengdu is not a frenetic city; from Mao's statue it is possible to stroll around some of the most interesting areas on foot, or you can rent **bicycles**. Two convenient bicycle rental places are the Jiaotong Hotel by Xinnanmen Bus Station, or the shop located behind a gap in the wall past the Sichuan Provincial Government Foreign Affairs Office on Renmin Nan Lu Er Duan, if approaching from the direction of the Jinjiang Hotel (take no notice of the 'Bicycle Renting & Repair Dept' sign closer to the Jinjiang Hotel, which identifies the shop's previous location). Travellers have managed to rent them from the large bicycle parking lot directly outside the Jinjiang Hotel. For local trips, there are also **pedicabs** (bicycle-rickshaws) outside the hotels,

bus and railway stations, and major road junctions; you should give your destination and agree on a price in advance. As a rule of thumb, the ride from the Jinjiang Hotel to the shopping district around Qingnian Lu should not cost more than four to five *yuan*.

Sights in Chengdu

WENSHU YUAN

This temple is located about one and a half kilometres (one mile) south of the railway station, down Wenshu Yuan Jie running east off Renmin Zhong Lu. The narrow approach, lined with a jumble of stalls purveying all the paraphernalia of worship—incense, 'hell money' for burnt offerings, red candles, firecrackers—is a fascinating manifestation of the popularity of religion in China today but also its more down-to-earth commercial possibilities. Mahjong sets, far from striking an incongruous note, seem perfectly in keeping with the other wares on sale.

Wenshu the God of Wisdom or, by his Sanskrit name, Manjusri, does not seem to be the pre-eminent object of worship at the eponymous temple. The principal shrines are dedicated to Maitreya (the Buddha to Come), Sakyamuni and Avalokitesvara (or Guanyin, the Goddess of Mercy). The devotion of Chinese Buddhists to their favourite bodhisattva, Guanyin, has been exhibited in many ways, but perhaps none more ardent than the masochistic act of an 18th-century adherent, who embroidered a picture of the goddess, not with silk thread but with hair pulled from her own head; this piece of embroidery is among the treasured relics at Wenshu Yuan.

Those shrines take up three of the five halls built along a central axis stretching from the temple entrance, the last two being used for preaching and for the storage of sutras (Buddhist scriptures), of which there is quite a collection. The temple is particularly proud of the three books written by fanatic monks in their own blood around 1836. Apparently the authors used to sit down to their task every morning by dipping their brushes in blood from their self-lacerated tongues.

Forming a rectangular enclosure around the central halls are long monastery buildings, for Wenshu Yuan is the Sichuan headquarters of the Chan (Zen) Buddhist sect and an active seminary. Novices and monks eat in a gloomy refectory furnished with rows of trestle tables and benches all facing a central aisle. One recent visitor counted 60 place settings, each with three bowls and a pair of chopsticks, which may give a clue to the size of the clergy serving here.

Although the monastery was founded earlier, its buildings date from 1697–1706 and are typical of the architecture of their time.

Chairman Mao's statue, Chengdu

LOTUS POOL CHINESE MEDICINE MARKET

One of the most interesting places to visit in Chengdu, when historical monuments pall, is the Lotus Pool Chinese Medicine Market (Hehua Chi Zhongyao Shichang). There, in the north of the city, close to the railway station (Beizhan), is a vast hangar-like building, open at the sides and heaped with every ingredient of the Chinese pharmacopoeia, both animal and vegetable. The temperate slopes of Sichuan's high mountains abound in herbs, roots and plants with a variety of curative properties, and, judging from what is available here, huge supplies of these find their way to this wholesale emporium. Gunnysacks surround each stall, their contents pungent with a mixture of sweet, woody, or sharply acrid aromas. The most extraordinary things spill from them: there are whole monkey skeletons, slabs of tree bark and sticks of twigs, porcupine quills, deer antlers, shiny green and matt brown striped snakes coiled and tied, dried seahorses and black knobbly slug-like caterpillar fungus. More appealing to the eye are the bright red seeds of Chinese wolfberry, claret-coloured dried jujubes, orange peel and the pearly kernels of different fruits. Then there are the more familiar cinnamon, liquorice and ginseng. Behind the stands, women knit or cuddle their children, and at the back of the building, clinics are conveniently located to provide on-the-spot prescriptions.

ZHAOJUE MONASTERY AND CHENGDU ZOO

More than two hundred monks serve at the Zhaojue Si, a surprising fact when not so long ago this monastery lay in ruins as a result of damage during the Cultural Revolution (1966–76).

Zhaojue Monastery was founded in the seventh century and harboured many an eminent monk. The monks were adherents of various sects, although the monastery is now closely associated with Chan Buddhism and, given its location in southwest China, with the Yellow Hat sect of Tibetan Buddhism. The monastery is certainly large enough to accommodate all kinds of practices and rites. Since the State Council's decision in 1986 to restore it, several main halls have been given a facelift and more reconstruction work is in progress.

Behind the red painted walls are several courtyards and shrines. With an ancient tree and an iron bell tower in front of it, the main hall rises two storeys on a framework of painted pillars and carved beams. Restoration work on this huge hall was completed in 1990. Inside, a massive Buddha seated on a lotus and displaying a swastika on his chest is flanked by two other Buddhas.

Before reaching the main hall, a small shrine behind a courtyard, the Guanyin Ge, is worth a peep. This is heralded by a small iron bell tower; like the one in front of the main hall, the clappers hanging from the bells are fish-shaped. To the left and right of the gate are grottoes dedicated to Guanyin, the Goddess of Mercy, filled with smouldering incense sticks and faded flowers and Buddha figures galore.

The monastery complex stands in the northeastern suburbs of the city, just beside **Chengdu Zoo**. Few travellers who visit the zoo do more than take a look at the giant and lesser pandas, the zoo's pride and joy. Pandas have been bred here by artificial insemination (see page 121).

Wang Jian's Tomb

Wang Jian (847–918) was a local ruler during one of those recurrent periods of disunity in China's imperial past when a centralized state broke into short-lived regional kingdoms. In this case it was the interval between the fall of the Tang and the rise of the Northern Song known as the Five Dynasties period (907–960). Wang Jian's tomb, discovered in 1942, lies in a cold, damp, arched vault under a grassy mound. The raised stone grave is supported by 12 effigies; along three sides of the platform is a frieze of dancing girls and musicians performing on lutes, clappers and drums. The redeeming feature of this depressing site is the pretty garden below the mound (to which a separate two-*jiao* ticket gains admittance), where there is a popular teahouse.

Du Fu's Thatched Cottage

Du Fu (712–770) is regarded by most Chinese scholars as China's greatest poet. In the year 759, with help from a relative, Du Fu came to Chengdu. There, by a small stream in the west of the city, he built himself a cottage and off and on for the next four years passed one of the most peaceful and carefree periods of his hard life, tilling the land, tending his fruit trees and writing some 240 poems. One of the poems refers to his rural retreat by a limpid brook, with its wicket gate opening onto a rutted country lane, where, living in remoteness, he could be nonchalant about his shabby gown. The poetry he wrote here is full of leisurely observations of the changing seasons—the red earth after spring rains, swallows chasing in and out of his house, the scent of loquats ripening on a tree, dewdrops on the tips of bamboo leaves, autumn gales tearing the thatch off his roof. A vein of sadness, about ill health, disappointments and life's brevity, also runs through it, but there is serenity, too, as when he watches his wife cut paper for a chessboard, and his son fashion a fish hook from a needle.

Du Fu's cottage has long since vanished. Instead, a symbolic thatched pavilion— the Shaolin Caotang—stands amidst the luxuriant greenery of a commemorative park. The very stream by which Du Fu built his humble house faces the park entrance. It was in the 11th century that a shrine to the poet was first established. Today the grounds embrace several buildings, some containing exhibitions of the poet's work, others given over to the selling of refreshments. But most people seem to come here to stroll in the gardens and sit in the teahouse to the left of the entrance.

Du Fu

China's Greatest Poet

Du Fu, the son of an official, was born in 712 in present-day Henan Province, central China. He started writing poetry at a very young age but, despite his talents and a classical Confucian education, failed the imperial examination by which officials were selected for the government bureaucracy. Deprived of the conventional career for men of his background, Du Fu spent several years travelling through the eastern and northern regions of China, in 744 meeting the poet Li Bo, for whom he was to develop an enduring admiration.

Still hopeful of a civil service appointment, Du Fu reached the capital, Chang'an (modern Xi'an), in 746. His petitions failed to win him influence at court. Without patronage or money, he had to send his wife and two sons to live in the country. A third son died of starvation afterwards.

By the time Du Fu finally secured an official position, the capital and the imperial house were caught in a rebellion which precipitated the flight of Emperor Minhuang to temporary exile in Sichuan and eventually brought about the downfall of the Tang Dynasty. He had already written 'The Ballad of the Army Wagons', a poem about the horrors of forced conscription, in which he spoke of the bleached bones of dead men lying ungathered where ghosts wept under a dark, rain-drenched sky. The An Lushan rebellion of 756 was to inspire some of Du Fu's best poetry against war and, in particular, to call up his most profound compassion for its victims.

It is thought that Du Fu fled before rebels stormed the capital, but was captured by them and taken back to Chang'an. He escaped to join the fugitive court, where he was appointed to a minor post, but his performance failed to find favour, and before long he was on the road again, impoverished and now ill, and trailing from one place to another in search of a livelihood.

His wanderings took him to Chengdu in the winter of 759, where a cousin was the subprefect, and for four years Du Fu seemed to set aspirations of public service aside, coming to terms with his failure in the eyes of his fellow men. It was a tremendously energetic period in which his frustrated ambitions found an outlet in poetry.

It was not to last. A new emperor on the throne and political changes in the provinces set him adrift again, travelling downriver on the Yangzi as 'a single gull between earth and sky'. For a time he settled in Guizhou where a local governor helped him to acquire a farm. He was now dogged by illness (he was consumptive and had become deaf in one ear); perhaps it was to seek a healthier climate that he moved again, southwards, to Jingzhou in Hubei Province. From then on he lived intermittently on a boat and it was while he was floating on the Xiang River, south of the Yangzi, that he died in 770.

Western scholars have found the highly compressed language of Du Fu's poetry difficult to translate, but whether literary or literal, such translations as have been published leave in no doubt Du Fu's intensely personal response to his times, be it the anguish caused by political turmoil or the joy of returning to the intimate circle of his family. Even if his technique and erudition elude us, Du Fu's poems have a universal appeal as the many editions of his work in Chinese and in translation attest.

The two characters read 'Caotang'—the 'Thatched Cottage'

WUHOU CI

Statesman and strategist Zhuge Liang (181–234), adviser to Liu Bei who founded the kingdom of Shu Han (present-day Sichuan), was given the posthumous title of Marquis of Wu (Wuhou). Reluctant statesman though he was (see page 190), Zhuge Liang served two kings—Liu Bei and his son—with honour and total dedication, and so highly did later generations esteem him that a shrine was erected to his memory. (It is said that the Sichuan farmers' white head-cloths are worn in perpetual mourning for Zhuge Liang.) The date of the original shrine is not recorded, but we do know from a poem by Du Fu, written in the eighth century, that it nestled in a glade of cypresses outside the 'Brocade City'.

Lost to a fire in the 17th century, Wuhou Ci was completely rebuilt in the early Qing Dynasty (1644–1911). Its grounds in the southwest corner of the city now form the **Southern Suburbs Park** (Nanjiao Gongyuan), but unless you have bags of time, it is hardly worth making a special trip to this rather dingy site.

Engraved steles line the approach to a series of halls, one behind another. The first hall commemorates Liu Bei, whose statue looks out to a Ming-dynasty iron cauldron, embossed with dragons, in the centre of the paved courtyard in front. Two corridors, one filled with the sculpted figures of 14 civil officials and the other with 14 military commanders, enclose the courtyard to the east and west. Liu Bei's tomb is nearby, west of a lotus pond.

The hall to Zhuge Liang stands at the rear, framed by the graceful upturned double roofs of a bell tower to its right, and a drum tower to its left. A low stone balustrade is decorated with carved images of bears, lions, gibbons and the furled hands of the Buddha. Within the hall, the gilded statues of three generations of the Zhuge clan sit side by side. The biggest of the three bronze drums in front of them, its lid studded with six crouching frogs, is said to date from the seventh century.

PROVINCIAL MUSEUM

From the skull fossil of Ziyang Man (c. 30,000 BC) to the photograph of communist leaders Deng Xiaoping and Liu Bocheng in conference during the southwest liberation campaign in November 1949, the collection at this museum gives a useful overview of Sichuan's long history.

Situated just south of the city ring road (Yihuan Lu Nan San Duan), the museum is a two-storey building divided into a historical section on ground level and a revolutionary section on the upper floor. Cultural relics from the area's earliest settlements include pottery from Daxi (see page 197) and bronzes dated to the Ba and the Shu kingdoms, notably a set of chime-bells from the Warring States period (475–221 BC). From the Han empire (206 BC–AD 220) the earthenware tomb figures and stone bas-reliefs are probably the most striking exhibits (reproductions of the former and rubbings of the latter are sold by the museum shop). These were all found in ancient tombs around the Chengdu area. Han tombs typically had their chamber walls inlaid with carved panels illustrating scenes of everyday activity, from harvesting and spinning to lifting brine from salt wells. Paradoxically, the craftsmen involved lavished their skill upon an art intended not for the living but the dead. Towards the end of the Han period, Sichuan lacquerware, which was regularly sent as tribute to the imperial household, also reached a high standard of artistry; one example is the cup with ear-shaped handles from the Western Han (206 BC–AD 8).

It was in the Tang Dynasty that funerary sculpture attained aesthetic perfection, as can be seen in the celadon figures unearthed from a tomb near Wanxian. There are also Song (960–1279) examples, such as the clay model of a house found in Meishan, south of Chengdu, in 1978.

The most riveting exhibit downstairs is an enormous loom contrived almost entirely of bamboo and wood. This early 19th-century machine stands four metres (13 feet) high and measures five metres (16 feet) from end to end. Sichuan's celebrated brocade used to be woven on it. Among the fabrics on display are some fine Qing-dynasty pieces, the most gorgeous of which is an embroidered panel covered with butterflies, flowers and leaves. There are more modern examples as well—a length of brocade with a fan-shaped pattern shot through with gold and silver threads, and one on which peonies and birds are picked out in a lovely colour scheme of greens, dark brown, cream and deep purple.

Minority culture is represented by Yi jewellery—chunky silver bracelets and earrings—and Tibetan tinder boxes, swords and robes.

The revolutionary struggles of the Communist Party, including the Long March (see page 143), are recorded in photographs and documents on the floor above.

The museum is open Monday to Saturday, 9 am–4 pm.

OTHER DIVERSIONS IN CHENGDU

There are other museums in Chengdu. The City or **Municipal Museum** is located in a former Confucian temple on Shudu Dadao. It has a permanent collection of artefacts excavated in the vicinity of the city, such as carved bricks, but recently, financial problems have forced it to open only irregularly. If you are in the vicinity (southeast of the city centre, near Wangjiang Park), the **Sichuan University Museum**, which holds a large collection (40,000 items) started by an American scholar, is worth a look, particularly if you are interested in Chinese calligraphy and folk art. Its advertised opening times are Monday to Saturday, 9 am–noon and 2.30–5.30 pm. The **University** itself is impressive, with its exceptionally well tended vegetation and classroom buildings bisected by wide walkways crowded with students. This would be a good place to meet people.

Chinese armour, one of the exhibits of the Sichuan University Museum

Parks in China are usually somewhat dusty and far from tranquil places. Chengdu's **People's Park** (Renmin Gongyuan) is no exception, but it is worth a brief visit for a cup of *cha* at the large teahouse within the grounds. An obelisk overlooks a funfair area providing rides and merry-go-rounds for children. The obelisk is a monument to the patriots who were killed trying to maintain Chinese authority over the Chengdu–Chongqing railway in 1911. This clash resulted from the Qing government's cession of control over the railway to British, French, German and American interests in exchange for loans.

Another park lies to the southwest of the city. The park is named after the **River Viewing Pavilion** (Wangjiang Lou), which stands beside the Jinjiang River. Shortly after entering, one is greeted by an avenue of arching bamboo, and in fact Wangjiang Park is chiefly noted for its 100 species of bamboo as well as some not very interesting relics associated with a Tang-dynasty poetess, Xue Tao. The pavilion itself has some fine carving.

Taoists in Chengdu worship at **Qingyang Gong** (Bronze Goats Temple) west of the city centre. The bronze goats in question can be seen in their own enclosures in the Hall of Three Purities (Sanqing Dian); they have obviously been smoothed by the many hands that have attempted to touch them for good luck. The goat with a single horn is meant to be an amalgamation of the 12 animals named in the Chinese lunar calendar. This hall, as well as the others in the complex, was first constructed in the Tang Dynasty, subsequently destroyed and rebuilt in the Qing.

Chengdu crafts include the weaving of Shu brocade, which has been made for more than 2,000 years and can be seen at the **Chengdu Shu Brocade Factory** at 105 Caotang Dong Lu. At most souvenir shops, you will find examples of porcelain covered with bamboo ware, such as vases and tea sets. They are produced by the **Chengdu Woven Bamboo Ware Factory** at 12 Jiefang Bei Lu Yi Duan.

Sights outside Chengdu

Dujiangyan Irrigation System

One of the world's most impressive hydraulic engineering projects lies 55 kilometres (34 miles) northwest of Chengdu, near a town called **Guanxian**. This irrigation system is all the more remarkable for having been in use for more than 2,200 years.

Before the project was executed, the Chengdu Plain was an old lake bed, alternately flooded in summer when mountain streams gushed across it, and vulnerable to drought in winter. The principal river flowing into the plain is the Minjiang, and it was this torrent

Bridge at Dujiangyan

that a local governor in the third century BC harnessed to transform the whole valley into the well-drained and richly fertile farmland that it has become.

Li Bing, the governor, began the project in around 256 BC, later passing the task to his son Erlang. What he did was to divide the Minjiang into two by building a midstream weir; from here, at **Fish Mouth** (Yuzui), the Minjiang splits into the Outer River, which runs in its old bed, and the Inner River, which Li Bing had diverted to a new course on the east. The Inner River was in turn divided at Lidui Hill, a man-made embankment; the right-hand (west) stream linked with the Outer River through **Flying Sands Spillway** (Feisha Yan), and the left-hand stream squeezed through **Precious Bottleneck Channel** (Baoping Kou) to feed a grid of irrigation canals now watering over 6,500 square kilometres (2,500 square miles) of the Chengdu Plain. The whole system made it possible for the water intake at Precious Bottleneck Channel to be controlled. As an aid to gauging high and low water levels, stone figures were placed at three different places as markers, and sometime in the Ming Dynasty (1368–1644), three iron bars were buried in the riverbed above Precious Bottleneck Channel as an indication of the depth to which it should be dredged. 'Dig the beds deep; keep the dikes low', Li Bing had warned. With the ex-

A Bizarre Experience

'C'est très bizarre, non?' I said as I emerged. 'Mais non,' cried the Frenchman, throwing up his hands wildly. 'Au Black Coffee Hôtel à Chengdu, c'est plus bizarre.' This I did not doubt. Already I had heard a great deal about this infamous place, an unrenovated air-raid shelter that now served as a $1.50-a-night bordello where beds were laid out in the windowless corridors and guests could reach the bathroom only by crawling through a hatch. In the lobby of this now legendary underground haunt, a rock-and-roll band serenaded drunken couples, while well-fed sixteen-year-old girls spread themselves languorously out on couches. Keys, of course, were strictly forbidden. 'Une fois,' began my roommate, 'je devrais attendre trente minutes parce que la gardienne lavait ses mains.'

Sobered by that cautionary tale, we decided to minimize our comings and goings, as well as to synchronize them. Since it was now dinnertime, we quickly put this policy to the test, ventured out into the corridor in search of the dining room, sticking as close to one another as members of a chain gang. As we edged through the winding hallways, we found them crowded with other guests waiting to be admitted to their rooms. Finally, after many curses and collisions, we arrived at a huge assembly hall of a dining room. A sweet-faced girl was seated at a desk outside. She directed our attention to a piece of paper that said 'Airpot Hotel.' Below that curious inscription were eight rows of Chinese characters. We stared at the list for a while in despair, and then the girl smiled back her understanding and motioned us to follow her into the kitchen. Proudly, she pointed to a bowl of chicken and a bowl of vegetables. And what could we have to drink? 'Yes,' she said, smiling brightly. 'Beer.'

> 'Would it be possible to have some tea, please?'
>
> 'Yes, yes,' she said, pointing to a bottle. 'Beer.'
>
> 'Thank you. But do you have tea, please? Tea.' I did an unworthy imitation of the dainty movements of a deb at Brown's Hotel. The girl looked crestfallen. Deciding that it might be undiplomatic to remind her that Tibetans, according to Heinrich Harrer, drink two hundred cups of tea a day, I tried another tack.
>
> 'Does the Airpot Hotel have any soft drinks?' She looked confused. 'Coke? Fanta? Lemon?'
>
> Suddenly, her face brightened. 'Beer,' she pronounced agreeably. 'Yes!'
>
> 'Do you have water?'
>
> She was now the picture of happiness. 'Yes, yes! Beer.'
>
> Pico Iyer, Video Night in Kathmandu, 1988

ception of periods of civil war, this principle has been observed and the spillway and channels kept in good order ever since.

Dujiangyan makes a thoroughly worthwhile day excursion from Chengdu. Once at the site, you can approach Li Bing's waterworks either from Lidui Hill or, upstream, from the high terrace behind Two Princes Temple. If you go there by taxi from Chengdu, you can ask to be dropped at the entrance of **Lidui Park** and to be met later behind the temple. Lidui Park holds little interest; **Fulong Guan**, the temple in the midst of it, marks the legendary spot where Li Bing was supposed to have subdued a troublesome dragon. A track to the left, as you face the temple, leads across the Flying Sands Spillway towards a suspension bridge. Sudden flooding in summer can submerge the spillway in torrents of water, as happened in 1986. The more usual route to Two Princes Temple is therefore along the far bank, under the lee of **Yulei Hill**: cross the bridge to the right of Fulong Guan; at the T-junction with Xinfu Lu, turn left into the path that ascends by steps between scattered pavilions snuggled into the hillside. The walk to Two Princes Temple takes about half an hour.

A dramatic **suspension bridge** spans the Outer and Inner rivers and leads to Two Princes Temple. Composed of thick bamboo cables floored with transverse wooden planks, the bridge swings wildly from side to side as pedestrians walk or wheel their bicycles to the opposite bank. There, ranged below the temple, a line of food stalls send up mouthwatering smells of dumplings on the boil, or fish being fried, or hot *dan dan* noodles flavoured with chilli sauce.

Two Princes Temple (Erwang Miao) is dedicated to Li Bing and his son, Erlang. They were given honorific titles for their great waterworks legacy to the people of Sichuan. The temple itself, a fifth-century foundation, is little more than a repository for inscribed tablets left by illustrious visitors down the centuries, and for two statues—of Li Bing and Erlang—in the main halls. Behind, a steep climb up a wooded slope takes you past more pavilions to a terrace built to mark a visit to Dujiangyan by Chairman Mao in 1958. A sweeping view of the Minjiang's diverted channel unfolds beneath the terrace.

You could combine a visit to Dujiangyan with hiking on **Qingcheng Shan**, 15 kilometres (9 miles) southwest of Guanxian and 65 kilometres (40 miles) west of Chengdu. This mountain is sprinkled with caves and shrines venerated by Taoists.

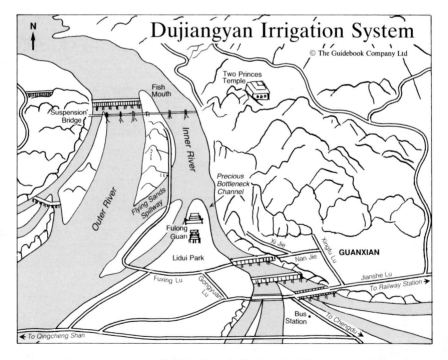

Sheli Pagoda at the Precious Light Monastery outside Chengdu

The four-hour climb on a clearly-marked stepped path to Shangqing Gong Temple, 1,600 metres (5,250 feet) above the sea, is a pleasant respite from city sightseeing, marred only by the persistence of the *huagan* (chair litter) porters at the entrance to the site.

PRECIOUS LIGHT MONASTERY (BAOGUANG SI)

The entrance to this temple is often the scene of much hilarity. *Fu*, the character for 'Good Fortune', is etched in red on an outside wall, and some ten or so paces in front, local visitors, their eyes tightly shut and their arms stretched out, take turns to stagger their way hopefully towards the luck-giving word. It is surprising how few manage to make contact.

Immediately inside the temple, the 1,000-year old **Sheli Pagoda** stands 30 metres (98 feet) high. This square tower rises in 13 levels—punctuated by eaves gently uptilted at the corners—to a gilded finial. It is a structure of plain and satisfying symmetry although, if you look up on entering the temple, you will be able to see that the top eight storeys lean slightly to the left. Twelve niches for Buddha icons pierce each level, and bronze bells hang from the corners of the eaves. The Sheli Pagoda is a stupa, a repository for 13 relics of the Buddha which were found buried in a box, as the legend goes, by Tang emperor Xizong during his exile in Sichuan (see page 166).

At that time a temple already existed on the site; in fact Baoguang Si is believed to have been founded in the Eastern Han (AD 25–220), but, destroyed by fire, it was totally rebuilt in the 17th century. The **Luohan Hall**, though, was a more recent addition, being erected in 1851. Dimly illuminated by natural light and candles, it contains 500 slightly larger than life-size gilded effigies of the disciples of the Buddha, whose range of expressions—leering, startled, grimacing or laughing—contribute in no small degree to the creepy atmosphere. Perhaps none of them is as gruesome as the *luohan* shown in the act of ripping open his belly to display a Buddha inside. The statue in the centre of the hall is of the many-armed Guanyin, the Goddess of Mercy.

Baoguang Si is 18 kilometres (11 miles) north of Chengdu in a suburb known as **Xindu**. Depending on traffic conditions, the drive there takes anything from 30 minutes to an hour.

Emei Shan: Sacred Mountain of Buddhism

Emei Shan is more than a mountain; it is a frame of mind. That is not just because looking up at monumental heights induces in the beholder a sense of his own frailty and insignificance. It is also because for centuries Chinese belief has endowed Nature with a mystical influence on man's character, and Nature is supremely exemplified by mountains. Mixed up with this tradition was the ancient folk belief that mountains were the magical habitations of immortals. Although Taoist in origin, these ideas have been gathered into the Chinese Buddhist's view of the universe like much else of the indigenous cult.

China has several famous sacred mountains, both Buddhist and Taoist. Why they came to be venerated no longer matters; their sacred character has been thoroughly institutionalized by the many temples and places of pilgrimage established on their slopes since antiquity. Emei Shan's first temples were Taoist; later it became known as one of the four most holy mountains of Buddhism (the others are Jiuhua in Anhui Province, Wutai in Shanxi and Putuo in Zhejiang).

There are at least two interpretations of the mountain's name. Some people say that 'Emei' derived from the first two syllables of 'Amituofo', the deity invoked in the Pure Land Buddhist prayer in which the repeated utterance of the holy name is supposed to help speed the pious to paradise. But since legends cling to practically every cave, streamlet and pinnacle, so the entire mountain has spawned a fable of its own. Emei means 'moth eyebrows', a poetic term for beautiful women, and the peaks of Emei, it is said, were originally four celestial maidens.

As the story goes, there used to be a temple outside the west gate of the town. A monk of this temple once gave shelter to a painter, who repaid his hospitality with four pictures, each one of an elegant and lovely young girl. The artist imposed one condition, however. Those paintings, he said, must be put away in a trunk for 49 days after his departure. Too impressed and delighted to heed the artist, the monk hung them on the wall. When he returned in the evening, he was astounded to find four girls chatting and giggling away in the hall, while the pictures were, of course, completely blank. As the truth dawned on him, he saw the girls run out of the room. Giving chase, he was only quick enough to grab hold of the skirt of the youngest girl. The desperate girl escaped his clutches by instant transmogrification into a pinnacle. Her sisters, loath to abandon the youngest, did likewise—which is why Emei Shan has three peaks close together, while a fourth stands a little distance apart.

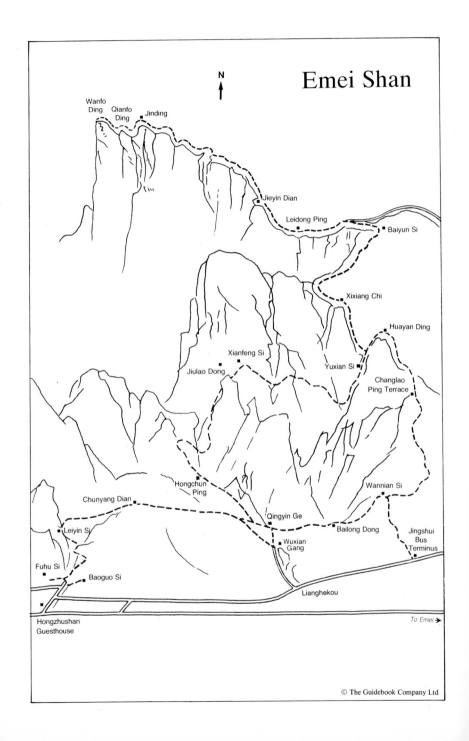

Emei Shan

N

Wanfo Ding
Qianfo Ding
Jinding

Jieyin Dian

Leidong Ping

Baiyun Si

Xixiang Chi

Huayan Ding

Xianfeng Si

Yuxian Si

Jiulao Dong

Changlao Ping Terrace

Hongchun Ping

Wannian Si

Chunyang Dian

Qingyin Ge

Leiyin Si

Bailong Dong

Jingshui Bus Terminus

Wuxian Gang

Fuhu Si

Baoguo Si

Lianghekou

To Emei ➤

Hongzhushan Guesthouse

© The Guidebook Company Ltd

Wanfo Ding (Myriad Buddhas Peak), the highest point on Emei Shan, is 3,099 metres (10,165 feet) above the sea. Below it the western face of the mountain slopes down in a series of inclines while eastwards the drop is almost perpendicular. Topped by a curiously truncated summit, the mountain with its ungainly silhouette is exactly the sort of geographical oddity which appeals to the Chinese, whose appreciation of Nature is often tinged with a particular fondness for its freakier aspects.

Travellers' reports of climbing Emei Shan have varied from enthusiastic recollections to a catalogue of woes. Much hinges on the weather. While the cooler heights make for a welcome interlude from the summer humidity and heat of the Chengdu Plain, frequent rain and low hovering clouds can turn the experience into a sodden endurance test. Early winter, when the mountain top is transformed by the first dusting of snow, can be a superb time to visit provided that you come armour-plated against the cold.

To climb to the top and witness Buddha's Aureole (see below) is the fulfilment of a Buddhist's dream. Inevitably, alongside the pilgrims, there are increasing numbers of tourists, from cadres on pre-retirement jaunts and People's Liberation Army soldiers on R and R, to young Hong Kong backpackers and Taiwanese groups. One of the nicest aspects of the excursion may be the acquaintances you make on the way. There is a tendency for visitors who climb at the same speed to cluster together; after some hours of keeping in step, or resting at the same monasteries, you are likely to start swapping not only snacks but life stories as well.

The advent of tourism has prompted the construction of motor roads and now, for the convenience of less than ardent hikers, there are buses to Wuxian Gang (for Qingyin Ge), Jingshui (for Wannian Si) and Leidong Ping (for Jieyin Dian), as well as a cable car to Jinding (Golden Summit). Be warned that you may have to wait in line for up to two hours to get on the cable car. When all else fails, porters are on hand with chair litters (*huagan*) at key points along the way.

ROUTES

If you are fit and properly-shod, and assuming that you are prepared to cheat a little (by taking a bus to Jingshui), the ascent and return can be done in two and a half to three days. You are the best judge of whether to add to this timetable by staying overnight near the Golden Summit in order to see the sunrise from the peak. The trail is mostly paved, with some quite steep steps in places. A common **route** from Jingshui, which we shall call (**A**), is: Wannian Si–Changlao Ping–Huayan Ding–Xixiang Chi–Leidong Ping–Jieyin Dian–Jinding, probably with an overnight stop at Xixiang Chi. This route has been estimated at 30 kilometres (19 miles).

A longer **route** (**B**) loops round from Wannian Si to Qingyin Ge, then proceeds as follows: Hongchun Ping–Jiulao Dong–Xianfeng Si–Yuxian Si, merging with route

A at Huayan Ding below Xixiang Chi. Total distance is about 52 kilometres (32 miles). This is the more scenic route. Alternatively, a bus plies between Baoguo Si and Wuxian Gang, close to Qingyin Ge, so you can start your ascent by route B from that point without going via Wannian Si. The majority of climbers ascend by route A and descend by route B.

Those who want a taste of the mountain without knocking themselves out may like to consider this **compromise**: take the bus to Wuxian Gang for Qingyin Ge, walk up to Hongchun Ping and stay the night. The next day, simply walk down the same way again, after which a bus and cable car can be taken to the summit. Since the monastery at Hongchun Ping is not strategically positioned for a climb up the entire mountain, it is generally not crowded with tourists. The monastery has well-preserved architecture and a serene courtyard.

For those who want to go the whole hog and start from the bottom, the route is Baoguo Si–Fuhu Si–Leiyin Si–Huayan Si–Chunyang Dian–Qingyin Ge; from Qingyin Ge either walk on to Wannian Si and then climb by route A, or you can take route B, to the top.

FOOD AND LODGINGS

As pilgrims have done for centuries, today's hikers must accept the spartan accommodation and vegetarian fare offered by Emei Shan's temples if they lodge overnight on the mountain. Travellers have come back with horror tales of leaky roofs, voracious rats under rotted floorboards, dirty dining rooms and inedible food. Others have found the sensation of waking up at dawn to tolling bells and the muffled chants of monks more than adequate compensation for the discomfort of the night.

A list of the places on Emei Shan providing lodgings or meals follows. They are all much the same, with dormitory beds at rates averaging Rmb 10, outside latrines, rudimentary plumbing, and dim electric lighting supplemented by candles. One or two of them have single or double rooms. You usually register at a window or counter just to the side of the main hall or gate pavilion. Set-menu meals are normally charged at the rate of Rmb 2–4 for breakfast, and Rmb 4–6 for lunch or dinner. There are also wayside stalls selling drinks, biscuits, nuts or cooked snacks.

Baoguo Si Single rooms and three-, four- or five-bed dormitories; dining hall. This is one of the cleanest monasteries.

Fuhu Si Accommodation separates local tourists from foreigners; dining facilities.

Wannian Si Two classes of dormitory accommodation; dining facilities.

Chunyang Dian Basic bed and board.

Guangfu Si (just below Qingyin Ge) Four classes of beds; set meals.

Xixin Suo (roughly halfway between Wannian Si and Huayan Ding) Basic bed space and meals.

'Sea of Clouds', Emei Shan

Hongchun Ping Dormitory accommodation; possible to have a shower here; set meals.

Xianfeng Si Single and double rooms; set meals.

Xixiang Chi Two classes of dormitory beds; set meals. Well patronized by hikers because of its location.

Jieyin Dian Bed and board.

Woyun An Near Jinding; bed and board; single and double rooms available.

Metereological Station Zhaodaisuo Jinding. Double rooms available; meals.

A new hostel has been constructed just below Jinding. Travellers' reports suggest that it is grotty and expensive.

After a night or two on the mountain, the hot baths and clean sheets at **Hong-zhushan Guesthouse**, back at base, will make one feel the most pampered of sybarites. This hotel, a short walk from the bus terminal at Baoguo Si, sprawls in its own grounds in a villa-style complex of seven buildings including Number Four, which was once occupied by Chiang Kai-shek but is now open to guests despite its recently proclaimed status as a historical monument. A cream-coloured timbered bungalow wrapped around on all four sides by a wide verandah, it housed Chiang Kai-shek in the summer of 1935. Number One Building, in the innermost corner of the grounds, has the most plushly appointed accommodation. A separate building contains the dining hall and kitchens.

Temples and Sights

Baoguo Si and Fuhu Si are the most frequently visited temples around the foothills. Before their ascent climbers can be seen inspecting the variously decorated walking sticks sold beside the road. A staff seems as much part of the image of the toiling pilgrim as the straw overshoes and rosary beads, numerous strings of which are also for sale. You can equip yourself with a map of the trails here.

Baoguo Si (Temple of Dedication to the Country), the gateway to the holy mountain, is confusingly the name used for the nearby bus terminal too. Actually the temple is entered a short distance higher up on the opposite side of the road from Hongzhushan Guesthouse. Founded in the 17th century, Baoguo Si was extended in the early Qing period (1866) and is fairly typical of all the temples on Emei Shan. Four imposing halls snuggle into the hill slope one behind another, the last being a library for sutras. Through the gate pavilion, you come to a large courtyard flanked by the monks' quarters with its upper-storey gallery more than likely festooned with drying towels. The main hall of the temple stands at the far end, its roof rearing up above huge wooden beams. Beyond it is the Seven-Buddha Hall dedicated to the six Buddhas of the past and Maitreya, the Buddha of the future. The most treasured relic of this temple is found behind Seven-Buddha Hall: this is the porcelain Buddha, a 2.4-metre (nearly seven-foot) figure fired in the kilns of the capital of chinaware, Jingdezhen in Jiangxi Province, in 1415.

Puxian Hall is the centrepiece of this temple complex. Incense smoke and the swelling chant of monks from some concealed recess greet you as you reach the entrance. Inside, pennants and draperies dangle from the rafters. Many of them are of red silk, embroidered or appliquéd with figures of monks, dragons and Chinese characters. A red silk drum like an enormous lampshade hangs between tasselled pennants sewn with tiny copper bells. Perhaps it is a lampshade, for a bare electric bulb diffuses a feeble light inside it. The crimson of the silk is echoed in the lac-quered pillars flanking the altar, and in the faded satin kneelers in front of it. Spreading his benevolence about him, Puxian glitters from inside a glass case, looking more Indian than Chinese with his gilt head-dress. The tutelary deity of Emei Shan, Pu-xian (Samantabhadra in Sanskrit) is sculpted in his customary pose, sitting cross-legged on a white elephant. One candlewick in a bowl of oil winks from his altar. A monk in padded grey habit, knee-length leggings and black cloth shoes sits below the altar in a wicker chair, his eyes straying from the scriptures he is reading when-ever a worshipper approaches the collection box. He acknowledges each donation by striking a gong.

Further uphill on the tarmacked road, a stone-flagged pathway to the left is all but concealed in bamboo groves. Spanning a peacefully trickling mountain brook, the Tiger Stream, it leads to **Fuhu Si** (Subduing Tiger Temple). A legend relates how a fierce black tiger once terrorized the neighbourhood. One day three sisters, a little bored with studying Taoism on the mountain, came to the stream. Being Taoist novices, these girls were rather eager to wield their magic on the notorious tiger, but their powers proved unequal to the task, and it was their brother, dropping from the sky at an opportune moment, who finally tamed the beast. A bridge was later built to mark the tiger's defeat.

Up a flight of stairs and beyond a spacious courtyard, the nicely-kept main hall is dominated by three Buddha figures. Within the dim chancel area fenced off by a low wooden railing, an elderly nun or monk might be fitfully dozing, undisturbed by the genuflections of pilgrims and tourists passing in front of the altar. A few worshippers sink to their knees, but most of them perform a quick triple bow from the waist. Joss sticks in their clasped hands smoulder and give off a musty fragrance. In the dark, hushed hall (much less of a tourist trap than Baoguo Si), two oil lamps, though lit, do nothing to lift the gloom, although the pair of enormous drums on either side of the altar stand out clearly enough. The altar is decorated with vases of pine branches and a potted bonsai (which, on closer inspection, proves to be plastic).

Fuhu Si was founded during the Southern Song Dynasty (1127–1279). However, the Huayan Pagoda to the left of the main hall, an unusual 13-tier bronze structure whose surface is covered with 4,700 Buddha images and the text of the Huayan Sutra, dates from the end of the 16th century (late Ming Dynasty).

Other mountain streams meander between rocks down the wooded slopes. Past Leiyin Si (Thunder Temple), a mid-19th-century establishment, and Chunyang Dian at 940 metres (3,080 feet), you drop down to Shuang Feiqiao (Double Flying Bridges) straddling two little rivers which, tumbling down a miniature waterfall just above, meet at an outcrop of rock called Niuxin Shi (Ox Heart Stone). Named for the 'singing' waters, Qingyin Ge (Clear Sound Pavilion) stands above the bridges among luxuriant vegetation at the junction of two paths, one to Hongchun Ping, the other to Wannian Si. As there is a bus service to Wuxian Gang, an easy two-kilometre (one-and-a-quarter-mile) walk from Qingyin Ge, this is a busy crossroads for climbers.

Wannian Si, 1,020 metres (3,345 feet) in altitude, is where most visitors start their ascent, since a shortcut by bus to Jingshui, a ride of 40 minutes or so from Baoguo Si station, takes you quite close to it. From Jingshui bus terminus it is only a walk of three to four kilometres (two to two and a half miles) to the temple along a cement track, stepped in places, with enough way-stations for drinks and things to look at to make it an enjoyable amble.

Wayside hawkers display their wares under straw matting or ragged tarpaulin, regaling passers-by with bottled drinks, snacks and medicinal herbs. Plucked from the higher slopes and grown for centuries around monasteries, the numerous medic-

Light at the End of the Tunnel

The railway halt at Emei was at the end of a long muddy road, and a market nearby sold fruit and peanuts to the pilgrims waiting patiently, leaning on their walking-sticks, for the train. And then, above the sound of sparrows and the whispers of bamboos, a train whistle blew. I like these country stations, and it seemed perfect to sit there among the rice fields in the hills of Sichuan until, right on schedule, the big wheezing train arrived to take me away, south into Yunnan. It was twenty-four hours to Kunming, and the train was uncharacteristically empty: I had a compartment to myself, and this one—because of the intense and humid heat—had straw mats instead of cushions.

'There are 200 tunnels between here and Kunming,' the conductor said when he clipped my ticket. No sooner had he got the words out of his mouth than we were standing in darkness: the first tunnel.

We were among tall conical hills that were so steep they were terraced and cultivated only half-way up. That was unusual in China where land economy was almost an obsession. And the day was so overcast that waterfalls spilled out of the low clouds and paths zigzagged upwards and disappeared in the mist.

So many tunnels meant that we would be among mountains the whole way—and hills and valleys, and narrow swinging footbridges slung across the gorges. The ravines were spectacular and steep, and the mountians were close together, so the valleys were very narrow. All of these magnificent geographical features had meant that the railway line had been difficult. In fact many of the engineering problems had been regarded as almost insurmountable until the early seventies when, with a combination of soldiers and convicts—a labour-force that could be shot for not working—the line was finally finished.

The line could not go through the mountains of the Daxue range, and so it crept around their sides, pierced their flanks, and rose higher and circled until it had doubled back upon itself. Then you looked down and saw the tunnel entrances beneath you and realized that you had not advanced but had only climbed higher. Then the train was in a new valley, descending to the river once again. The river was called the Dadu He, 'Big Crossing'. It was wide and greyer than the sky above it. For most of its length it was full of boulders. Fishermen with long rods or ancient fish-traps sat on its banks.

These were the densest, steepest mountains I had seen so far, and the train was never more than a few minutes from a tunnel. So, in order to read or write, I had to leave the lights burning in the compartment. One moment there was a bright valley with great white streaks of rock down its sides, and gardens near the bottom and vegetable patches sloping at an angle of forty-five degrees, and the next moment the train would be roaring through a black tunnel, scattering the bats that hung against the walls. This was one of the routes where pepole complained of the length of the trip. But it was easily one of the most beautiful train-trips in China. I could not understand why tourists went from city to city, on a forced march of sightseeing. China existed in all the in-between places that were reachable only by train.

Paul Theroux, Riding the Iron Rooster, 1988

inal plants on Emei Shan have given it a nationwide reputation for producing some of the most highly valued drugs in China. Alongside a booth stacked with roots and bark and wizened furry objects, a doctor holds a consultation while his patient—a baby almost totally swaddled in layers of blankets—cries plaintively on its mother's lap. Further uphill, another doctor peers into his patient's eyes and murmurs his diagnosis. What seems like an incredibly small consultation fee changes hands, and the patient goes off with a prescription.

By and by you may overtake a string of porters carrying preposterous loads of bricks on their backs; every now and then they lean slightly backwards on their T-bar staves to prop up their burdens and take the weight off their shoulders. Like the tea-brick coolies of Kangding (see page 129), these men each carry some 100 kilograms (220 pounds) at a time—in some spheres of life very little seems to have changed in 50 years.

The use of *huagan*, in which pilgrims too feeble to walk are borne up the mountain by porters, has certainly persisted. The eagerness of past pilgrims to reach the summit without exertion spawned a profession that lives on today, perpetuated by those overseas Chinese for whom a visit to Emei Shan (or Qingcheng Shan outside Chengdu) is incomplete without sampling this experience. A *huagan* is a simplified sedan chair made of a bamboo-slatted seat slung on a light rectangular frame, in which the rider not so much sits upright as lolls. Protection against rain is assured by a canvas awning. The 19th-century and early 20th-century Western writers who came upon these 'chair-litters' always remarked on their bearers' surefootedness. One of them found the whole procedure strange and grotesque, and 'shuddered to think what would happen were the porter to stumble and send the pilgrim hurtling into the void . . . To keep step on the uneven mountain paths, the tandem porters sang a duet, the headman warning and the rear responding . . .'

Founded in the third century, **Wannian Si** (Temple of a Myriad Years) is probably the oldest surviving monastery on Emei Shan. The holy mountain's patron saint, Puxian, is honoured here in the most arresting religious building on Emei Shan. This is a square brick hall surmounted by a stupa-decorated dome. Rather more suggestive of Indian shrines than of Chinese ones, the hall is composed of brick and stone only, and is beamless. Its purpose is to enclose a magnificent bronze statue of Puxian and his mount, a six-tusked elephant with its feet planted in lotuses. At least three disastrous fires have demolished Wannian Si since the statue was wrought in the tenth century, and each time this image has escaped more or less unscathed. The hall is not very large, so that Puxian and his elephant, together measuring more than eight metres (26 feet) high, seem to fill it all. If you peer more closely, however, you will see that the interior walls are shelved and set with a multitude of fired-clay Buddha figures. Emperor Wanli's mother, who came to Emei Shan on pilgrimage, is supposed to have ordered the shrine to be built in 1580. It is also said that twice a year, at the solstices, the sun shines through a hole in the dome and strikes the bodhisattva's forehead.

In a side hall, to which visitors are admitted if permission is first sought by an official guide, four other treasures belonging to the monastery are normally locked away in a safe. (The unspoken condition for taking them out is a generous donation to the temple funds.) The treasures are: a small jade Buddha from Burma; a manuscript, closely written with scriptures, consisting of a sheaf of more than 400 narrow palm-leaf pages; a Ming-dynasty imperial seal; and a tooth of the Buddha. The last is a most curious relic, about 30 centimetres (a foot) long, rather less in width and some 8 centimetres (three inches) thick, a lump of smooth veined yellow ivory which came into the temple's possession during the Southern Song period (1127–1279).

A tough haul up a winding trail, and the next stop for bearings is **Huayan Ding**, where the two routes converge. Downhill to the left, as you face the summit, are **Xianfeng Si** (Immortal Peak Temple) and **Jiulao Dong** (Nine Ancients Cave), sites formerly revered by Taoists. A Chinese version of the Rip van Winkle story is told about these sites. One day an abbot of Xianfeng Monastery met nine old men near the cave. Invited to join them for a game of chess, the abbot whiled away a few pleasant hours. Only when he returned to the monastery did he realize that the few hours were actually 60 years—had he stayed, he would have achieved immortality. He rushed back to the cave at once, but no trace of the immortals remained.

Emei Shan's notorious and ferocious monkeys lurk around here, scampering out of the undergrowth to extort food from passers-by. Local people say that you should show your empty palms to them if you want to avoid their importunate pestering. They bite, too, so give them a wide berth. To the right the path goes up to **Xixiang Chi** (Elephant Bathing Pool), a popular overnight stop for climbers before their assault on the summit. Climbers have now reached the temperate zone, and will notice the subtropical vegetation of the lower slopes giving way to rhododendrons and other species of deciduous shrubs and trees. The temple at Xixiang Chi, in a lofty position on the edge of a precipice, is named after the legendary wash of Puxian's white elephant, although it would be hard to imagine anything of that size having much of a bath in the meagre tank of water here.

Above Xixiang Chi, the path zigzags up to a plateau at the rear of the summit. At this altitude the air is perceptibly colder, and in winter the slopes are blanketed with snow. It can be startlingly beautiful at that time, when all around the branches of trees are frosty sheaths of ice, while at your feet the undergrowth thrusts out fingers of sparkling crystal. Every puff of wind sends a tremor through the trees, sweeping the ice and snow to the ground with a faint whispering rustle.

Four hours' hike from Xixiang Chi, **Leidong Ping** (Thundering Cave Terrace) marks the end of the motor road (the drive up from Hongzhushan Guesthouse takes around two hours). Crowds of vendors here offer padded greatcoats for hire (Rmb 2) and straw overshoes (Rmb 1 a pair) to combat the slippery stairs. *Huagan* porters press their litters on elderly visitors for the last 15-minute lap to the cable car. From **Jieyin Dian** (Reception Hall) the cable car (for which there may be a long queue) lurches over treetops to deposit you at an elevation of 3,077 metres (10,092 feet). It starts operating early enough for the sunrise, a glorious spectacle of orange gaudiness if you catch it.

The path from Leidong Ping to the summit (a climb of about an hour and a half) includes two very steep flights of stairs. Once at the top, you can walk on to **Wanfo Ding** (Myriad Buddhas Peak) on the western edge, the highest point on Emei Shan. Such facilities as exist on the peak, though, are concentrated at **Jinding** (Golden Summit), 3,077 metres (10,092 feet) in altitude. These include a **meteorological station** (Emei Shan Qixiang Zhan) and a newly restored temple perched on a bluff. Otherwise, except in clear weather, the summit is something of an anticlimax. The original Golden Summit Temple, which by all accounts was as resplendent a structure as one can imagine, was gutted by fire in the 1880s. Financed by subscriptions from provincial officials as well as Tibetan Buddhists, it was a shining monument clad in tiles of iron and bronze and ornamented with thousands of Buddha figures covered with gold. These days Tibetans still regard the mountain as holy, coming on pilgrimages and leaving a few scattered prayer flags fraying on poles.

Besides sunrise and sunset, the celebrated sights of Jinding are the **Sea of Clouds** and **Buddha's Aureole** (also called Buddha's Glory). Clouds are all too prevalent on the summit, sometimes robbing climbers of their hard-earned views by enveloping everything in an opaque whiteness. On a sunny afternoon, though, when the clouds hug the lower slopes, leaving the summit clear, a curious effect of light can be seen, most often between two and four o'clock. Then, shadows cast by objects on the summit upon the clouds below take on a bright halo of rainbow colours. Although the mirage is a natural phenomenon, caused by the rays of sun being refracted through water-laden air, pilgrims in the past thought it a manifestation of the Buddha and some of them would leap from the cliff in ecstatic wonder. This practice was frowned upon, and chain railings and walls were put up at Self-sacrifice Crag to forestall further losses of life.

Fan Chengda (1126–93), a poet and scholar from Jiangsu Province, came to worship on Emei Shan and left this record of his impressions: 'The rounded gauze cloud spread out below the cliff, rose brilliant and beautiful, came within a few *zhang* [a Chinese measure of length] of the cliff, and stood there. It was unbroken and shone like polished gems. At the time minute drops of rain were falling, as at the

In the main hall of a Buddhist temple on Emei Shan

finishing of a shower. I leaned forward and gazed upon the centre of the cliff; there was a great aureole resting upon the level cloud; outside this was a triple halo, having the colours of ultramarine, yellow, red and green. The glory was in the centre, like bright space, serenely clear. Each person looking saw the image of himself in the empty place exactly as in a mirror, and there was not an infinitesimal part obscure. If I lifted my hand or moved my foot the image followed the motion, but I could not see the person standing by my side.'

The greatest sight of all, though, is not one of the traditional vistas of Emei Shan. To the west the land lifts towards the Tibetan plateau, and the distance before it is filled with mountains. At first feathery clouds hide the farthest peaks; as the sun rises higher, the scene is gradually tinged with blue. Bluer and bluer it becomes, and then the white incandescent crest of **Gongga Shan** (see page 136) appears. Two plateaux flank the pinnacle to the right and left, absolutely flat as if the tops had been sliced off. Momentarily the view is shut out by clouds being drawn up by the sun, but just as suddenly it re-emerges, this time more sharply in focus. To Fan Chengda the snow on the mountains of the 'western countries' was bright as polished silver. 'The mountains extend into India and other foreign countries, and beyond I know not how far,' he wrote, 'but they are seen as distinctly as though upon the table before me—a marvellous and incomparable sight; a diadem for a whole lifetime.'

Meishan: Shrine to a Literary Family

Meishan, a town 80 kilometres (50 miles) south of Chengdu, was the birthplace of Su Shi, also known as Su Dongpo (1036–1101), a distinguished poet and essayist as well as a painter and calligrapher. His was a classic literati upbringing. His father, Su Xun, and his brother, Su Ziyou, were also well-known men of letters. Having acquitted himself brilliantly in the imperial civil service examination, Su Dongpo served as an official until disagreement with the reforms of Wang Anshi, prime minister to the emperor, led to his banishment to Hubei Province in 1079. For a time he also languished in the southern province of Guangdong, but was recalled to office shortly before his death. Su Dongpo is best known as a master of *ci* poetry. This was a lyrical style based on the verse form of previously popular songs. Su and other contemporary poets developed and raised it to the level of a major genre.

The **Su family ancestral hall** (Sansu Ci) in Meishan is now a memorial museum. Some tour buses make a brief stop here. Although it hardly merits a special trip, the shrine is worth a visit if you are in the vicinity. Its exhibits, mostly documents and examples of calligraphy, are of rather esoteric interest, but the site is redeemed by its leafy park and lotus pond. Couplets celebrating the illustrious trio run across and down the lintels and pillars of the pavilions. Behind the main hall is a lovely courtyard filled with old trees—gingko, camellia, osmanthus, *nanmu* and camphor. All around are curved bamboo panels inscribed with lines of *ci*.

Leshan: The Great Buddha

At 71 metres (nearly 233 feet) high and 28 metres (92 feet) broad, the Great Buddha of Leshan (Leshan Dafo) is unquestionably enormous; in fact it is the largest carved Buddha in the world. Although it is also monumentally hideous, as Sichuan's most famous man-made curiosity it should not be missed.

Leshan, 31 kilometres (19 miles) east of Emei Town, nestles at the confluence of three rivers—the Minjiang, the Dadu He and the Qingyi Jiang. The town was a prosperous centre of silk weaving and white wax production. White wax trees (*baila shu*), which abounded in the area, were the basis of an extraordinary industry. Farmers engaged in it used the trees as repositories for the eggs of a scale insect which, once hatched, secreted a wax that coated the branches. The wax was then scraped off, melted in boiling water and collected, to be used in the manufacture of candles and as a polish.

The days of silk and wax are over, but Leshan remains a lively town. Travellers have enjoyed wandering around it, particularly the streets (Dong Dajie, Yutang Jie and Xian Jie) leading from the jetty to the Jiazhou Hotel. Parallel to these is a charming, narrow alley following the line of the Dadu River waterfront and bounded by the old city walls. At the bend of the Minjiang, directly opposite the jetty, are five or six residential lanes running parallel to one another that seem to belong to another century. Leshan's markets have some of the finest fruit and vegetables encountered anywhere in Sichuan. If you have given Meishan a miss, there are plenty of reminders of Su Dongpo in the examples of his calligraphy and poetry displayed on pillars and chiselled into rock all over Leshan.

Most visitors, however, make only a perfunctory call at Leshan, going straight to the pier for a boat trip to Wuyou Shan. This takes them past the Great Buddha in his rocky niche for a full-frontal view. Leaving from the pier on Binjiang Lu, regular ferry boats make the 25-minute trip to Wuyou Shan until 5.30 pm. This short ride gives passengers plenty of time, while the boat dawdles in front of the Great Buddha, to take photographs of themselves with the Buddha in the background.

Back in the eighth century, the turbulent waters of the three rivers converging just below Leshan made navigation so difficult that many a boat capsized in the current. Haitong, a Buddhist monk, conceived the idea of carving a Buddha figure above the spot to protect river craft from danger. One of those fanatic Buddhists who resorted to self-mutilation to demonstrate their piety, Haitong went so far as to blind himself. The sculpture was a labour of nearly a century. Down the years there has been some erosion of the reddish brown sandstone in which the seated Buddha is carved, but considering that it is well over a thousand years old the statue is remarkably intact. This can be attributed to the hidden drainage network incorporated into its design. Still, some water does seep through, and lichen and weeds sprout grotesquely from the cracks. A fuzz of grass covers the Buddha's lap, his chest is green with ferns, while some yellow flowers struggle for existence on his pate.

Sitting with his back against Lingyun Shan, the Giant Buddha is flanked by two guardian figures, much smaller at eight metres (26 feet) high, while behind him the hill is dotted with pavilions. The most stunning—raised as it is on the crest—is Lingbao Pagoda. A ladder-like staircase coils up the cliff-side to the Buddha's right. From the front the statue looks clearly out of proportion. Its nose is said to be 5.6 metres (18 feet) long, and a hundred people can sit in a circle on one foot. Tourists like to be photographed on one of Buddha's toes.

Wuyou Shan, once part of the mainland, was cut adrift when Li Bing (see page 57) dug an overflow channel to divert the Dadu River floods in the third century BC. It is now linked by suspension bridge to Lingyun Shan, although it can also be

Foreign Devils

And over against these remembrances of an otherwise forgotten age, there was this last development of modern days, this station of the China Inland Mission... Mr Horsburgh's party is expected to live upon forty pounds a year, and to have an ideal before it, that is to be accomplished on twenty pounds a year. But this last they are not sure yet is quite practicable. People who know say it could be done at Ta-chien-lu. And let people, who think missionaries come to China for what they can get, try a summer regimen of pork and chicken by way of meat, Chinese sugar that has to be washed before it can be used, local blue-green salt and all those other delicacies that are to be had for forty pounds a year, where carriage from Shanghai is about thrice as expensive as from England to Shanghai. And let those who think it is undertaken from a love of travel and adventure try a four years' confinement to any Chinese city of their acquaintance, for the same two young men, who started the China Inland Mission there four years before, were still stationed there.

Never before had a woman in European dress walked through the street of Kiating (Leshan), but only in one place did the people seek to annoy us; then they painted a cross on a flight of steps, fancying we should be unable to walk back over it. When missionaries first came here the people fancied they would steal their children and do all manner of dreadful things, so they used to pin crosses on to their children's clothes, thinking that Christians would not then dare to touch them. There was a Roman Catholic station there also of course, and one of the Fathers said when he first came to Szechuan twenty-eight years before, about one per cent—certainly not more than three per cent—smoked opium. He estimated that about a quarter of the population then did. But this was the very lowest estimate we heard, and must, one would think, be under the mark. He seemed to think the people were killing themselves as fast as they could.

Mrs Archibald Little, In the Land of the Blue Gown, 1912

reached by boat. From the pier, a shaded pathway leads to **Wuyou Si**, a temple founded in the eighth century, which affords nice views of the river from its terraces. A newly renovated Luohan Hall is filled with shiny statues of the Buddha's followers. Behind the hall is a pleasant garden. If you decide to eat at the temple, you will pass a calligraphy studio, still in use, alongside the steps leading up to its unpretentious vegetarian restaurant. The last boat back to Leshan leaves at 6 pm.

There are three approaches to **Lingyun Shan**. You can cross the bridge from Wuyou Si, take a direct ferry from Leshan or reach the back of it by road. The road ends close to the 13-tiered **Lingbao Pagoda**, standing on a knoll hard by the car park. From here it is only a short walk to **Dafo Si** (Great Buddha Temple), entered from a spacious courtyard off which an unpretentious hotel, **Nanlou Binguan**, is located. Nanlou Binguan, with only 30 beds, is a charming place to stay, combining as it does simplicity and modern conveniences. Through Dafo Si's Hall of Guardians, in which Maitreya (the Buddha to Come) is depicted in the traditional image of a fat-bellied, grinning deity, you come to an open area level with the Great Buddha's right ear. It teems with photographers' stands. To meditate upon Su Dongpo, unquestionably the presiding genius of Leshan and its environs, go to the part of the hill around the **Dongpo Studio**. There are gardens, walkways, and old buildings decorated with intricate woodwork. Su Dongpo, it is said, came here to drink and contemplate the moon. One of his poems, written on the night of the Mid-autumn Festival in 1076,

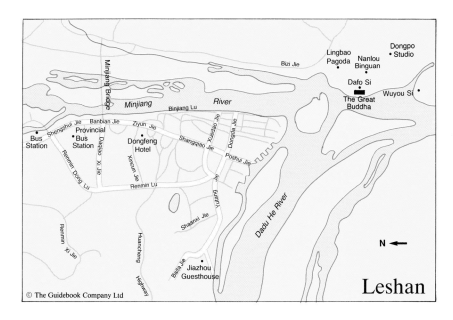

chastises the moon in one verse:

> Rounding the red pavilion,
> Stooping to look through gauze windows,
> She shines on the sleepless;
> The moon should know no sadness;
> Why, then, is she always full when dear ones are parted . . . .

(Translated by Yang Xianyi and Gladys Yang)

Descend by the **Nine-twists Stairway** (Jiuqu Zhandao), past numerous carved niches, along the Buddha's right side. The steps, cut into the cliff, are quite steep in places, but a solid metal railing prevents people from falling off onto Dafo's toenails below.

From the Buddha's feet, more steps to the left wind uphill between bamboo, banana trees and caves (in one of these Haitong apparently lived after blinding himself). These steps will take you back to Dafo Si. Along the way, the river Minjiang is always in view, its surface broken by floating logs and sampans midstream. A haze often hangs over it, but the outline of Wuyou Shan in the near distance, lacy with foliage on the cliffs, is usually visible.

From the top of Dafo Si, drop into the **Forest of Steles** (Beilin) if you are interested in Chinese calligraphy. There are many steles here covered with rows of Chinese characters in varous scripts. At the main gate several food stalls do a roaring trade in noodles and other snacks.

Getting There

BY RAIL

Emei Town is on the Chengdu–Kunming line. The most convenient trains to take are the special express 93, departing **Chengdu** 4.15 pm, arriving **Emei Town** 6.46 pm daily; and number 389, departing 7.49 am, arriving 10.43 am daily. Buses meet the trains and take passengers either to Emei Town (only a few kilometres from the railway station) or direct to **Baoguo Si** at the foot of Emei Shan (ten kilometres or six miles distant). There is usually no reason to go to Emei Town. There are also trains from Chengdu to **Jiajiang**, the railhead for **Leshan** 33 kilometres (21 miles) away, but if you intend visiting Leshan before Emei Shan, it may be simpler to get there by long-distance bus from Chengdu (see below); otherwise go by train to Emei Shan and then by bus from Baoguo Si to Leshan.

In the reverse direction (Kunming–Emei–Chengdu), special express 94 departs Kunming 11.30 am, the following day arrives Emei Town at 6.20 am and Chengdu

At the feet of the Great Buddha of Leshan (above);
descending by the Nine-twists Stairway alongside the Great Buddha (below)

at 9.15 am; passenger express number 390 departs Kunming 7 pm, arrives the next day in Emei Town at 3.53 pm and Chengdu at 7.17 pm.

BY ROAD

Long-distance buses leave six times a day from Chengdu's North Railway Station (Beizhan) to **Baoguo Si**, Emei Shan, taking around five hours for the journey. Five scheduled buses to **Leshan** are also available, with the service starting at 7 am and ending at 1 pm. The 165-kilometre (103-mile) journey takes about five hours. Emei Shan and Leshan are only 31 kilometres (about 19 miles) apart, and buses ply between the two throughout the day. Many Leshan buses go direct to Baoguo Si. In addition to scheduled public buses, there are tourist buses laid on by Chengdu-based travel agents between May and October (see page 21); they all combine the two destinations of Emei Shan and Leshan. Some may also make a stop at **Meishan**, a town 80 kilometres (50 miles) south of Chengdu and mid-way between Chengdu and Leshan.

LOCAL TRANSPORT

If you do not wish to climb the whole way up Emei Shan, privately operated minibuses zip round from **Baoguo Si** to **Jingshui** (near the site of Wannian Si) or **Leidong Ping** (the end of the road, just below the cable-car terminus). Another service from Baoguo Si goes to just below **Qingyin Ge**. These services are fairly regular during daylight hours in summer but obviously more sporadic in the winter months. Buses congregate in the square in front of Baoguo Si; you will almost certainly have to bargain over the fare (locals are charged Rmb 3 for the ride to Jingshui, but a foreigner might be asked for a lot more). These buses leave as soon as enough passengers have boarded. In the busy summer season there is usually no trouble filling them; in winter months they tend to hang around rather longer and tout for customers at every likely spot en route.

Motorized three-wheelers with a covered trailer to provide passenger seating ply between Baoguo Si bus station and Emei Town.

Northern Sichuan

Northern Sichuan shares frontiers with (from east to west) the provinces of Shaanxi, Gansu and Qinghai. To the west lies a plateau and the fountainhead of great rivers, the borderlands of old where nomads still wander the vast swampy grasslands of Aba in search of pasture for their yaks. This world remains very distant from our own. To the east, the boundary marches with the serried ridges of **Daba Shan** and **Micang Shan**, a continuous chain of mountains that meets the foothills of the **Minshan** massif at the point where the river Jialing drains into the province to join the Yangzi at Chongqing (see page 148). Beyond those peripheral highlands what we think of as north China begins—red earth shades into yellow loess.

Jianmen: The Ancient Road to Shu

The passage cut by the **Jialing River** (Jialing Jiang) is one of the ancient roads to Shu, as Sichuan was known in ancient times. As late as the third decade of this century camel caravans could still be seen along it, bringing wheat, tobacco and sheepskins from the north to exchange for the rice, coal, salt and—no doubt—contraband opium of the south. We know that back in the Qing Dynasty (1644–1911), salt merchants of Shaanxi Province regularly traversed this route (see page 205). And apart from the road, there is the river itself, navigable from Chongqing right up to Sichuan's northern frontier and beyond.

These days the Jialing valley is as vital an artery of communications as in former times. Nowhere is this fact more evident than at Guangyuan, a city just within Sichuan's borders. Lying on the river's southern bank, it straddles the junction of two highways—one into Gansu Province to the northwest, the other into Shaanxi Province to the northeast.

Penetrating Sichuan's mountain fastness was not always so effortless, though. In a famous poem, Li Bo (701–762) described the approach as fraught with danger. Although the poem's most quoted lines remain the first two, it also makes a memorable allusion to Sword Pass, a perpendicular cleft in the mountains south of Guangyuan:

> Oh how dangerous, how high! How hard is the road to Shu!
> It is as hard as the road to Heaven . . .
>
> From peak to peak, each hardly a hand's breadth from the sky,
> Withered pines hang over chasms
> Filled with the contending roar of torrents . . .

What takes you, travellers from afar, this long, weary way
So filled with perils?

Sword Pass is so steep and narrow,
That one man could hold it against ten thousand.
And sometimes its defenders
Are not mortal men but wolves and jackals . . .

We may follow the **ancient road to Shu** today and see the undulating country of the Red Basin in all its agricultural richness. Our journey will be in the opposite direction, however, starting in Chengdu.

As the suburbs are left behind, the city unravels into a landscape of market gardens, mud-coloured villages, roadside teahouses and cone-shaped lime kilns. Behind these straggling frontages lies some of Sichuan's most fertile farmland.

At least two staple crops are harvested annually: summer rice and winter wheat. In spring, flowering rape shimmers a bright yellow among the emerald green of rice seedlings. And other bounties reaped from the fields are evident everywhere—rows of corn-on-the-cob hanging from the shadowy eaves of roadside farms, hot sweet potatoes sold from makeshift ovens, long-jointed sugarcane chewed for its sweet juice, and the variety of seasonal vegetables in the markets. But the rich alluvium of the Chengdu Plain is being eaten away by creeping urbanization, as rural land is everywhere; each year some 40,000 hectares (100,000 acres) are lost.

The city comes to the village most palpably in the form of traffic jams. Trucks and buses, some with ducks and hens pinioned on their roof-racks, vie for road space with much recourse to blaring horns. 'Observe Road Safety'—warnings are daubed on an occasional whitewashed wall, but, with their chipped paint and mud-spattered outlines, they seem merely half-hearted. The ancient thoroughfare continues to bulge with the kind of transport inherited from a pre-industrial age. Trishaws ferry everything from cabbages to a sad, trussed-up pig; creaky carts, so overladen that the men hauling them are bent almost double, transfer bricks and steel girders from factories to construction sites. In every other incident encountered on the road you see the colossal triumph of Chinese muscle power over crushingly limited resources.

(Left) *Blossom in the soft early morning light on the road to Jianmen*
(Above) *Corn on the cob drying under eaves*

Mianyang is 130 kilometres or so (about 80 miles) from Chengdu. This industrial town is notable only for being the birthplace of Ouyang Xiu (1001–72), a Song-dynasty scholar and man of letters. Another 60 kilometres (37 miles) on, past **Zitong**, the road begins to climb. The terraced fields below fall away in a swirl of mist. In the sheltered valley the mulberry trees peeping above the grey tiled roofs of farmhouses appear misshapen and ghostly in the haze. Equally eerie is the sudden apparition of a moving bush, until, close up, one sees that it is a bundle of kindling, so tall as almost to obscure the farmer underneath it. Only the white bandeau encircling his brow stands out against the dark, towering burden on his back. Such headgear is to be seen again and again in Sichuan. Its origin is said to date from the third century, when three warring generals succeeded in splitting the empire into independent kingdoms (see page 190). Zhuge Liang, an adviser to one of those generals, emerged as the hero of the hour, for with his help General Liu Bei founded Shu Han, the kingdom around which present-day Sichuan is based. Transmuted into legend by the 14th-century historical novel, *Romance of the Three Kingdoms*, Zhuge Liang was endowed with such prowess that his name became a byword for great wisdom and cunning. The white turban is worn in mourning for this hero—or so the story goes.

On the crest of the hill, **Qiqu Temple** nestles amidst ancient cypresses. Its decaying halls were first built in the Yuan Dynasty (1279–1368) and added to later. According to historical records an extensive forest of cypresses was planted on the hill by order of a third-century emperor. A huge number were lost to the hunger for timber; and later generations probably found the wood oil tree (also known as the tung tree), and the endlessly versatile bamboo, more commercially worthwhile. Copses of these line the road as it descends. Wood oil, extracted from seeds, was a valuable export from Sichuan until the 1940s. Its most widespread use was in the caulking of boats. Of the bamboo, the Jesuit missionary and translator of Matteo Ricci's journals, Nicolas Trigault, wrote in 1615: 'The Chinese use it for pillars, shafts of lances, and for 600 other domestic purposes.' This is scarcely less true today. Most attractively fashioned into the teahouse chairs seen all over Sichuan, bamboo is also spliced for waterpipes, lashed together as rafts, woven into mats, plaited into rope, and the tender tips of its shoots are edible.

If you hit any village on market day, prepare to slow your pace as you weave between the mounds of produce on sale. All around is a sea of blue and khaki tunics, white turbans, red capsicums, straw baskets, pink radishes and every shade of green from the pale lime of blanched chives to the milky jade of *qingsun*, a tuber eaten both raw and cooked. Market day is the highlight of the week; in all likelihood many of the villagers have come with nothing more than a bag of chillies each, and buy little else besides a pair of shoelaces or a new thermos flask. But perhaps, between sips of tea, one or two of them can catch up on a bit of local gossip, while another concludes arrangements for a marriage in the family. You know you have come upon a wedding by the red cloth and silk rosettes which custom requires to be draped across the portal of the nuptial home.

The county town of **Jiange** is 87 kilometres (54 miles) from Zitong. From Jiange to Sword Pass it is a further 30 kilometres (19 miles). This short stretch, shaded by the funereal foliage of more cypresses, was so important for defensive purposes that at one time courier posts were established at intervals along it to expedite the transmission of despatches.

The sheer brown walls of **Sword Pass** (Jianmen Guan), bare of grass and scrub except on the summit and lower slopes, rear themselves up above the road like gaunt sentinels. Although the pass was widened in 1936 to enable the Sichuan–Shaanxi highway to be pushed through, it still retains a strong sense of lofty impregnability. For a small entrance fee, payable at a concrete shack by the road, visitors may make the vertiginous ascent up the right-hand cliff. The stone staircase then drops sharply down to the rocky bed of a little stream. In a grassy hollow beside the water's edge, the tangle of wild flowers in summer makes a startling contrast to the rugged backdrop of the surrounding hills.

These hills still harbour some half-forgotten relics of battles fought long ago. Among them is the grave of Jiang Wei, a Shu Han general who held Sword Pass against the 100,000 crack troops of the rival kingdom of Wei (see page 190). Not far distant, there is apparently a tablet erected in memory of the communist Red Army's capture of this strategic defile. But nothing marks the path taken by Zhuge Liang and the army of Shu Han, nor the invasion by the forces of Qin, sweeping down from their Shaanxi base to claim the southwestern hinterland for the empire. Yet they must have come this way, their pennants drooping in the billowing dust as they hacked a trail across the narrow pass.

We learn from another famous poem, 'The Song of Eternal Sorrow' by Bai Juyi (772–846), that the Tang emperor Minhuang also came along the difficult road to Shu. The poet tells us that Minhuang, fleeing from rebels in 756, retreated to Sichuan through Sword Pass. He would have done so by a *zhandao*, a twisting plank footbridge laid across the facade of the cliff. (The holes for inserting supports for such pathways pierce the many precipices of Sichuan still, as can be seen along the gorges of the Yangzi, for example.) A somewhat elaborate version of a *zhandao*, complete with balustrade, is depicted for us by an anonymous artist in a richly detailed landscape painting, 'The Emperor Minhuang's Journey to Shu', now in the collection of the National Palace Museum in Taiwan. The picture is dominated by the convoluted silhouettes of mist-wreathed mountains, their jagged outlines broken by dark-foliaged trees (could they be cypresses?). On the right, the emperor and his retinue of mounted guards have emerged from the pass and are approaching a bridge. After resting themselves and their horses, they ascend the mountains to the left, picking their way along the *zhandao* that clings to the slopes. This beautiful scroll is believed to be a Song copy of a ninth-century original. As for Minhuang, who nearly lost his empire for the love of a favourite concubine—Yang Guifei— Sichuan proved a temporary refuge, for his throne was restored to him. He returned to the capital a broken man, though, haunted by his irrevocable loss on the road to Shu, where Yang Guifei was killed in front of the horses of his mutinous guards.

Guangyuan, 57 kilometres (35 miles) from Sword Pass, is the last city before Sichuan dwindles to a stop at the frontier with Shaanxi Province. It is a grey, bustling centre sliced in two by a railway line. Hugging the north bank of the Jialing River is another railway, the Chengdu–Baoji line to Xi'an and beyond. West of its tracks, the halls of **Huangze Si** (Imperial Beneficence Temple) sit recessed in a low hill. The imperial connection derives from Wu Zetian (625–705), the only woman sovereign in Chinese history. She was born in Guangyuan, became a junior concubine at court, and eventually usurped the throne from her own son. There is a stone statue of the empress in the temple, with a face so impassive that not a hint of her murderous career is detectable. Of far more interest is the 'forest of steles', a collection of inscribed stone tablets which record the establishment of three soviets at Guangyuan by the Fourth Front Red Army in 1933–5. Pavilion follows pavilion up the hillside. One of them is a hotel, the Empress Mountain Villa, but it is not recommended for prospective guests burdened with heavy luggage.

On the opposite bank of the river, the road leading out of Guangyuan takes you past the **Thousand Buddha Cave** carvings, one of which, a now headless Sakyamuni sleeping under a tree, greets you as you arrive. The cliff is honeycombed with some 400 niches, these being filled with more than 7,000 figures, all that remain of the original 17,000 which made this site a Mecca equal to Dazu (see page 161). Over half were destroyed in the course of constructing the Sichuan–Shaanxi highway in 1936. Pilgrims would have found the whole group of greater artistic interest than Dazu, including as it did a variety of sculptural styles spanning an extensive period from the Northern Wei (fourth to sixth century) to the Qing Dynasty (1644–1911). There is little Northern Wei sculpture left; some of the Tang pieces, the secular female figures in contemporary dress in particular, are worth a look.

Jiuzhaigou: Nine Stockade Gully

Northeast of Guangyuan the road to Gansu Province follows a Jialing tributary and cuts through a valley with pitched green slopes on one side and the churning brown river on the other. Landslides are a common occurence along this dramatic, gorge-

Waterfall at Jiuzhaigou

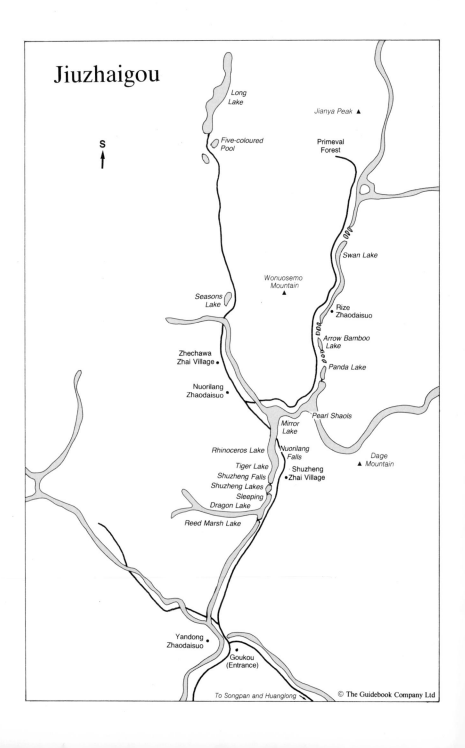

Jiuzhaigou

S
↑

Long Lake

Five-coloured Pool

Jianya Peak ▲

Primeval Forest

Swan Lake

Wonuosemo Mountain ▲

Seasons Lake

Rize Zhaodaisuo

Arrow Bamboo Lake

Zhechawa Zhai Village •

Panda Lake

Nuorilang Zhaodaisuo •

Pearl Shaols

Mirror Lake

Rhinoceros Lake

Nuorilang Falls

Dage Mountain ▲

Tiger Lake

Shuzheng Falls

Shuzheng Zhai Village

Shuzheng Lakes

Sleeping Dragon Lake

Reed Marsh Lake

Yandong Zhaodaisuo •

Goukou (Entrance) •

To Songpan and Huanglong

© The Guidebook Company Ltd

like stretch. After Shazhou the road slices through a southern projection of Gansu, re-enters Sichuan at Shuanghegou, wends northwestwards to **Nanping** and finally traces an arc up to Jiuzhaigou, our next destination. Just before Nanping, a temple perched incredibly like an eagle's eyrie on the summit of a bluff comes into view.

This is an unusual approach to Jiuzhaigou. For most travellers the standard route is from Chengdu (see page 100).

Jiuzhaigou is a nature reserve speckled with crystalline lakes, foaming waterfalls and Tibetan hamlets. It covers an area of 720 square kilometres (278 square miles) spread over a broad Y-shaped ravine about 30 kilometres (18.6 miles) long. Being in a high valley at elevations of 2,000 to 3,100 metres (6,500 to 10,000 feet), the reserve is filled with flora of a richness which has long excited botanists. The scenery is stunning.

Before the violent deformation of the earth's crust some 40 to 50 million years ago, when a collision of the Indian subcontinent with the rest of south Asia caused a massive crinkling along the line of what is now the Himalaya, much of south China lay under an ocean. The collision lifted the ocean bed and created mountain ranges which ramified as far as western Sichuan. One result of these upheavals, as well as of subsequent geological changes, was the necklace of alpine lakes which, perhaps more than any other feature, is the glory of Jiuzhaigou.

Tinted turquoise, blue, purple, emerald and amber by their mineral content, the waters of these lakes defy description. Tibetans call the lakes *haizi*, literally 'sea', but they vary in size from the 66 hectares (163 acres) of Long Lake to only 20th of a hectare (598 square yards). Some of the small ones are spanned by a narrow plank bridge, others are so shallow that small plants sprouting from driftwood lying on their beds trace a delicate pattern of green across their rippling surfaces. All of them are fringed by shrubs and trees rising in layers up the slopes of snow-domed mountains. There is no definitive explanation of how the lakes came to be formed. While most geologists agree that they are barrier lakes created by dikes of calcium carbonate deposited on the flotsam brought down by mountain streams, a minority view holds that they are glacial or corrosion lakes, such as would be found in limestone areas.

Tibetan lore has it that these lakes were the panes of broken glass from Goddess Wonuosemo's mirror. It happened this way: long, long ago, Jiuzhaigou was visited by such calamities that the mountains collapsed, the trees and flowers withered, and its inhabitants fled. Alighting upon this scene of devastation, the goddess Wonuosemo decided to restore the valley to its former beauty. Dage, a handsome god, had the same idea, and from their respective mountain abodes they accomplished the miracle. Rivers flowed again, forests sprang up, birds returned to nest, and previously abandoned villages filled up with people. It was inevitable that Wonuosemo and

Dage should meet, fall in love and live ever after in celestial bliss, but not until they had foiled a vicious demon who tried to separate them. United at last, the lovers pledged their affection with an exchange of gifts. Wonuosemo wove and embroidered for her swain a white woollen coat. Dage ground and polished a bright, gleaming mirror with which he hoped to show to his sweetheart her perfect loveliness. In her delight, though, she loosened her grasp, and the mirror slipped from her hand. They searched the gully, but the mirror was not to be found. Instead they kept coming across luminous pools of water, throwing back at them the mirror-images of trees, mountains and clouds. All at once they understood, and so the 108 fragments of Wonuosemo's splintered looking-glass have remained at Jiuzhaigou ever since.

Entering Jiuzhaigou, you follow a limpid stream which, by early summer, is trickling with snowmelt from the Minshan range. Behind the wooded foothills and cultivated banks the snow on the distant peaks to the left glistens a dazzling white. With the arrival of warmer temperatures the rhododendrons for which Jiuzhaigou is famous begin to bloom. Clusters of white, yellow, pink and lilac flowers dapple the hillsides from late June. The naturalist E H Wilson, who made four plant-hunting expeditions to China in the early 1900s (see page 99), had this to say about rhododendrons: '. . . in Western China, [they] are a special feature. The genus is the largest recorded from China, no fewer than 160 species being known . . . Rhododendrons commence at sea-level, but do not become really abundant until 8,000 feet is reached. They extend up to the limits of ligneous vegetation (c. 15,000 feet). These plants are gregarious in habit and nearly every species has a well-defined altitudinal limit. In size they vary from alpine plants only a few inches high to trees 40 feet and more tall . . . no finer sight can possibly be imagined than mile upon mile of mountain-side covered with rhododendrons in full flower.'

Beside the magnificent rhododendrons the flowers of other shrubs and plants appear less showy; there is, nevertheless, an astonishing variety of them: the common rose, weigela, clematis, mock orange, cotoneaster, honeysuckle, wild ginger and violet and many more.

With a change of seasons Jiuzhaigou shows another face as the ravishing autumnal hues of the maple and the common smoketree clothe its lower slopes. Golden larch, oak, poplar, and birch also abound, while at higher altitudes forests of spruce, fir, pine and weeping cypress loom darkly over the flame-coloured leaves. The layered zones of vegetation are quite distinct.

Jiuzhaigou is named for the nine Tibetan settlements in the mountain valley. Around them will be found the sacred symbols of Tibetan Buddhism. These may be cairns of *mani* stones inscribed with the mantra 'Om mani padme hum', or a *chorten*, a white or ochre-painted cone surmounted by a tapering spire and standing on a square pedestal. Most ubiquitous are prayer flags—long strips of printed cloth hoist-

Five-coloured Pool, Jiuzhaigou

ed on poles—wafting mantras to heaven. The passage of time has turned many of them into tattered rags. Around the larger settlements, at Zechawa Zhai and Shuzheng Zhai for instance, inhabitants have constructed several Tibetan-style hostelries to welcome tourists to Jiuzhaigou. Built of stone and wood with fretted ornamentation, they are pleasing to the eye. These inns provide meals too: hearty helpings of Chinese dishes washed down with, if you wish, yak butter tea.

Goukou Entrance to Nuorilang

As one would expect, **Goukou** is where lodgings, souvenir stores, ticket office (entrance fee Rmb 20 at the time of writing), tourist information and car park are to be found. From here buses run three times a day in peak tourist season to Nuorilang, at 9 am, 1 pm and 4.30 pm, and, in the other direction, at 10.30 am, 2.30 pm and 6.30 pm. This timetable is to be interpreted loosely, though, as the buses tend to leave as soon as they are full. Nuorilang, being at the point where the valley forks, is the most convenient place to stay within the reserve. It is also, of course, the least tranquil.

The hostel complex at **Nuorilang Zhaodaisuo** consists of barrack-like blocks of double or triple rooms grouped around some buildings from which services such as registration, meals, hot water, and tourist information are dispensed. Some of the rooms have been hooked up to a system of running water and individual bathrooms. One of the reception halls resounds to the beat of dance music after dinner; anyone can join in for the price of an entrance ticket (Rmb 3). Some of the young Tibetans from the villages come in all their colourful finery.

If you can afford the time to walk, spend three to four hours covering the distance (14 kilometres or 8.7 miles) from Goukou to Nuorilang, passing **Reed Marsh Lake** (Luwei Hai), the first *haizi* and home to many waterfowl; **Sleeping Dragon Lake** (Wolong Hai); the group of lakes and waterfalls at **Shuzheng**; **Rhinoceros Lake** (Xiniu Hai) and **Nuorilang Falls**. Strictly speaking, Sleeping Dragon Lake is part of the Shuzheng Lake complex. Just breaking the surface of its waters is a pale yellow embankment, to which local people point as the relic of a legendary evil dragon, forever imprisoned in the lake after being soundly defeated by Dage. At Shuzheng, rushing water swirls between clumps of mosses and splashes down a series of natural dikes to spill in cascades down to willow-bordered pools. Rotated by the flow, Tibetan prayer wheels spin an endless stream of invocations to the mountain tops. There is a village across the road, from which **Shuzheng Falls**, the longest drop here at 20 metres or so (66 feet), can be seen. Further on, Rhinoceros Lake has been made into a recreation area: you may swim or paddle a canoe here, overlooked by **Wonuosemo Mountain** to the north.

Nuorilang Falls plunges 30 metres (nearly 100 feet), its drop broken here and there by jutting rock. This cataract is aptly named, for 'Nuorilang' is Tibetan for 'magnificent'.

Nuorilang to Rizegou

Bus services on this stretch leave at 8 am and 2.30 pm, returning at noon and 5 pm. To walk the entire length (17 kilometres or 10.6 miles) with stops on the way allow five hours.

The road runs alongside a string of lakes. Pandas used to roam here, as attested by the names of two **lakes—Panda** (Xiongmao Hai) and **Arrow Bamboo** (Jianzhu Hai). Human encroachment has made Jiuzhaigou untenable as a panda reserve (the local population of these animals was estimated to have declined to less than ten by 1987). North of Arrow Bamboo Lake the **Rize Zhaodaisuo** offers basic accommodation and a restaurant. From the hostel one daily bus service makes the round trip to the primeval forest at 9 am, returning at 11 am, provided that there are enough passengers to justify it. Otherwise local tours seldom go beyond this point, and for this reason the far uplands of Rizegou, more than 3,000 metres (10,000 feet) above sea level, are ideal for quiet communion with nature. Some ten kilometres (six miles) from the hostel the long narrow **Swan Lake** (Tian'e Hai) is tucked away between steep cliffs, and only the wild ducks weaving among its luxuriant growth of reeds disturb its secluded splendour. The road ends at a **primeval forest**, behind which hulks the lone peak of **Jianya**.

The biggest draw along Nuorilang–Rizegou, though, is **Pearl Shoals** (Zhenzhu Tan), an extraordinary stepped slope across which a torrent rushes in eddies and rapids before tipping over down the largest waterfall at Jiuzhaigou. It is the spray, or perhaps the bubbles, which are said to resemble pearls. Be that as it may, the water is icy, but some enterprising villagers have outsize rubber boots for hire, so wading through the flooded expanse is fun rather than numbing. At your feet the floor of moss makes for a slippery progress. Embedded in the shallower spots, hardy water plants, some of them threaded with flowers, struggle for possession against the current. Alongside the shoals, a stepped pathway descends through dense vegetation to the bottom of the falls; from below the view of the vertical sheets of frothing spume, cross-cut with the ridge lines of deep blue mountains on the horizon, is magical.

NUORILANG TO LONG LAKE

About 18 kilometres (11 miles) long, the western branch of Jiuzhaigou has the valley's largest and smallest lakes. An irregular bus serves the route but, again, it will operate only if there is demand.

Zechawa Zhai, bedecked with prayer flags like all villages in the valley, makes a convenient base for a hike up to Long Lake (Chang Hai) at the terminus of the road. Visitors may stay here, or have a meal. There is nowhere else offering such facilities beyond Zechawa, so hikers should carry food and drink and allow plenty of time to return to base.

Nestled in a glade of birches and firs, the **Five-coloured Pool** (Wucai Chi) appears as a sheet of turquoise glass from the road above. Its water at different depths covers a colour spectrum from pale blue through aquamarine to emerald green. Geologists may attribute the phenomenon to mineral concentration, but local lore claims that the pool is tinted in such beautiful shades because Wonuosemo washes her face in it.

Long Lake, 3,100 metres (9,840 feet) above the sea, offers another perspective. The eye is irresistibly drawn across its calm blue expanse towards the snow-flecked peaks that mark the limit of the view, and then back again to the dark triangular reflections of the nearer hills. On the bank, an oddly shaped cypress with sparse horizontal branches growing only on the right side of its trunk poses an interesting counterpoint to the immensity of those distant mountains. The tree, too, has a story to tell. In Long Lake there used to dwell a black dragon whose depredations upon the land and its inhabitants caused great misery. One day a kind-hearted hunter set forth to kill it. In the struggle which ensued, the dragon bit off the hunter's left arm. Wonuosemo intervened in the nick of time, before he lost another limb, but more

TRAVELLERS IN A BOTANICAL PARADISE
Plant-hunting in Sichuan

Tea roses, peonies, chrysanthemums, azaleas, camellias—flowers familiar in European and American gardens—were unknown outside the Far East until introduced from China by plant collectors in the 18th and 19th centuries. The first European plant collectors were missionaries and merchants, notably officers in the service of the British trading concern, the East India Company. As foreign commerce in China was initially confined to the southern port of Canton (Guangzhou), their shipments contained only subtropical plants that were cultivated in local gardens. The situation changed dramatically when, in the second half of the 19th century, as a result of treaties terminating a series of wars, other ports in China were opened to foreign commerce and residence. Subjects of the European treaty powers were then allowed to travel to the interior. Many sailed up the Yangzi River to Chongqing. From there they penetrated western Sichuan, northwest Yunnan and beyond. A vast temperate region with a wealth of wild flora unequalled anywhere else in the world lay before them. That region became the hunting ground of botanists.

Sichuan particularly compelled botanic exploration because of its highly diverse topography. Between its basin and its peaks, the province presented vertically demarcated zones of vegetation from the cultivated crops of warm, wet farmlands to the myriad varieties of herbs and flowers of alpine meadows. Much of it was virgin territory undefiled by the hand of man. Primitive communications meant, though, that plant-collectors faced near-insuperable obstacles in reaching the most rewarding areas. They walked enormous distances or, at best, bumped along in a bamboo chair, known as *huagan*, borne on the shoulders of coolies. At night they either camped or slept in stinking shacks, sharing them with cattle. Bad weather could set all their efforts at nought, for unless kept clean and dry, specimens could be easily destroyed by mould. Sometimes they found themselves fording raging torrents, hacking through impenetrable forests, plodding up jagged mountains, and even being set upon by bandits and hostile tribesmen.

They rose to the challenge. Some of them had the opportunity anyway, being stationed on the spot as consular officials or missionaries; others were specialists in natural history who made the long journey and stayed at least a whole season so that they might gather seeds for planting at home. They are remembered through the plants that bear their names. Augustine Henry (1856–1930), a medical officer with the Chinese Maritime Customs in Yichang on the Yangzi, took to plant-collecting out of boredom with expatriate life. During periods of leave he wandered in Hubei and Sichuan, sending the herbarium material and seeds gathered with the help of Chinese assistants to the Royal Botanic Gardens at Kew in London. Towards the end of his tenure in China Dr Henry was posted to Yunnan, another province rich in flora. He was instrumental in introducing such garden plants as *Rhododendron Augustinii* and *Viburnum Henryi*. He also reported sighting the dove tree, an ancient plant growing wild only in China.

At that time the French Catholic missionary effort was gaining a foothold in western China. Dedicated priests of the Mission Etrangères spent long lonely years in the interior, hardly ever seeing another European. Père Jean Pierre Armand David (1826–1900) was an assiduous botanist and zoologist. During a two-year expedition from Chongqing through Chengdu to Sichuan's northwestern corner, he found his first specimen of the dove tree, growing at an altitude of 1,830 metres (6,000 feet). It was subsequently named after him—*Davidia involucrata*. This tree, besides being rare, is exceptionally ornamental. Two large pure white bracts sprout under each tightly-packed flower-head, so that, when in bloom, a tree conjures the illusion that a flock of doves with outstretched wings has alighted on its branches. David did not stay long enough in the area to collect any seeds; that was left to E H Wilson, the most outstanding plant-hunter of western China.

Jean André Soulié (1858–1905) was another missionary. From his base in Kangding (or Tachienlu as the town was designated in early European travelogues) this plant-collector sent to the Museum of Botany in Paris a prolific harvest including *Primula Souliéi* and *Buddleia variabilis*. Later he went farther afield towards Tibet, and it was near the frontier, at Batang, that he was captured and shot by Tibetan monks in 1905.

Although better known for his studies of the Naxi tribe in western Yunnan, Joseph F Rock (1884–1962) also travelled extensively in the Sichuan borderlands and introduced innumerable plant species to the Western world. An Austrian born in Vienna, he went to the United States in 1905

(*continued*)

and later proceeded to Honolulu where, in between teaching Latin and natural history at a school, he made himself an expert on the flora of the Hawaiian islands. His first expedition to China, in 1922, was under the auspices of the US Department of Agriculture. Not only did he collect plants; the bird life and the peoples of western China also fascinated him. Before long his insatiable curiosity had taken him into regions hitherto unexplored by foreigners—the corners of Sichuan, Yunnan, Gansu and Qinghai provinces inhabited by Tibetans. In time Rock's activities in botany were displaced by an interest in ethnological research. He never published anything on Chinese flora, but he did leave an invaluable written and photographic record of the minority peoples among whom he lived.

Rhododendrons, which grow best on high ground,
cover the hillsides of Sichuan from late May

Such was the European rage for new exotic species that the field covered by amateur botanists was soon invaded by professional collectors, thanks to their sponsorship by private nurseries, botanical gardens and institutions like the Horticultural Society of London. Ernest Henry Wilson (1876–1930) was both by training and temperament the epitome of the meticulous plant-collector. In 11 years of travelling in central and western China he sent to England and America a botanical and horticultural cornucopia comprising 65,000 specimens of some 5,000 species and the seeds of about 1,500 different plants.

Wilson, born in the English county of Gloucestershire, left school very young and became an apprentice in a nursery garden. Later he attended botany classes at a technical college in Birmingham. His bent for botany was recognized by the Director of Kew Gardens, and it was while Wilson was there that his name was put forward to the nursery firm of James Veitch & Sons to go to China on their behalf. Besides a general brief to search for plants to introduce into English gardens, his main quest was to be, quite specifically, the elusive dove tree.

On his first expedition (1899–1901) Wilson travelled by way of the United States, where he called on Professor C S Sargent at the Arnold Arboretum in Boston. In China he made a detour to consult Augustine Henry in Yunnan, and then embarked upon a thorough survey of the mountains and valleys along the Hubei–Sichuan border, which indeed yielded not only *Davidia involucrata* but a veritable bounty of seeds, herbarium material, bulbs and roots.

Wilson made four journeys to China altogether. During his second sojourn the patch he made uniquely his own was Sichuan. He covered an enormous area, from present-day Leshan to the far northwest, going twice to Songpan. He also made a thorough investigation of the flora on Emei Shan.

In 1907 he was again in Hubei and Sichuan, this time for the Arnold Arboretum, concentrating on woody plants. It was on his last visit to China that he made his greatest discovery—the Regal Lily. His description of the flower reveals nothing of the excitement he must have felt on finding it, yet it is typical of his factual style: 'In the Min Valley the charming *Lilium regale* luxuriates in rocky crevices, sun-baked throughout the greater part of the year. It grows 3 to 5 feet tall, and has slender leaves crowded on stems bearing several large funnel-shaped flowers, red-purple without, ivory-white suffused with canary-yellow within, often with the red-purple reflected through, and is deliciously fragrant.'

than that, she gave him a powerful sword, and this he wielded for seven days and seven nights, finally succeeding in severing the dragon's tail and claw. The wounded beast retreated to the depths of the lake; lest it should reappear, the hunter, with his sword raised in readiness, has stood perennial guard ever since.

GETTING TO JIUZHAIGOU

An excursion to Jiuzhaigou can be contemplated only between late March and October, when the area is not sealed off by snow. During the rainy season, too, it is essential to check with CITS (see page 32) or other travel agencies beforehand, since flooding and landslides could make access roads impassable. Jiuzhaigou receives most rain between June and August.

Only about a third of the 480-kilometre (300-mile) journey from Chengdu is on a tarmacked road, and car tyres take a terrible hammering on the rest of the route. In view of the poor condition of parts of the road, travellers are advised to set aside five days for the journey there and back, excluding time spent in the nature reserve. Those who take in Huanglong as well (see below) should allow another two days. Be prepared for a heart-stopping drive on dirt switchbacks snaking up steep mountains, for sudden descents of thick mists on high passes, for breakdowns and delays, for altitude sickness. But you will also glimpse some of the most spectacular scenery in China, such as rarely encountered in the lowlands.

There are several ways to go to Jiuzhaigou from Chengdu. If you wish to go under your own steam rather than join a tour, the most convenient form of transport is by the direct buses which ply regularly between the destinations during the peak tourist season.

VIA NANPING

Direct 'soft seat' tour buses run from late spring to autumn from Chengdu's Ximen bus terminus to Nanping, with an overnight stop on the way (usually Maowen), reaching Jiuzhaigou on the evening of the following day. Buses leave early in the morning, and tickets should be bought in advance. There are regular scheduled buses to Nanping as well, but these are more crowded and involve changes en route. Minibuses make the transfer from Jiuzhaigou to Huanglong (see below) during the summer months. Otherwise you need to go to Songpan and pick up another bus (inquire at the Foreign Affairs section, Songpan County Government Office).

VIA HUANGLONG

The Aba Autonomous Prefecture administers a fleet of minibuses which cover the Chengdu–Huanglong–Jiuzhaigou run. They vary in size, the smallest being 11-seaters. From the Ximen bus station in Chengdu it takes only one day to reach Songpan, around 300 kilometres (186 miles) away. Stopping overnight in Songpan, the bus leaves early the next morning for Jiuzhaigou, arriving at Goukou sometime after midday. The route involves crossing over a pass 4,100 metres (13,500 feet) above sea level. Alternatively, at Songpan you can arrange to visit Huanglong first, and from there—if time and transport availability permit—go on to Jiuzhaigou.

VIA JIANGYOU

From Chengdu take the train to **Zhongba** station in **Jiangyou County** (the station is on the Chengdu–Baoji line). Thereafter transfer to a long-distance bus to **Pingwu**. Several buses a day cover the 135-kilometre (84-mile) distance. Overnight in Pingwu. Next day resume by bus for another 108 kilometres (67 miles) to Nanping. From Nanping connect with one of several regular buses to Jiuzhaigou.

Once arrived at your destination, it is advisable to buy your return or onward ticket straight away. They are usually sold up to three days in advance.

TOURS

Six-day, seven-day and eight-day tours to Jiuzhaigou and Huanglong are organized by several travel agents in Chengdu. Prices and standards vary considerably. It is worth checking out a few packages (they may or may not include accommodation and meals en route) and comparing them with anything that CITS or CTS offers. As the Jinjiang Hotel in Chengdu is packed with travel companies, getting information there is a simple matter. It is also worth dropping in on the kiosks at Beizhan (see page 21).

LAND CRUISER OR JEEP HIRE

Arranging your own transport through a Chengdu travel agent will cost around Rmb 600–700 a day. The package comes with a driver and a guide.

Huanglong Si: Yellow Dragon Temple

This scenic valley was designated a nature reserve in 1983. To visit it, you must pay an entrance fee (Rmb 15 in early 1992). 'Huanglong' means Yellow Dragon, and there are several stories of how the area came to be thus named. One of them tells of a Buddhist monk called Huanglong whose saintly acts included rendering a great service to **Yu**, founder of the mythical Xia Dynasty (see also page 184). In Chinese tradition the Xia Dynasty is supposed to have reigned for several centuries in the prehistorical period. Its most illustrious ruler, Yu, tamed the flood that had devastated the lowlands of central and southern China. Indeed there are few rivers or waterways in the country with which Yu is not associated by way of legends or myths. With the monk's help Yu was able to create the channel of the Min River (Minjiang), directing its course past Maowen and southwards down to the Yangzi. Eventually the monk became an immortal, and it was to his memory that later generations erected Huanglong Temple (Huanglong Si).

Another version of the origin of Huanglong simply represents the whole site as the incarnation of a yellow dragon, its head thrust into the snowy crags, its scaly body transformed into overlapping tiers of flashing, silvery pools, and its coiled tail turned into the Fu River that flows along the bottom of the valley. Formerly temples stood where the tail, the back and the head were said to be. The first of these, the so-called Front Temple of Huanglong, was northeast of the **Fuyuan Bridge**, not far from the entrance to the reserve. It no longer exists.

Once the valley lay under a glacier. Since time immemorial carbonate-saturated snowmelt and spring water, gushing through cracks in the stone, has tumbled down the gently descending slope, leaving in its wake a fantastic karst terrain of pale honey-coloured ledges punctuated by pools and waterfalls. Karst formations occur where slightly acidic water, in which carbonate easily dissolves, runs over limestone rock and deposits its sediment of yellow-white calcium carbonate. In most karst areas, the strange topography is characterized by caves and underground streams. It is only infrequently found above ground, as it is here at Huanglong.

The banks on either side are thickly wooded. There are profuse stands of spruce, fir and pine as well as birch, the most common broadleaved species at Huanglong. Like Jiuzhaigou, the area is rich in alpine flora. To the east, **Xuebaoding**, the main **peak** of the Minshan range, towers 5,588 metres (18,440 feet).

Dense forests, both around Huanglong and Jiuzhaigou, provide cover for a variety of wildlife. Rare fauna under protection include the giant and lesser panda, golden-haired monkey, takin, musk deer, Temminck's tragopan, Tibetan-eared pheasant and Chinese monal.

The high valley of Huanglong stretches for about nine kilometres (just over five and a half miles). There is a plank footbridge up the slope, linked by little pavilions where the hiker might want to linger to admire a particularly beautiful view, or merely to rest. Beneath the footbridge, tiny streams slither over rocks and mosses, sending a light, cool spray into the shaded undergrowth. It should take no more than four hours to trek up to the valley head and back, although it is as well to remember that the air is a little thin here, and to regulate the pace so as to avoid getting short of breath.

Here and there mineral- and algae-laden water has collected in shallow stepped pools. By some play of light they seem suffused with colour, as if actually dyed in

Limestone pool at Huanglong Si

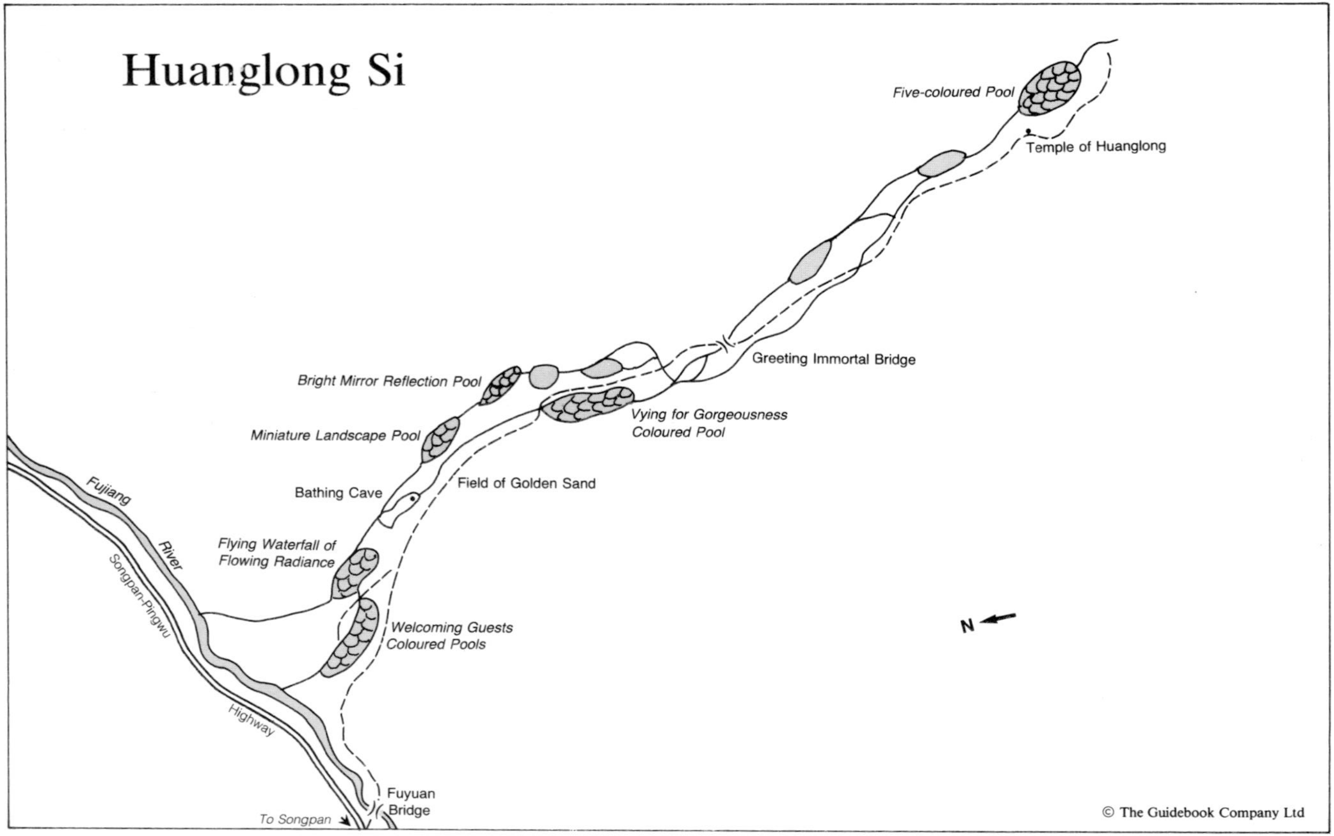
Huanglong Si
Five-coloured Pool
Temple of Huanglong
Greeting Immortal Bridge
Bright Mirror Reflection Pool
Vying for Gorgeousness
Coloured Pool
Miniature Landscape Pool
Bathing Cave
Field of Golden Sand
Flying Waterfall of
Flowing Radiance
Welcoming Guests
Coloured Pools
Fujiang
River
Songpan-Pingwu
Highway
To Songpan
Fuyuan
Bridge
N
© The Guidebook Company Ltd

pigments of green, blue and orange. Over the years deposits of lime have built up low crescent-shaped barriers and coated the fallen twigs strewn across the milky yellow beds. The first cluster of pools, named **Welcoming Guests Coloured Pools** (Yingbin Caichi), is fed by the **Flying Waterfall of Flowing Radiance** (Feipu Liuhui) some ten metres (33 feet) above. Higher up to the right the small **Bathing Cave** (Xishen Dong) hides behind yet another waterfall. Magic attaches to the cave as surely as gods are believed to inhabit the mountains nearby. Tradition has it that Huanglong the monk bathed in it before his transformation into a celestial being. It was also said that for ordinary mortals, a wash here will not only cure all sorts of diseases, but also restore fertility to barren women.

The **Bathing Cave Waterfall** is the overflow from an extraordinary stretch of limestone strata, the **Field of Golden Sand** (Jinsha Pudi). If the entire valley is a yellow dragon, this is the dragon's back. The rounded protuberances of lime-encrusted rock have also been likened to a dragon's scales. For part of the year the amber-coloured staircase is dry, and even in late spring drifts of snow cling here and there, concealing the hollows in the lumpy, contorted terrain. Waterfalls are frozen stalactites of ice. Then, when the thaw finally comes in summer, they turn into rippling curtains of spray, the pools fill and the whole area awakes in a riot of colour.

Zigzagging up the slope are more pools in clusters: the **Miniature Landscape Pool** (Penjing Chi), the **Vying for Gorgeousness Coloured Pool** (Zhengyan Caichi) and **Bright Mirror Reflection Pool** (Mingjing Daoying Chi) among them. Over the **Greeting Immortal Bridge** (Jiexian Qiao), treading where Huanglong the monk once passed, you arrive at the site of the Midway Temple of Huanglong. Of the original five buildings put up in the Ming Dynasty (1368–1644), only ruins remain. Alongside, the **Jade Coloured Pool** (Yucui Caichi) is a corrugated sheet of translucent green.

The **Back Temple of Huanglong** had fallen on hard times, particularly during the Cultural Revolution (1966–76), and what was left after wanton destruction was finished off by neglect. It has since been restored. Now, for three days every year from the 15th day of the sixth lunar month (roughly between July and August), it becomes the venue for a temple fair. Crowds of Tibetans, people of the Qiang nationality and of course Han (ethnic) Chinese come then to camp around its modest premises for a spot of worship and fun. Their revels include singing, dancing and, at the end of the fair, a horse-race in Songpan before returning to their homes.

The temple itself is chiefly remarkable for its setting. It stands at an altitude of 3,588 metres (11,768 feet). Behind the roof-line of its second storey, mountain peaks enclose a glorious view to the south. A statue of the eponymous monk is found inside the main hall.

Nearby, **Five-coloured Pool** (Wucai Chi), made up of some 400 lesser pools, marks the valley head. Arguably Huanglong's most spectacular pool, it makes a suitable climax to the uphill trek. Under the right conditions, the mineral-rich water glows in hues of creamy white, silvery grey, amber, pink and blue. Sunk in its limestone bed are two small pagodas (hence the pool's earlier name, Stone Pagodas Guarding the Sea or Shita Zhenhai). They reputedly stand over the graves of Cheng Sichang, grandson of a famous Tang-dynasty general, and of his wife.

Although most visitors stay in Songpan, 55 kilometres (34 miles) away, it is possible, and certainly more exciting, to spend the night in Huanglong. Foreigners are required to fill in a registration form of temporary residence. To the right of the entrance a hostel (the Se'ercuo Zhai Guesthouse) run by the Huanglong Scenic Site Administration Office offers basic accommodation. It has double and triple bedrooms at an extremely modest price. However, it has no washing facilities apart from an enamel washbowl and a flask of hot water, and communal toilets are housed in a shed across the dirt road. It does boast a wonderful dining room, though. Furnished with round tables and stools, this separate restaurant is a rafterred structure of painted wood with a gallery around the sides. A new Tibetan-style hotel stands behind it.

GETTING TO HUANGLONG
Much of the transport information given for Jiuzhaigou applies (see page 100). Huanglong and Jiuzhaigou both feature on tours from Chengdu organized by various travel agencies in the summer months. Direct public buses also run to Songpan from Chengdu.

Visitors to Huanglong may suffer from mountain or altitude sickness (see page 34). Symptoms such as a headache and nausea will dissipate on return to lower altitudes; meanwhile aspirins and rest should ease the discomfort slightly.

Over the Pass: Jiuzhaigou to Huanglong

For all the picturesque scenery of Huanglong and Jiuzhaigou, the best part of the journey actually lies in between. To reach one from the other it is necessary to drive along a dirt road winding zigzag up a precipitous escarpment until it goes over a col 4,100 metres (13,450 feet) above sea level. It is all but single-track, a narrow, boulder-strewn passage of shale and loose grit cut out of the mountain-side. Bedevilled by erosion and landslides, it is positively treacherous in heavy rain and snow, and where melting ice trickles across its course, the track virtually disappears in a mass of slush and mud.

Before the pass is reached, the road from Jiuzhaigou to Huanglong enters a wide highland valley. It is a green-brown amphitheatre of scrubland, empty and bleak

Fortress-like Tibetan houses with small windows outlined in white paint

except for 'dzos' cropping the twiggy shrubs on the slopes. A dzo is a hybrid breed, offspring of yak and ordinary cattle. Even in summer, the air is cold at this altitude and the valley floor crunches with frost. A line of stunted trees flanks the margins of this desolate moor. Then, ahead, blobs of white appear in the distance. They turn out to be the tents of an isolated encampment of nomadic Tibetans. Pitched way off the road, these white tents are piped in black along the folds, with here and there a flap of peacock blue. One or two of them are further decorated with a pelmet of appliquéd cloth. In their midst, the silence of this remote place is broken by the continuous low chant of '*Om mani padme hum*' ('Praise to the Jewel at the heart of the Lotus'). This devotional murmur rises and falls from the nomads as, at a little distance from the tents, they repeatedly throw themselves full length on the ground, up and down across the stony turf. Everyday Tibetan life is filled with such religious preoccupations, and, like the pilgrims who prostrate themselves outside a lamasery, the worshippers here are quite oblivious of the dirt. A grinning monk, resplendent in his robe of reddish-brown serge with a crumpled magenta sash across the shoulders, does the honours of showing visitors around the encampment. He exudes the pungent smell of yak butter.

There is scant traffic on the road, which affords only transitory glimpses of passing Tibetans—on ponies, in trucks and on foot. Those who are not riding are more often than not twirling prayer wheels in their hands. All of them are arrestingly dressed, with silver amulets hung round their necks and flint-boxes dangling from their waists. The women, especially, are a fine sight. Although their basic garment is a shapeless long black or brown coat lined with sheepskin, it is quite commonly edged with multi-coloured facings and braid round the collar and hem. They sport aprons and sashes of bright green, blue, red or a striped material woven in different colours. Turbans and scarves cover their heads. Underneath, the hair is piled in a thick plait coiled round the crown. A circle of enormous smooth nuggets of opaque amber threaded together with a leather thong might complete the exotic head-dress. Or they ornament their coiffure with crude turquoise and coral beads. Both men and women like to wear their coats off one shoulder, with the sleeve pulled round and tucked into a girdle of twisted fabric in vivid contrasting hues. They are shod in boots of felt and yak-hide.

Some of these travellers are probably making for the Bonpo **Monastery of Gamel** further along. There it sits in the dun-coloured landscape, flaunting its fresh paint, for it has been renovated only recently. Through the gatehouse (at which an entrance donation of a few *jiao* will probably be asked for), the main hall is straight ahead. A three-storey edifice graced by tiled roofs with curled-up eaves, it is entered through a recessed porch glowing with colour from lacquered vermilion pillars, brackets decorated in designs of a distinctly Chinese stamp, and a back wall covered with murals of guardian demons and flowers, painted in crimson, azure blue, orange, gold and green. (The demons originated in Bon beliefs and were later absorbed by Tibetan Buddhism.) In front and to the right, the prayer hall is an equally impressive building. It, too, spans three storeys and its second-floor balcony is draped with a simple *thangka* banner embroidered with a wheel and the geometric endless knot, two of the eight sacred symbols. Above the balcony, on the finials of slanting roofs, are brass emblems polished to gleaming perfection—the *dharma* wheel and a pair of deer among them. Also gleaming are the prayer wheels set shoulder-high all round the ground-level gallery. There are perhaps 30 of these golden embossed cylinders on each side. Worshippers revolve them with their left hands as they walk round the hall.

Going up to the pass, the view is awe-inspiring all the way. As far as the eye can see, ranges deeply shadowed on their flanks and tipped with eternal snow rise up into puffs of clouds hanging just above the serrated peaks. Those clouds, and the mountains too, seem very close at this height. The pass itself, a dark and lonely spot, is swathed in mist. Once over it you drop fairly rapidly down to Huanglong.

Songpan: Hui Town

At the junction of the Huanglong–Songpan roads, near a village called **Yuanba**, a statue raised on top of a hillock reminds passers-by that the Red Army came this way on its historic Long March (see page 143). The statue, of a soldier lifting his rifle, rests on a high plinth emblazoned with a red star. It is the centrepiece of several other revolutionary sculptures, and people actually pay to go into the park where they are placed. Tibetans in the car park outside ply visitors with trinkets.

The town we call Songpan is, strictly speaking, Songzhou, the seat of Songpan County. These distinctions are only important for administrative purposes and most maps use the name 'Songpan' for the town anyway. The County of Songpan is in turn under the jurisdiction the **Aba Tibetan Autonomous Prefecture**, although Muslims, who are known as 'Hui' in China, predominate in its mixed population. Their ancestors probably migrated from Gansu just over the provincial border, where the population includes people of central Asian origin. That is not to say that the Hui around Songpan are ethnically distinguishable from the Han Chinese who make up over 90 per cent of China's total population. Hui are officially classified, though, as a minority, enjoying a certain degree of say in running their own affairs including freedom to practise their faith. In Songpan, as indeed elsewhere in China,

Bon

Indigenous Tibetan Religion

Bon or Bonpo is the name of Tibet's first known religion. It is a shamanist cult, the worship of spirits, gods and demons which are believed to be present everywhere—in valleys and mountains, rivers and springs, rocks and trees. Those harmful spirits need to be propitiated by offerings which included the sacrifice of humans in an earlier age. Bon priests or shamans preside over such rites, being credited with magical powers which enable them to communicate with the spirit world. When, early in its history, Tibet was ruled by kings, they were regarded by followers of Bon as the human incarnation of a deity and therefore divine.

Buddhism was introduced to Tibet in the seventh century during the reign of the 33rd king, Songtsen Gampo, two of whose consorts were respectively Nepalese and Chinese. Later, his grandson, the 37th king, invited the Indian Tantric sage Padmasambhava to Tibet. According to legend, Padmasambhava fought and subdued the spirits and demons of Bon, but he also converted them into guardians of the Buddhist doctrine. The religion that emerged from all this, which has been called Lamaism, was a mixture of Buddhism and Bon: Bon adopted certain Buddhist forms while Buddhism absorbed and modified some ritual practices of Bon including its taste for the supernatural. Emblems such as prayer flags probably derived from Bon. The idea of divine kings has also remained tenacious; one of the most singular characteristics of Tibetan Buddhism is the fusion of spiritual and temporal authority in the person of the Dalai Lama.

they are recognizable by their close-fitting white caps (reminiscent of the headgear of surgeons) as they mill around their **mosque**, known as 'Qingzhen Si' in Chinese, at the northern end of town.

With its mixed population, Songpan provides many opportunities for people-watching. Renmin Lu, threading through the North and South gates (Beimen and Nanmen), is the main thoroughfare of this ramshackle walled town. Tibetan mastiffs scrounge for scraps around the food stalls; they are ugly, fierce-looking creatures, even if 'Songpan dog' is a local pejorative for someone who is all bark and no bite. Many of the old houses are of wood, and the presence of a timber trade in this high narrow valley is apparent everywhere. Logs float downriver on the Minjiang, which wends through the town in a sweeping curve. Songpan's surrounding slopes,

Though subsumed under Tibetan Buddhism, Bon persists as a sect, having added to its own deities a borrowed pantheon of Buddhas and bodhisattvas, now scarcely differentiated from their originals except in nomenclature. Instead of the mantra 'Om mani padme hum', Bon adherents chant 'Om ma-tri-mu-ye-sa-le-du'. Opposite to Buddhist practice, they circumambulate their temples and rotate their prayer wheels anticlockwise. The motif of the swastika, too, is found drawn on walls and floors going in an anti-clockwise direction. Otherwise, to all intents and purposes, the modern Bon faith is little more than an offshoot of Tibetan Buddhism, especially for lay people.

Out of a religious reform movement initiated in the 12th century the Gelugpa or Yellow Hat school (the order of the Dalai and the Panchen Lamas) emerged as the dominant Buddhist sect in Tibet. Its popularity has driven Bon to the border areas where the Gelugpa's influence is weaker. In Sichuan's western region, it is not at all unusual to find large prosperous Bonpo monasteries in areas like Aba, Huanglong and Ma'erkang, whereas they do not exist in and around Lhasa. Many Western travellers find Bon iconography rich and intriguing, with its brilliantly colourful depictions of terrifying demons, humans being devoured by evil spirits, and abundance of skulls and other representations of death. They may also discover that the followers of Bon are often the only Tibetans who are uninterested in photographs of the Dalai Lama.

though, have long been denuded of its namesake *song* (pines). Deforestation remains a cause for concern judging from the slogans scrawled on the walls of villages nearby —'Protect Forestry Resources', 'Treasure the Nation's Timber' and so on.

Historically the administrative headquarters of the grasslands to the west, Songpan was a thriving entrepôt where pastoral and nomadic tribesmen, bringing with them pelts and medicines, bartered for tea and barley. The medicines would have included Chinese caterpillar fungus, fritillary and gastrodia, herbs still widely prized today. Songpan was also garrisoned, for the grasslands were once the haunt of lawless bandits who paid little heed to Chinese authority.

At Songpan, it is possible to rent horses to visit the neighbouring valleys, Erdaohai and the Zhaga waterfall. Travellers have reported that this involves camping overnight.

Maowen: Qiang Town

Originally a nomadic people who have lived alternately under the sway of Tibetans and Han Chinese since the seventh century, the Qiang are a minority group found in northwest Sichuan. A census in the early 1980s put their population at just over 100,000. Their centre is the **Maowen Qiang Autonomous County** (also known as **Maoxian**), within the Aba Tibetan Autonomous Prefecture, about halfway between Songpan and Chengdu. They now live by farming and animal husbandry.

Apple orchards line the approach and exit of their county town and herds of goats and oxen browse on the grassy slopes above it. Maowen itself is like countless other rural market towns in China: one main street with anonymous cement buildings housing shops which purvey the usual assortment of groceries, cloth, shoes, thermos flasks, enamel basins and medicinal herbs. The Qiang Nationality Handicrafts Shop is disappointing, offering little in the way of the embroidery and cross-stitch needlepoint in which Qiang women are skilled. Young Qiang women are attractively attired in long, brightly coloured dresses slit up to the waist like a Vietnamese *cheongsam*, under which peep blue or black trousers. Often the collar and lapels of the dress are embroidered, as are headbands securing the cloth turbans which most Qiang people wear. Generally the turban is white or black, but sometimes it is a more decorative affair of square, floral patterned headscarves tucked under coils of plaited hair. In winter a sleeveless sheepskin jacket is worn by both men and women.

There is a tradition that Qiang men are particularly fine stonemasons. When they settled in these parts, they lost no time in putting up tall chimney-like watchtowers above their villages and solid flat-roofed houses with thick walls to shelter themselves as well as their goats and cattle. A few of these towers can still be seen today; they are reputed to be 500 years old. Perched on the crests of hills, these stark and sturdy bastions have the air of medieval keeps.

The road south to Chengdu, through **Wenchuan**, hugs the Minjiang closely. At intervals along the river the banks are linked by **suspension bridges** made to a design going back hundreds of years. They consist of nothing more elaborate than a framework of thick bamboo ropes, firmly anchored at the bridgeheads, across which planks of wood are laid to form a walkway. At either side of this walkway, higher up, are stretched more riggings. These serve as handrails for pedestrians, who appear to step across the oscillating bridge with complete sang-froid. At the narrower points, people cross by an even more hair-raising contraption. A cable of bamboo fibre is slung from winches on the banks. It is fitted with a metal ring and pulley, from which a sort of rope seat dangles. The rider simply secures himself to the seat, holds

The young abbot of a Bonpo monastery with his personal bodyguards, photographed by Joseph Rock in southern Sichuan, 1924

tight to the supporting rope, and slides across the river, dipping precariously as he reaches the middle. If the momentum of the downward slide does not carry him right across, the rider has to haul himself hand over hand, unless a friendly passer-by on the opposite bank helps by tugging another rope laced through the pulley to heave him up the last sagging stretch.

The Aba Grasslands: Northern Marshes

The first European to penetrate the region around Songpan is believed to be Captain W J Gill (in 1877); he wrote about a land of aborigines called Man-tzu and Sifan. The Chinese originals of these names (which would be romanized nowadays in *pinyin* as Manzi and Xifan) give no clue as to who these people were, for they only translate as 'savages' and 'western aliens'. Sir Eric Teichmen, an English consul, referred in the early 1900s to the Goloks, a wild nomad tribe inhabiting a remote, little-known territory bounded by today's Songpan, Kangding, Ganzi and Xining (in Qinghai). Another explorer, encountering a band of Goloks near Ganzi in 1940, described them as 'picturesque barbarians' with long hair falling straight down to their shoulders, their ears pierced with large silver rings. They were armed to the teeth with swords and rifles. Other travellers seemed to think that the terms were interchangeable and used them very loosely for any eastern Tibetan they met.

Despite the ethnological confusion, the accounts do agree that several different tribes with their own dialects occupied the fringes of northern Sichuan's settled valleys. These tribesmen were a menace, habitually preying on the caravans that travelled between China's border outposts. Far from recognizing Chinese rule, they retained their own chieftains until well into this century. They also warred among themselves, and there was nothing the Chinese, their nominal overlords, could do to impose order. As Teichmen had noted, the Goloks recognized the temporal authority of the Lhasa Tibetans as little as they did that of the Chinese.

The Aba Tibetan Autonomous Prefecture, enclosing a huge expanse of high-altitude grasslands, is roamed over by the Goloks still. They remain fiercely independent, speaking their own dialect which is unintelligible to other Tibetans less than a day's march away. Yet a common heritage based on deep religious belief binds all Tibetans. Age-old practices are still in evidence: the monasteries remain the repository of learning, providing the only formal education that most Goloks receive; and, as is the custom, a large number of boys spend several years as monks, usually until their late teens. Those who remain become ordained and some of these will make their solitary way across the grasslands from clan to clan, taking nothing from

A Tibetan woman, with a head-dress of amber and coloured beads, shopping in Songpan

the monasteries but their clothes, rosary, prayer wheel and bowl. They inspire intense devotion from the nomads. For their part, the nomads are generous givers of alms and perform a truly prodigious number of prostrations whenever they find themselves in the vicinity of a monastery.

The everyday life of the nomads is focused on their extensive herds of yaks from which milk, butter, meat, cheese and skins are derived. Government policy requires each family to care for 30 yaks, any number beyond that being designated as personal property. Surplus yak products can therefore be exchanged in the towns for things like *tsampa* (parched barley), the staple of a Tibetan's diet. Through the summer the nomads' black tents of beaten yak-hair are pitched on pastures some 4,000 metres (13,000 feet) in altitude, in a landscape of alpine meadows rustling with grass and wild flowers in bloom; in the bitter winter months the herdsmen and their flocks move down to the lower valleys. Every now and then, long-running disputes over traditional grazing rights break out in open fights between the clans. Old tensions have been aggravated in recent years by the faster depletion of forage as more private herds are raised.

The grasslands, some 15,000 square kilometres (5,800 square miles) in size, lie at an average height of 3,500 metres (11,500 feet). From the western extremity of Songpan County, they extend just beyond the town of **Ruo'ergai** to the north, **Hongyuan** to the west, and their southern tip is roughly on the same parallel as the town of **Mao'ergai**. Two rivers, the White (Bai He) and the Black (Hei He), meander sluggishly across them, tracing tortuous courses between flat-topped hummocks. Poor drainage leaves the land soggy at the best of times; during the rains from May to September, it becomes pitted with a maze of marshes. Coarse sedges fill these marshes, and on their borders of grassy meadow, gentians, hemlock and iris soften the landscape in summer. Over this weird, unearthly terrain the sun would blaze one minute and a hailstorm descend the next; but generally it is cold and humid, and in the long winter season the ground is hoary with frost.

Apart from the nomads, possibly no-one else before or since has gained as intimate an acquaintaince with the harsh realities of the grasslands as the First Front Red Army which traversed them in August 1935 (see page 145). Over a period of seven to ten days they trudged across the miry wastes, soaked from perpetual rain and frozen at night for lack of shelter; many lost their bearings and were sucked into deep swamps. An estimated 500 soldiers lost their lives.

Today, the nearest a traveller gets to the grasslands is **Hongyuan** (Red Plain, named for its Long March associations). Chengdu-based travel agents offer nine-day tours to Jiuzhaigou, Huanglong and Hongyuan by coach. Adventurous travellers have made it by a combination of public bus and hitch-hiking. With its dirt roads, horses and yaks hitched in front of shops, and rifle-toting Tibetans in felt cowboy hats, Hongyuan has all the rawness of a new frontier town. The Tibetan menfolk sport interesting hairstyles: braids, dreadlocks or topknots. Some of them appear to have simply taken random swipes with a razor. They can look intimidating but smile readily and love having their photographs taken (although one should always ask permission). The women are bedecked with strings of gorgeous turquoise and coral. The Grasslands Research Institute is located in Hongyuan. In September 1989 a Sino-Swedish joint venture research team did preliminary fieldwork on the feasibility of burning grassland peat as fuel.

There are several monasteries in the area, including the **Mi'er Lamasery**, the principal one in this part of the grasslands. First drive to Amukehe (Amiko in Tibetan), about 18 kilometres (11 miles) north of Hongyuan. There will be a small gravel road branching off right, parallel to a stream. Follow this for about five or six kilometres (three to four miles). Clusters of prayer banners flutter by the wayside. The cement buildings along here are the nomads' winter lodgings. The lamasery is a large one with more than a thousand monks attached to it. Although the buildings themselves are constructed in Chinese style (contemporary concrete crossed with reproduction Qing-dynasty ornamentation) and there are no relics to see, the religious atmosphere is strong, especially during prayer sessions at daybreak, when hundreds of monks seated crosslegged in the great hall intone their monotonous chant in the murky glow cast by the flames of numerous yak butter lamps.

A hundred and eighty kilometres (110 miles) south of Hongyuan, **Ma'erkang** (spelt 'Barkam' on old maps) is the administrative capital of the Aba prefecture. It is an industrial town with a population of 18,000. Several lamaseries are located within a day's trek of its centre, including some established by the Bonpo sect, but they are relatively new and not of great interest.

Western Sichuan

Tibetans had been settled for many centuries in the territory which now forms part of the provinces of Qinghai and Sichuan before a Sino-Tibetan political frontier was formally defined during the reign of Qing emperor Kangxi (1662–1722). By this agreed demarcation the territory west of the upper Yangzi, a section known as the **Jinsha Jiang** (the River of Golden Sand), was formally acknowledged to be governed by Lhasa, while all that lay to the east of it became the domain of the Chinese empire. Even so, in practice the frontier was a fluid one; semi-independent Tibetan tribes in the border regions more or less carried on as before, submitting to the authority of their chieftains rather than to the Chinese officials appointed over them. Although Chinese garrisons were stationed at Kangding (formerly Tachienlu) and other points along the road to Lhasa, domination of the rugged highlands west of the Red Basin remained tenuous. There were sporadic Sino-Tibetan conflicts, inter-tribal skirmishes and nomad raids on Chinese settlements. This state of affairs continued despite the creation of a buffer province, **Xikang** (see page 136) in 1928.

Xikang has disappeared from the maps but western Sichuan still seems a world apart. Geographically it is a grand and savage region made up of tremendous mountain ranges and deeply eroded canyons. Three great rivers and their tributaries cut through it roughly from north to south—the Jinsha Jiang, the **Yalong Jiang** and the **Dadu He**. Culturally it is Tibetan: the 1,000-kilometre (620-mile) highway from Chengdu to the border of Tibet passes through the heartland of Kham, one of Tibet's three traditional regions.

The nomads here, known as **Khampas**, are great fighters: it has long been said that of all Tibetans the Khampas make the best killers and the greatest saints. Not so long ago they were divided into clans and tiny kingdoms only loosely controlled by Lhasa, and were feared throughout Tibet and the border regions as unruly bandits. Since then Kham has been subsumed by Sichuan: the present **Ganzi Tibetan Autonomous Prefecture** corresponds in area to a large portion of the original tribal territory. In the 1950s, smouldering resentment of the Chinese government's collectivization programme—anathema to a spirited, independent people such as the Khampas—flared up in violent armed resistance. A wave of guerrilla warfare rolled across Kham and into central Tibet, sparking a popular uprising in March 1959. Many Tibetan-Buddhist monasteries were destroyed in the fighting. As the world knows, this revolt was suppressed and the Dalai Lama—put to flight from Lhasa to India—remains in exile.

Khampas still wrest a living from their wild and desolate enclave. They can graze their yaks, sheep and horses on the high-altitude pastures, but much of the terrain is

A nomadic way of life is still practised on the high-altitude pastures of Sichuan

unfit for human habitation. The landscape consists of long stretches of wilderness broken by frozen rivers, and lofty mountains whose deforested slopes are covered with shale and rock. Against this backdrop a lone rider on a caparisoned horse may suddenly appear on the horizon, as proud and dashing a figure as one imagines his bandit forebears to have been. Khampa men are tall and muscular, wearing their hair in braids over which wide-brimmed hats are pulled down on foreheads. Feet are shod in brightly coloured boots, and a knife dangles from the belt securing a volumi-nous skeepskin coat worn, Tibetan-style, with one sleeve hanging loose from the shoulder. If at first all this looks intimidating, a flashing smile revealing a single gold front tooth soon dispels the effect.

Few places on earth are as difficult to visit as the Ganzi hinterland. Travellers have penetrated it by public bus, or by hitching rides on trucks—it is mostly con-voys of trucks that make that journey across western Sichuan. The drivers of these trucks are tough, spending as they do hour after hour jolting and slithering all over the road. From time to time the highway is put out of action by avalanches.

If the road is passable, **Dege**, the last town on the highway before it enters Tibet, can be reached in five days. This highland settlement has two monasteries belonging to the Saskyapa sect, whose early exponents were particularly active in translating Buddhist literature from Sanskrit. Dege's Bakong Scripture Printing House has been reproducing copies from the pages of the 333 volumes of the Tibetan Buddhist can-on, the *Kanjur* and the *Tanjur*, for 250 years. Besides Buddhist classics, these vol-umes contain all the commentaries as well as works on medicine and astrology. Printing is done by hand from wooden blocks, more than 210,000 of them, on which the text is carved. Catalogued and numbered, this collection of blocks is stored in an enormous building lined with shelves. Printed sheets are stacked as loose leaves between wooden slates that are often decorated with carvings or paint-ings. There is an increasing demand for these 'books', and pious devotees come to buy them and to touch the ink dripping from the roller presses.

Even though much of the Ganzi region is too remote for most travellers, it is possible to potter along the edges of it, at centres such as Wolong, Luding, Kangding and halts en route. Most places in Sichuan west of Chengdu, except for Ya'an, are officially closed to foreigners, but the policy is not by any means rigorously imple-mented. Travel permits to officially closed areas can be obtained from the Chengdu Public Security Bureau (see page 28). Unless they attract attention to themselves, though, independent foreign travellers have rarely been accosted for travel-permit checks in recent years. Most local security officials seem to make a distinction be-tween 'passing through' and 'staying overnight' in a closed area, generally making no fuss over the former, although even the latter is increasingly winked at. The odd *zhaodaisuo* (see page 35) receptionist may raise a murmur, but she can usually be placated by a promise to stay only one night. Most travellers' experience suggests that the farther they get from Chengdu the less scrupulously are the 'open areas' rules enforced. A pass to visit Wolong can be obtained from the Department of Forestry (see below).

Wolong Nature Reserve: Last Sanctuary of the Giant Panda

If Sichuan has an international reputation, it is as the home of the giant panda, the cuddly animal adopted as the logo of the World Wide Fund for Nature (WWF). We also see giant pandas replicated as soft woolly toys, turned into brand names and embroidered on silk. These animals are so popular that the birth of a baby giant panda in a zoo is international news.

Although they used to be found in almost all the southern provinces and even as far north as Hebei, giant pandas have now retreated to only a few forests in Sichuan, Gansu and Shaanxi. The Wolong Nature Reserve, all 2,000 square kilometres (770 square miles) of it, was established in 1975 to conserve the largest concentration of these rare and beautiful creatures in all of China. In 1980 a field research centre was set up there in cooperation with the WWF.

Entering Wolong from the east, you follow the **Pitiao River**, a tributary of the Minjiang, past a row of empty houses standing forlornly in a clearing, spurned by the intended tenants who had apparently refused to move there from inside the reserve. On past rhododendron-clad slopes blurred by mist, then across a bridge under which the Pitiao flows fast and furious, the **Hetaoping breeding station** stands in a wooded ravine sprayed by small waterfalls. It was set up in 1983 and has ten captive pandas. The Chinese habit of expressing endearment to a child by repeating one character from his or her name has long been applied to pandas: the ones here are called Quan Quan, Tao Tao, Li Li and so on. Li Li and her companions loll in their individual cells either munching or sleeping. They look a little sad, but perhaps it is their distinctive markings—black rings around eyes emerging from a white furry face—that give them such a woeful expression.

China's total giant panda population is believed to have declined to fewer than 1,000. Research at the breeding station is aimed at improving the reproduction rate so that more cubs can be bred and eventually introduced back into the wild. All visitors to the station must undergo a disinfection process at the gate. But the endangered panda's greatest enemy is still the relentless deforestation that goes on hereabouts. Logging trucks thundering along the edges of the reserve threaten to destroy what would otherwise be a sublimely peaceful and carefully preserved ecosystem which harbours not only the giant panda but other rare fauna and flora.

Scattered in the area are Qiang (see page 113) and Tibetan villages surrounded by vegetable plots and shaded by magnolias. The valley floor, though high, has a warm and humid climate in which subtropical crops flourish.

Shawan, 40 kilometres (25 miles) from the reserve entrance, is the visitors' centre and where the **Wolong Museum of Natural History** is located. English-language brochures sold by the museum supplement the information posted in the entrance hall; exhibit captions, however, display only Chinese and Latin names. The exhibits fall into two groups: animal life and botanical specimens. In the first section you see glass cases filled with stuffed birds—warblers, pheasants and other game birds with variegated plumage like the red-breasted Temminck's tragopan. There are, as well, beautiful butterflies and snakes all preserved in various ways. Taxidermists have also been at work on a serow (Asiatic antelope) and a takin (a horned beast known collo-quially as *yeniu*, 'wild cattle'), both of which used to be hunted. Nearly a hundred species of animals, 230 species of birds and 4,000 species of plants have been found at Wolong. In the botanical section, photographs and pressed leaves and flowers guide the visitor through the belts of vegetation occuring at different altitudes, from the mixed evergreen and deciduous broadleaved forests of the lower slopes to the alpine shrubs and herbs at 3,500 metres (11,500 feet) and above.

Going up to Balangshan Pass, above Wolong

One plant which enjoys 'first-priority protection' under China's national register of endangered wildlife is Père David's dove tree (see page 97), now increasingly rare in the wild. Two species of bamboo, the umbrella bamboo and the arrow bamboo, are essential to the panda's survival. Not only do seedlings take at least ten years to become mature enough as suitable feed, but every 50 to 60 years these species flower and seed *en masse*, after which the bamboo dies and the pandas starve. A wealth of flora can be seen at close quarters at **Silver**

In the Wolong Nature Reserve

Mine Gully (Yinchanggou) and **Heroes Gully** (Yingxionggou), where wet, slippery trails lead between dense thickets of bamboo interspersed with birch, maple and fir. Wild flowers poke out of the undergrowth in tiny stipples of colour. Ferns sprout from the surrounding cliffs, moistened by mist and waterfalls. At the foot of those cliffs, flowering rhododendrons appear as smudges of pink, purple and yellow against the dark lustrous greenery.

GETTING TO WOLONG NATURE RESERVE

The Wolong Nature Reserve is within half a day's drive of Chengdu. The 136-kilometre (85-mile) route out of the city passes through Guanxian (see page 57) and

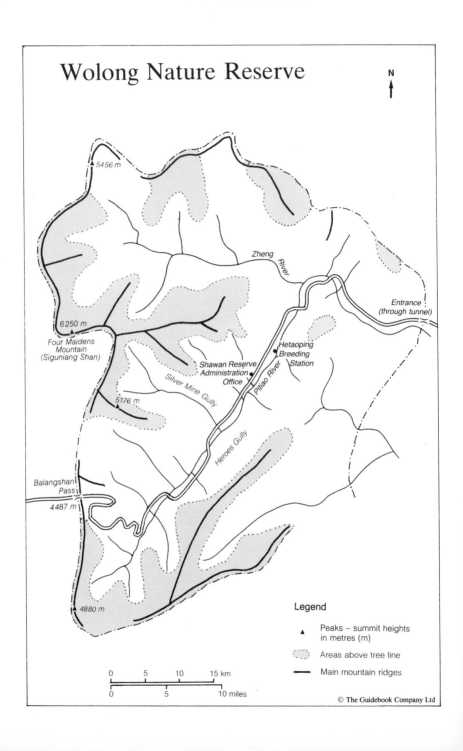

then, at **Yingxiuwan**, takes a left bend to advance westwards between hillsides studded with tall stone towers. While it is simplest to go to Wolong by hired car, public buses make the run between Guanxian and Shawan once a week (on Friday at the time of writing). There is also a local service from Yingxiuwan (daily except on Wednesday).

The **Wolong Nature Reserve Administration Office**, at Shawan, runs a hotel and restaurant. The officers here say that a permit to visit Wolong has to be obtained from the foreign affairs section, the **Sichuan Provincial Government Department of Forestry**, Jinhua Jie, off Renmin Bei Lu, Chengdu. It may be simpler to leave the arrangements to a travel agent.

If you plan on exploring the Yinchanggou or Yingxionggou trails, make sure you have a raincoat and shoes with a good grip on the soles.

Balangshan Pass: Wolong to Xiaojin

Leaving the Pitiao River on your left, you begin to climb by a series of giddy bends to Balangshan Pass, the barrier you must cross before proceeding further west. The dirt road, heavily used by logging trucks, is also prone to disintegration from landslips and is constantly under repair.

This exhilarating climb may be rather alarming for those with no head for heights; Balangshan Pass is 4,487 metres (14,701 feet) above sea level. As the top is reached the ramparts of snow-crowned peaks around it fade from sight and instead a cold fog grips the treeless cleft. You know from your map that in the misty distance to the north, a peak of the **Four Maidens Mountain** (Siguniang Shan) towers to a height of 6,250 metres (20,500 feet), the second tallest peak in Sichuan (the first is Gongga Shan, see page 136). Its lower valleys, accessible from **Rilong** town, have been opened to campers and trekkers.

Then the trail sweeps in a wide arc between gentler slopes. You see vestiges of human handiwork in a zigzag track straight up the cliff on the other side of the road. Only yaks seem to use it. The valley is plainly abandoned, but proof that people lived here lies scattered in the ruins of foundation stones, not to mention that curious zigzag path.

The small towns of Rilong and Dawei are on the road to Xiaojin. This is Qiang and Tibetan country, as the architecture of the turreted stone hillside houses attest. The sombre heavy facades of Tibetan dwellings, built to a slight trapezium elevation, are pierced by a few small windows outlined in white paint. They are also decorated with swastikas and the ancient protective symbols of a crescent moon cradling a sun. Above a gorge, Qiang watchtowers stand guard over the river approach.

Giant Pandas
Habits and Habitat

The giant panda has been called a living fossil, a relic of the glacial age. Nevertheless, despite having existed for three million years (as fossil evidence indicates), giant pandas face extinction unless their natural habitat of bamboo forests can be saved. Once these animals—peculiar to China—may have been spread throughout the southwestern provinces and even as far north as Hebei. Today, the beleaguered population of less than 1,000 survive in a few mountain ranges, mainly in 12 reserves including Wolong.

Zoologists in the West first learned about the giant panda from the French missionary Jean Pierre Armand David, who came across a pelt in western Sichuan in 1869. The first living giant panda seen in the West was taken to a United States zoo in 1936. More recently, widespread concern for its survival led to an international programme of research and conservation being established: in 1980 George Schaller of the New York Zoological Society was asked by the World Wildlife Fund (now the World Wide Fund for Nature) to take part in a study of pandas in the wild.

The Chinese name for the giant panda is *daxiongmao*, or 'big bear cat'. It is indeed both bear-like and cat-like, a barrel-shaped bundle which pads quietly through the cool damp mountains that are its habitat. A fully grown giant panda might be about one and a half metres (five feet) in length, weighing some 160 kilograms (350 pounds). Covered thickly all over with creamy-white fur marked with black on the ears, limbs, the shoulders and around the eyes, it is one of the most distinctive of mammals. The lesser or red panda, a smaller creature which resembles a racoon, seems altogether less attractive and loveable.

The chances of a casual visitor to Wolong seeing a panda in its natural habitat are virtually nil. The giant and the lesser pandas are both rather shy. Schaller saw his first giant panda at Wolong after two months there. Whenever he and his field director, Professor Hu Jinchu, caught one, they would fit it with a remote-controlled radio collar to help them track it and thus piece together a picture of the animal's feeding, sleeping and mating habits.

Although endowed with the digestive system of carnivores, giant pandas move far too ponderously to catch game. A certain type of high-altitude bamboo is what they seem to like best, but they can digest only a fraction of their food, and to extract the nourishment they need to consume as much as 20 kilograms (44 pounds) of stems and leaves a day. Their daily routine consists of foraging for several hours, taking a nap, and waking to forage again. In the spring months they will descend from above 3,000 metres (10,000 feet) where the arrow bamboo thrives, to a lower elevation where the umbrella bamboo is just putting forth its tender shoots, another panda delicacy. So fastidious is the giant panda that it will not forage in areas where forests have been felled, scorning the kind of bamboo that grows there for its thin stems and poor quality.

Powerful front legs and paws first tear apart the bamboo, and massive jaws and broad molars then make short work of it. With a special wristbone formation on each front paw which functions as a sixth digit, the giant panda is remarkably dexterous in manipulating the stems of bamboo.

It is rather less efficient at reproducing itself, though. Giant pandas tend to be solitary except during the short mating season in spring. A female panda will bear one offspring at most every two to three years. Gestation takes about four to five months. Usually only one cub is born; if there are two, one is abandoned since the mother cannot care for both at the same time. The birth will take place in the hollow of a tree or a concealed cave. A newborn panda is hairless and tiny, and spends its first month being carried everywhere by its mother until it is warmly furred and released into the nest. At 18 months or so it is able to lead an independent life.

Pandas in a display of rough-and-tumble

Xiaojin: Revolutionary Town

Xiaojin at the foot of **Jiajin Mountain** is a nice town. Clustering round a river-bend, the town rises up steep banks overlooked by a multi-coloured pagoda-topped building which has been recently completed to house government offices. The municipality headquarters remain in the former **Catholic church**, a grey brick edifice reached by a lane lined with saplings.

It was the Jiajin that the main body of the Red Army scaled to cross the Great Snowy Mountains range on their Long March north (see page 144). At Xiaojin (then known as Maogong) the weary soldiers joined forces with the Fourth Front Army, which had first reached Sichuan in 1932. Their reunion was celebrated on 21 June 1935 at the Maogong Catholic church, where cadres from the two armies, after addresses by Politburo member Bo Gu and Commander-in-Chief Zhu De, put on a programme of plays and songs. A plaque in the courtyard of the church marks the event.

Kangding: Gateway to Tibet

Kangding has a most dramatic situation. This interesting town is cradled in a narrow fold between steep, dark green mountains and lies at an elevation of over 2,500 metres (8,400 feet). A swift, foaming stream roars through its centre, sending up a constant rumble as the sound reverberates round the amphitheatre of hills. Frequently in deep shadow, for the mountains shut out sunlight, Kangding seems at once starkly grim and full of mystery.

Its approach from the west is heralded by village houses tucked into the hill slopes on which neat terraces have been cut to support a little cultivation. Barley is grown, and here and there you come upon cherry trees and peppercorn bushes. Ragged prayer flags and obelisk-like watchtowers can be seen en route. From Chengdu, the road to Kangding goes through Ya'an (see page 133).

At the beginning of the Republican period (1911), there was still a Tibetan king resident in Kangding. He was monarch of the Chala kingdom, but in reality no more than a Chinese puppet. When Zhao Erfeng overran western Sichuan (see page 136), the king was stripped of even his nominal powers. Kangding's motley population at that time also included French priests; in fact it was the seat of the bishop of the Mission Etrangères, a Paris-based organization. Many famous Frenchmen passed through Kangding, not least of whom was the Lazarist Père Huc, whose account of a remarkable expedition, *Souvenirs d'un voyage dans la Tartarie et le Tibet*, electrified

BRICK TEA
Kangding's Entrepôt Trade

Tibetans are great tea-drinkers, and their favourite brew is specially made from coarse leaves and sweepings mixed with twigs which are then steamed and compressed into bricks. This is how they drink it: a bit of the brick is snapped off and thrown into boiling water; the tea is left to infuse until the liquid is almost black. The infusion is usually flavoured with a pinch of salt, and sometimes a little ash is added to give it a pinkish colour. Strained from the pan into a churn, the tea is then laced with yak butter. After a thorough stirring, the mixture is finally decanted into a kettle or pot from which it is dispensed into bowls. Into the same bowls the owners might put some *tsampa*, a flour made from roasted barley. This barley meal is stirred with a little butter tea and kneaded until it becomes a dollop of dough, which is then eaten with more helpings of tea.

Brick tea has been exported from China to Tibet for centuries. Before the advent of motor roads the tea was transported by porters, mules and yaks. Kangding was a major go-between, serving as depot, packager and distributor all at once. Wrapped in sheets of red and gold paper on which Chinese and Tibetan labels were printed, the tea bricks started their journey in packs of four placed end to end in a tube of bamboo matting. Each porter would carry some ten or more of these tubes to Kangding, a load of 70 to 90 kilos (150 to 200 pounds)—more or less the weight that could be carried by a mule or pony. Pack-animals were less adept, though, at negotiating the steep and narrow paths the porters travelled.

In Kangding the commodity was either sold or stored in warehouses to await the caravans of Tibetan merchants. Various specialized groups took over at this stage: Tibetan packers who repackaged the tea in yak-hides, and women porters who had the monopoly of moving the tea from the warehouses to the caravans.

Untanned yak-hides made completely waterproof containers. They were soaked in water to make them soft, and then sewn tightly round the tea packets so that when dry, they turned into hard casings in which the bricks could be transported over the most difficult terrain and through the worst weather without damage. In this way brick tea would be carried hundreds of miles by mules and yaks to Lhasa and beyond.

France when it was published in 1850. Of the missionaries who later went there, most pursued their largely vain task of proselytization with great zealousness, dedicating their lives with very little expectation of ever returning to France again.

To early European observers Kangding marked the limit of China. Once out of its west gate, Tibet began. Indeed the outpost was for many of them the starting point of a journey to Tibet. They called it Tachienlu or Tatsienlu, a corruption of its Tibetan name, Dar-tsen-do. The very atmosphere of the town was Tibetan, for its importance resided in its being the emporium for brick tea, wool, hides, medicinal herbs and cloth, and there was a constant throng of muleteers, yaks, emissaries from Lhasa and red-robed lamas in the market square.

Today the square is dominated by an array of chunky concrete buildings. On the façade of one of these, a faded slogan rallies the proletarians of the world to unite. But more often than not the square is used for less serious purposes—either by the townspeople for dancing early in the morning, or for basketball matches. As the administrative centre of the **Ganzi Tibetan Autonomous Prefecture**, Kangding retains something of the civic importance it enjoyed when it was the capital of Xikang. Industrial progress has come in the form of textile and tea-processing factories and a hydroelectric plant. The 30,000 inhabitants are mostly Han (ethnic) Chinese, although Tibetans still wander its streets. On the main bridge a few hopeful pedlars display their wares: daggers chased with silver, a prayer rug or two, a turquoise ring. Tibetan women thread through the market, distinguishable from the Chinese by their ruddy cheeks and clothes. Down by the river, a network of channels takes the place of piped plumbing and brings the mountain stream right up to people's doorsteps. Housewives, using baskets as colanders, rinse vegetables in the stone runnels.

Walk down Dong Dajie, and you find yourself in an alley flanked by rickety timbered houses, their top storey tilting precariously forward over the clutter of baskets in the doorways. The shops and stalls are stocked with manufactured goods, all manner of Tibetan artefacts, and mass-produced underwear and children's clothes in fluorescent colours. The French fathers did not labour entirely in vain, judging by the small **Catholic church** on the south side of the river, easily found down a narrow alley once you catch sight of the cross mounted on its roof.

Kangding's lamasery (**Anjue Si**) is hard by the principal guesthouse (*zhaodaisuo*), on the north bank, its series of double roofs with upturned eaves rising up above the low stone buildings in front. Its façades have been painted a distinctive salmon pink. In an anteroom just inside the entrance a large painted prayer wheel waits to be rotated; while devotees file around it, they can gaze upon the pictures of the late Tenth Panchen Lama, who visited Kangding in 1986, stuck all over the walls. (The Panchen Lama, considered along with the Dalai Lama as a divine leader, traditionally presided over an area around the Tashilhunpo Monastery in Shigatse, Tibet.)

(preceding pages) *Kangding*

Three effigies form the centrepiece of the altar in the prayer hall, with the Buddha in the middle. But the most resplendent icon is a richly painted garuda, an echo from Hindu mythology and symbol of the sun. Some 30 monks currently serve in the monastery; their living quarters, ranged on two sides of the monastery courtyard, were recently restored.

In a corner of the monk's quarters, facing the main street, is 'The Snow-Covered Area Tibetan Restaurant', whose billboard advertises butter tea, milk curds, barley beer and other Tibetan delicacies. This is a small snack bar run by a young Tibetan and his wife, an interesting place to drop into one evening even if yak butter tea is not your cup of tea.

The high point in Kangding's calendar is the fair on **Horse-race Hill** (Paoma Shan) every year on the 18th day of the fourth lunar month (sometime between May and June). As the day draws near, tents and stalls spring up all over the slopes and Tibetans from far and wide converge for an exuberant round of trading, wrestling matches, tug-of-war contests, folk dancing and, of course, horse-racing. The public security authorities may be quite strict at this time over travel permits for foreigners, since Kangding is full to bursting during the festival and transport in and out of the town becomes oversubscribed.

Otherwise, Horse-race Hill is nothing exceptional. It is an easy walk up to the flat summit. There is a monastery on the hill, built in a mixture of styles—Chinese and Tibetan—and above it, a resplendent white stupa with a silver spire.

Ya'an: On the Edge of the Red Basin

Once Yan'an was visibly the last Chinese town before the Tibetan borderlands. Here coolies loaded up with Chinese brick tea began their ascent up mountain paths to Kangding, where Tibetan caravans awaited their precious merchandise. Today the contrast between Ya'an's countryside and the rockier land to the west of it is still striking, especially when one crosses the pass over **Erlang Shan**. The road out of Ya'an runs between patches of green fields dovetailed as in a jigsaw puzzle, then winds through a humid, misty valley lush with vegetation—rhododendrons cascading like strings of jewels down hillsides, wild strawberries jostling with rambling roses, and ancient trees dripping with moss. The Red Basin has been left behind by the time you cross Erlang Shan.

Ya'an is a pleasant country town displaying a touch of civic pride in the rows of plane trees and dinky bird-shaped street lamps lining its thoroughfares. The town centre, overlooked by the Youth Palace and a pagoda up on a low hill, is found on the south bank of the Qingyi River. Behind the principal street, Dong Dajie, tumble-down timber houses and open shop-fronts make for an interesting area to stroll in. There is a market on Xinkang Lu.

Luding: Bridge over River Dadu

Luding is hallowed in Chinese communist history for the crucial battle fought here to gain control of its bridge.

The **Dadu He** (River), a tributary of the Minjiang, plunges south between the precipitous walls of Sichuan's northwestern mountain ranges and then swings east-wards to merge with the Min waters at Leshan (see page 76). In the reign of Emper-or Kangxi (1662–1722) an iron chain bridge, constructed to a design that presaged the modern suspension bridge, was thrown across this turbulent stream. It spans 101 metres (331 feet) and consists of nine stout iron chains forming the bridge deck, across which is a plank walkway, with two more chains on either side acting as handrails. All 13 chains are sunk into stone abutments on the banks, above which simple pavilions with curved eaves stand on brick foundations rising from the river floor. A billboard in the bridgehouse at the western end recounts the action on Lu-ding Bridge on 29 May 1935, when 22 soldiers from the Fourth Regiment of the Second Division of the First Front Red Army captured the crossing from Kuomintang troops and secured the communists' escape route through northern Sichuan.

Control of the bridge was imperative for the Red Army, pinched as it was be-tween the Dadu River ahead and the Jinsha River behind, while Kuomintang troops were pressing closer to stop the Long March in its tracks. In a 24-hour forced march that covered an incredible 120 kilometres (nearly 75 miles), the Red regiment raced enemy reinforcements to Luding Bridge and took its western bank approaches in record time. It found that half of the planks had been removed from the span, so that the assault party, the 22 heroes, could make it across only by swinging from the links hand over hand. Machine-gun fire from the eastern bank swept them as they slowly moved forward, while the men behind them had to lay down planks at the same time as providing cover. As those that were hit fell into the river, more men replaced them; accounts vary as to how many of the vanguard died. At last the as-sault party landed on the opposite bank, followed by the plank-layers and the rest of the regiment. The battle that ensued was a short and decisive one. With Luding Bridge taken, Mao Zedong, Zhou Enlai and Commander-in-Chief Zhu De arrived soon after to lead the Red Army across the Dadu River.

Qiang women crossing a river by means of cable, pulley and plank platform (above);
Luding Bridge (below)

XIKANG

The Province That Never Was

The formation of Xikang (generally spelt Sikang) Province had its roots in the early days of the Manchu or Qing Dynasty (1644–1911). The present border between China and Tibet did not exist then, and the rugged hinterland stretching away to the west of Chengdu was the Tibetan region of Kham. Later, as imperialistic expansion under the Manchus forced Lhasa to yield large slices of its territories, the Chinese sphere of influence extended by the 18th century as far as the upper Yangzi valley, to a line traced by the Jinsha River.

Chinese suzerainty was challenged in 1904 when, following the invasion of Lhasa by the Younghusband expedition, a treaty was negotiated between Britain and Tibet. To prevent further damage to Chinese interests, the Manchus resolved on annexing Eastern Tibet. Their commanding officer, Zhao Erfeng, conducted the campaign with such ruthlessness that he earned himself the nickname of 'The Butcher of Monks'. He and his army swooped down on Kham, slaughtered the tribesmen there and pushed on to sack the lamasery at Batang, close to the Jinsha River. Two thousand of his troops marched on Lhasa, although when the advance guard reached the city they found that the Dalai Lama had fled to India.

Having subjugated Tibet, Zhao Erfeng unveiled a plan that was to consolidate the conquerors' domination. All of the Tibetan region of Kham up to Giamda, a mere 150 kilometres (93 miles) from Lhasa, would be swept up into a separate province—Xikang—with Batang as its capital. Before the plan could be implemented, however, the Manchu Dynasty fell in a revolution that plunged China into chaos. For the next decade and a half, Sichuan was too preoccupied with internal disorders for its governors to bother much about neighbouring Tibet. Rival Chinese warlords, not the Kuomintang (Nationalist) government in Nanjing, controlled the province.

Hailuogou: Conch Gully

Gongga Shan or, to call it by its Tibetan name, Minya Konka, is one of the highest peaks in the world. This 'Sublime White Mountain', as its Tibetan name translates, soars 7,556 metres (24,783 feet) above the eastern extension of the Tibetan Plateau, a spellbinding sight for anyone who sees it. Travellers to Kangding pass quite close to it, but the town lies so low in relation to its surrounding hills that any view of

Zhao Erfeng's project was revived in 1928. By then Tibet had recovered most of the annexed territory, and it was to retrieve lost ground that the Nationalist regime brought Xikang into being. The new province incorporated all the territory on Zhao's blueprint; or so Chinese cartographers had it. In reality Chinese influence was thinly distributed among the few garrison towns visited by caravans, and disputes continued to sour Sino-Tibetan relations. Rebellion in the borderlands broke out again in 1932. Liu Wenhui, a powerful Sichuan warlord, repelled the Tibetan army as far as the Jinsha River and was making ready to push westwards when he found himself threatened from the rear. It transpired that his nephew, Liu Xiang, also a warlord, was marching on Kangding in a bid for supremacy while the uncle was engaged elsewhere. Liu Wenhui had no alternative but to withdraw his troops and return to Kangding. In the aftermath of this confusing series of events an agreement was reached whereby the Tibetans relinquished the whole area east of the Jinsha River. The Nationalist government took no part in these negotiations.

Liu Wenhui lost the family quarrel and spent his later years more or less in exile as governor of Xikang, with his seat in Kangding. There he became a very devout Buddhist and was on good terms with the lamas. The uneasy truce between China and Tibet continued after the communist takeover in 1949. Xikang was abolished in 1955 and the frontier lines were re-drawn, but it survives on maps of China published in Taiwan and is still represented as a province in Taiwan's National Assembly.

Gongga is blocked by the nearer peaks. You are far more likely to see its eastern face fom the summit of Emei Shan (see page 63), the pass over Erlang Shan or at Hailuogou (see below). If the skies are clear Gongga appears as a graceful, slightly blunted pinnacle of white ice scintillating against a background of deepest blue. The simple purity of its outline is unforgettable.

Gongga has proved difficult to climb. There have been two successful attempts, one in 1939 by two Americans and another in 1957 by six Chinese mountaineers. In

1981 a group of Japanese climbers were foiled in their attempt when eight of them were killed by an avalanche. They were within 300 metres (984 feet) of the top. One of the survivors was later saved by some Yi herdsmen.

Mount Gongga has four glaciers: Hailuogou, Yanzigou, Dagongba and Xiaogongba. Hailuogou (Conch Gully), its largest and most impressive, slithers down Gongga's eastern flank through a belt of conifer forests and terminates at an elevation of 2,850 metres (9,350 feet), arguably the lowest glacier in Asia. Accessibility from the town of Moxi (which is serviced by a daily bus from Luding), and the mild weather prevailing through much of the year, made the area attractive to adventurous travellers. In the late 1980s the area was opened as the Hailuogou Glacier Park.

The glacier, believed to have been formed some 1,600 years ago, is considered 'modern' by geological standards. Climbing up to it should present no problems for the physically fit; you are only likely to get a little breathless as the air becomes thinner the higher you ascend. A stone-flagged trail cuts through the glacier park, weaving between thick stands of trees, abraded cliffs, hot springs and, as it rises towards the tongue of the glacier, ice-floe covered lakes. Wooden huts and chalets have been built at three campsites along the gradient to provide bed and board; although the accommodation is basic, the proximity of hot springs at the first two campsites does supply the luxury of hot water.

MOXI

In its mountain fastness at the foot of Gongga Shan, Moxi (also known as Moxi Xiang) appears to dawdle in an earlier age. Its narrow main street is bordered by wooden buildings. The shops supplying life's essentials include a street-front counter where an apothecary diagnoses and dispenses a few Western and Chinese drugs. Set back from the main street is—somewhat unexpectedly—a small Catholic church with a pagoda-shaped steeple painted in pastel green and yellow. It is a thriving church, a legacy of the dedicated French missionaries who brought Christianity to southwest China some 130 years ago. Built in the 1920s, the Moxi church continues to be attended by local people. Some 500 worshippers fill its red wooden pews at major festivals such as Christmas and Easter. The plaque in front of the building states that Mao Zedong stayed here during the Long March. At that time, there was still a priest here, living and working in the white two-storeyed building with red eaves and beams next to the church. The story goes that the incumbent left with the Long Marchers and was never seen again. Moxi's Catholics now rely on a visiting priest who comes once a month.

THE GLACIER PARK

It is 13 kilometres (eight miles) from Moxi to Hailuogou. Previously visitors had to

Hailuogou glacier

hire horses to reach the glacier park, but there is now a motor road. Independent travellers may hire horses still, on arrival in Moxi, or hitch a ride for the last stretch. Horses are now banned from the park itself. The park entrance, where you are required to register and pay a fee (Rmb 22.50 for foreigners), is found shortly after leaving Moxi. Covered in the fee is a ticket for a guide at the glacier, as well as two hot spring baths during your stay in the park. A fairly leisurely programme at Hailuogou might be to walk up to the second campsite from the end of the motor road on the first day, go on to the glacier the next day and descend on the third.

Campsite 1 is a one-kilometre (0.6-mile) walk from the end of the road. It is located 1,940 metres (6,363 feet) above sea level. This, like the other two camps further up, provides basic services—accommodation, food and drink. Porters are on hand to carry your pack from here, or carry *you* (in a *huagan*, the modern version of the sedan chair) if you find the walk too strenuous. Payment for porterage is either on a package-deal basis (say, three days paid for in advance), in which case the porters' supervisor rakes off a percentage straight away, or you can insist on a day-by-day hire (a course much discouraged by the supervisor but one that gives you and the porter concerned some flexibility on arrangments for subsequent days). There is a hot spring here but it is less inviting than the one at Campsite 2.

Campsite 2, at 2,620 metres (8,594 feet) in elevation and some five kilometres (three miles) from the base camp, is where you find the hot spring and a pool. Bring your swimming gear. The pool is really the communal bath.

Campsite 3 is four and a half kilometres (2.8 miles) further up and 2,940 metres (9,643 feet) above sea level. In early summer, the slopes splashed with blooming rhododendrons present a magical sight. Hailuogou is 1,800 metres (5,900 feet) below the snowline and endowed with a mild climate which means that the approach to the glacier passes through lush forests and abundant ground cover. Thousands of species of flora and fauna, some of them quite rare, are found here.

The tongue of the glacier is an easy hike (two kilometres or 1.2 miles) from the third campsite. A simple pavilion marks the spot. Down at your feet is a stupendous drift of ice and debris tumbled into a deep chasm edged with hardy firs. It is a greyish-blue expanse which belies the treacherous flow beneath. To see the ice fall, caves and seracs—huge irregular boulders of ice created by the intersection of crevasses—as well as Gongga Peak itself, one must walk down to the glacier tongue and follow it around to the right, a trek of around two hours to be undertaken with care and only with a guide.

The glacier, though spectacular, is only one of the many stunning sights one catches wherever one looks in Hailuogou Park. Gongga is part of an enormous range that includes 45 other snow-tipped peaks towering over 6,000 metres (19,680 feet).

Encampment in southern Sichuan, near the Yunnan border, with one of the main peaks of the Gongga range in the background; photographed by Joseph Rock, 1928

GETTING TO HAILUOGOU

Visitors to Hailuogou first make for Moxi, 52 kilometres (32 miles) south of Luding. Unless you arrange your own transport (jeep or land cruiser) from Chengdu, it is a two-day journey by public bus from Chengdu (Xinnanmen Bus Station) to Luding, 319 kilometres (198 miles) away. The journey includes an overnight stay in Ya'an or some other town en route. To reach Luding, vehicles have to keep to a strict time-table: only one-way traffic is allowed on the Erlang Shan pass for safety reasons, so there are designated times in the day for vehicles travelling in opposite directions. At Luding, the traveller must take another bus, which runs an early-morning service, to Moxi. An alternative to all this is joining one of the seven-day tours offered by travel agents in Chengdu in the summer months.

Combining train and bus is also possible. The Chengdu–Kunming train makes a brief stop at **Wusihe**, close to Luding. From Wusihe, one can proceed to Luding by local bus and finally to Moxi.

Temminck's tragopan, found in western Sichuan, is here shown in one of the 'Rare Birds of China' series of watercolours painted by J Fenwick Lansdowne

ACROSS TORRENTS, OVER MOUNTAINS AND THROUGH MARSHLAND
The Long March in Sichuan

In the winter of 1935 some 7,000 bedraggled revolutionaries led by Mao Zedong walked across Gansu's provincial border with Shaanxi into a blaze of glory. For this vanguard, the Long March, begun almost exactly a year earlier, was all but over.

The Long March started as a retreat from Jiangxi, a poor and backward province in China's southeast where a central soviet area had been built up since 1929. This base had to be abandoned in 1931 when Chiang Kai-shek, leader of the Nationalist Party (Kuomintang) and the strongest military and political figure in post-imperial China, launched the first of his campaigns to flush the communists out of their strongholds. For three years his troops were kept deployed away from fighting China's external enemy, Japan, whose invasion of Manchuria in 1931 and subsequent incursions in coastal provinces were all but ignored. Chiang's strategy was both simple and methodical—he built blockhouses equipped with machine guns to command all the routes out of the known soviet bases.

Yet the communists managed to break out of the blockade. Initially the evacuation of some 120,000 people, most of them soldiers in the First Front Red Army, was a shambles. Disorganized and ill-equipped, the Long March columns accomplished the first lap at enormous cost, with the army fighting every inch of the way. Casualties were believed to have reached 40,000–55,000. Chinese historians were to relate these failures to dissension within the central command of the Communist Party.

At a crucial conference held en route in Zunyi, Guizhou Province, these disagreements appeared to have been resolved when Mao Zedong emerged as leader. Now a new sense of purpose began to animate the march. It was transformed from a flight in disarray into a call to arms against Japanese aggression. And it was to lead to a communist base in Yan'an, in northern Shaanxi Province, by way of Sichuan. In Sichuan the core army could hope to reunite with the Fourth Front Army. The latter, commanded by a founder member of the Chinese Communist Party, Zhang Guotao, was originally concentrated in soviet areas in central China and had preceded the First Front Army to Sichuan in 1932.

(continued)

Striking northwest, the Long Marchers moved slowly towards their destination. Brilliant manoeuvres threw the Kuomintang troops off their scent. The Red Army advanced, doubled back on itself, wheeled round and resumed its forward thrust. In May 1935 it reached the Sichuan border.

The route lay through Yi country. A minority people who speak their own language, the Yi had no reason to love the Chinese. Nevertheless they were persuaded into granting the communists safe passage through their mountainous homeland, thanks to Red Army commander Liu Bocheng, a native Sichuanese who had once served in a warlord's army and had some experience of dealing with tribal people. Liu convinced the Yi chieftain that Red Chinese policy aimed at peaceful coexistence with, not oppression of, minority nationalities. He even swore blood brotherhood with the Yi chieftain, sealing his oath in the tribal tradition with a draught of chicken blood.

The next hurdle was the Dadu River. Crossing it was to be the single most critical action of the Long March. The men could not have done so by ferry boats, for the Dadu's current was too swift and progress would have been too slow. Meanwhile Kuomintang troops were converging on the opposite bank to cut them off at Luding Bridge. Seizure of the bridge on 25 May 1935 became another heroic incident in a story crowded with heroes. General Liu Bocheng, inspecting the bridge the following day, was reported to have exclaimed: 'We've given plenty of blood and energy to get you, Luding Bridge, but we've got you! We've won out!'

North of the river the Great Snowy Mountains (Daxue Shan) rear up to form a forbidding barrier. Local people said the mountains were haunted, for surely only supernatural beings could cross them. The Red Army now had to prove the locals wrong. When it was decided to proceed over the pass on Jiajin Mountain, the men, most of them southerners with no experience of icy terrain, were briefed on altitude sickness and snow blindness. They were told to keep warm by drinking a hot infusion of chillies and ginger. Each man was reminded to take care of his feet and have two pairs of shoes. Sound advice though it was, little of it could be put into effect. It was not as if the men had mountain boots; the common footgear was cloth shoes or straw sandals. Although it was June, a blizzard swept the heights and the climbers' thin cotton uniforms were quickly soaked.

The climb started before dawn. At first the ascent was easy, but as the men mounted, the rarefied air began to trouble them. One Long March veteran recalled how he had counted his steps, allowing himself a break to catch his breath after each hundred. Then he had to stop after every 50, until even that pace could not be sustained, and he had to drop to stints of 30. The less hardy ones just stopped breathing; others died from exposure or fell into deep crevasses. By the time the party reached the summit, some 4,100 metres (13,450 feet) above sea level, not a few had become what the locals called 'meat dumplings'—corpses enveloped in snow.

At the foot of the Jiajin, near the town of Maogong (now Xiaojin), the First Front Army found the Fourth Front Army waiting for them. In the first flush of excitement at their reunion, the rank and file could have had no inkling of the differences that divided their leaders. Yet a confrontation between Mao Zedong and Zhang Guotao was to take place here—over policy, ideology and power. Mao was later to describe the struggle as the darkest moment of his life. Still, faced with the exigencies of evading Chiang's pursuit the rivals compromised by mixing and dividing their troops into two main forces, the Left and Right Columns—the former to strike northwest towards Aba, the latter to cut through to Baxi across the great grasslands.

Supply squads went in search of food for the ten-day trek across the grasslands, but hostile local Tibetans had stripped their villages and lay in wait only to take pot shots at the intruders. A Tibetan guide was eventually pressed into leading the vanguard. Even so, the Right Column forces when they arrived could not always locate the signposts the vanguard had left. And not only were signposts submerged in mud; the men were soon falling into weed-concealed bogs themselves. Some of them drowned.

It was August, and the floral extravaganza of the grasslands was giving way to a scene of rain-soaked and hail-battered desolation. The marchers were alternately drenched or frozen. They could not light fires and so ate their grain rations raw. They drank from stagnant swamps and were stricken with dysentery. When the food ran out, they allayed hunger with wild berries, weeds and boiled leather belts. Countless men succumbed to the horrendous conditions and more than 500 died.

'Every man in the Red Army is a seed of revolution,' one Long March participant had said. Over a distance of 12,000 kilometres (7,500 miles) through 11 provinces the epic trek had touched the lives of 200 million Chinese. In the course of the next decade, from its headquarters in Yan'an, the communist movement grew, blossomed and bore fruit. Its harvest was reaped in 1949 when victory for the revolution was finally proclaimed.

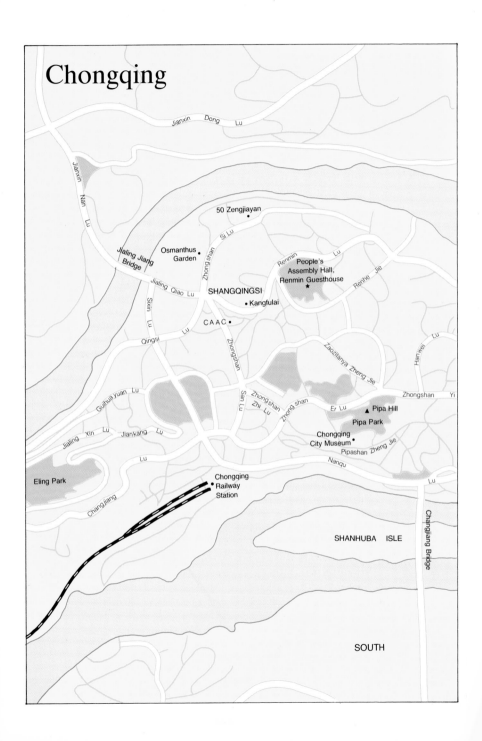

Chongqing

Jianxin Dong Lu

Jianxin Nan Lu

50 Zengjiayan

Osmanthus Garden

Si Lu

Zhongshan

Jialing Jiang Bridge

Renmin Lu

People's Assembly Hall, Renmin Guesthouse ★

Renhe Jie

Jialing Qiao Lu

SHANGQINGSI

Sixin Lu

Kangfulai

CAAC

Qingsi Lu

Zhongshan

Zaozilanya Zheng Jie

Hanwei Lu

Guihua yuan Lu

San Lu

Zhongshan Zhi Lu

Zhong shan

Er Lu

Zhongshan Yi

▲ Pipa Hill

Pipa Park

Jialing Xin Lu

Jiankang Lu

Chongqing City Museum •

Pipashan Zheng Jie

Nanqu Lu

Eling Park

Chang jiang

Chongqing Railway Station

SHANHUBA ISLE

Changjiang Bridge

SOUTH

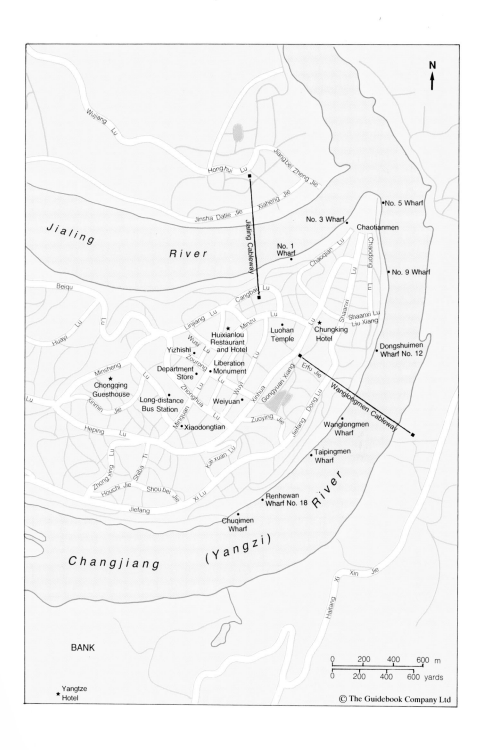

N

Wujiang Lu

Hong hui Lu

Jiangbei Zheng Jie

Xiaheng Jie

Jinsha Datie Jie

Jialing River

Jiling Cableway

No. 5 Wharf

No. 3 Wharf

Chaotianmen

No. 1 Wharf

Chaoqian Lu

Chaodong Lu

No. 9 Wharf

Cangbai Lu

Beigu Lu

Huayi Lu

Linjiang Lu

Minzu Lu

Luohan Temple

Shaanxi Lu

Shaanxi Lu

Liu Xiang

Chungking Hotel

Wusi Lu

★ Huixianlou Restaurant and Hotel

Yizhishi

Zourong Lu

Liberation Monument

Wuyi Lu

Dongshuimen Wharf No. 12

Minsheng Lu

Department Store

Zhonghua Lu

Ertu Jie

Wanglongmen Cableway

★ Chongqing Guesthouse

Xinmin Jie

Long-distance Bus Station

Minquan

Weiyuan

Xinhua Lu

Gongyuan xiang

Jiefang Dong Jie

Lu

Heping Lu

• Xiaodongtian

Zuoying Jie

Wanglongmen Wharf

Zhong xiang Lu

Kai xuan Lu

Taipingmen Wharf

Shiba Ti

Houchi Jie

Shou bei Jie

Xi Lu

Renhewan Wharf No. 18

Jiefang

Chuqimen Wharf

Changjiang (Yangzi) River

Haitang Xi

Xin Jie

BANK

0   200   400   600 m

0   200   400   600 yards

★ Yangtze Hotel

© The Guidebook Company Ltd

Chongqing: Mountain City

Hilly Chongqing is the principal inland port not only for Sichuan Province but for a huge hinterland encompassing Guizhou, Yunnan and eastern Tibet. It has a stunning location on a narrow, humped rock squeezed between the confluence of two rivers—the Yangzi to the south and east, and the tributary Jialing to the north. Known as 'Shancheng'—Mountain City—to locals, it is one of the few urban centres in China where the bicycle fails to come fully into its own.

This sandstone peninsula, though, is merely the old city. Like many others of similar stature, Chongqing was dignified by a wall of solid stone in the Ming Dynasty (1368–1644). All that remains of this wall today is the odd outcrop of masonry that props up a house here, or abuts a path there. For the city long ago burst its ancient boundaries: so extensively has it grown that its limits now embrace the suburbs and industrial zones to the southeast, as well as the northern shore (Jiangbei) of the Jialing River and the southern bank (Nan'an) of the Yangzi. Three million people live in the city, out of the nearly 14 million in the counties and districts within its jurisdiction.

Shrouded in fog for much of the winter, Chongqing on occasions attains a sombre picturesqueness when the mists begin to dissipate from the bluffs, and faint sunlight, piercing through the clouds, illuminates their steep faces. In the evaporating mists the tier upon tier of post-war apartment blocks, wooden houses with façades blackened by coal dust, and fragile bamboo structures sagging into their perches on the slopes, appear suspended in mid-air. The staircase streets winding uphill are barely visible, so tightly crammed are the houses around them. Across on the south bank, an arched window or some decorative brickwork marks a once-grand mansion previously occupied by a Kuomintang (Nationalist Party) official or foreign consul. Below, the hulks of passenger ships, tugs and ferries emerge from the brown sludge of the rivers, their foghorns silent now that the eddying murkiness has lifted; and, as the surrounding mountains float into view, the background is slowly sketched in with expanses of grey, blue or dull green.

It was the fog, of course, which saved Chongqing from being completely flattened by Japanese bombers in 1939–43. Generalissimo Chiang Kai-shek, leader of the Kuomintang (KMT), had retreated before the invading Japanese, coming across from eastern China, and set up government in Chongqing in 1938. The temporary capital bulged with refugees, many of them patriots with little idea of how they would aid the war effort apart from showing solidarity, somehow, with the KMT. They were soon to find themselves targets of air attacks. Through the first three summers (1939–41) of intensive air raids, Chongqing, with no anti-aircraft guns to speak of, suffered and endured a terrible scourging by fire. Misfortune bound together the disparate communities of exiles and natives otherwise split asunder by differences of class, dialect and experience. From all accounts the populace took the bombardment in its stride, withdrawing to dugouts burrowed into the rock whenever sirens shrieked out across the city.

Then the reverberations of Pearl Harbor reached Chongqing. This isolated river capital had already impressed the world at large, for its courage under bombardment was headline-grabbing news, and its image as a beleaguered city, staunchly upholding a Free China in a country overrun by the Japanese, was stirringly heroic. At the head of this unyielding resistance stood the stiff and god-like figure of Generalissimo Chiang Kai-shek, with his glamorous wife Soong May-ling intermittently at his side. Now, with the United States on the side of China against Japan, the tide of war turned. China's war was subsumed in a global conflict. To keep China in the war and Japanese troops deployed away from the Pacific theatre, Washington sent billions of dollars in aid and despatched General Joseph W Stilwell as Chief of Staff to Chiang. The achievements of this brilliant American soldier are well documented; so are his clashes with Chiang. Dedicated as Stilwell was to his mission of training Chinese soldiers into an efficient fighting force, he made no bones about his frustrations with the parlous state of China's military and administrative organization. At Chiang's request Stilwell was relieved of his command in October 1944. And, as the war dragged on in China, disenchantment set in. Somewhere along the line Chiang's supporters lost their faith in the KMT as the saviour of China.

In the meantime the communist guerrillas, in a fragile alliance with the KMT in the war of resistance, were gaining notable success in penetrating the rural areas behind Japanese lines. Their populist reforms rallied an increasing number of peasants to their cause. Chiang and his American allies were fully aware of that expansion. In fact, the united front of communists and Nationalists, ostensibly fighting shoulder to shoulder, was unravelling. At the prospect of renewed hostilities between them, President Roosevelt sent his representative, Patrick Hurley, to negotiate a settlement in 1944. Hurley held discussions with Chiang in Chongqing, and then with Mao Zedong in Yan'an (see page 143), but his efforts were to no avail. When Japan surrendered, the Chinese government returned to their earlier capital, Nanjing, but not for long. The KMT were back in Chongqing in the autumn of 1949, this time on the run from the communists. The mass killings of Communist Party members and liberals during this last desperate stand are remembered in the US-Chiang Kai-shek Criminal Acts Exhibition Hall. By winter the Liberation Army was in Sichuan (its political commissar was Deng Xiaoping), so within two months of their return the KMT once again abandoned Chongqing, first for Chengdu and finally for Taiwan.

The First Lady

I approached my first interview with Mme Chiang much less nervously than I had gone to Sassoon Road. A few Chinese had done their best to give me the fidgets, assuring me that I would find the First Lady of the land less 'human' than her eldest sister, but I wasn't impressed with the threat. What do people mean when they say 'human'? Everything or nothing. Sometimes it means that a public person is not without his little vices, but that isn't what the gossips meant about Mme Chiang and Mme Kung. I think it really means 'warmhearted'. Certainly Mayling's heart is kept cool. She would like to be entirely steely and without emotion, I suspect, except in a large and patriotic way. She doesn't think that public personages should have any use for individualistic orgies of sentiment, either in love or anything else; she is as severe with her heart as a New Englander. That is what I thought after our first conversation . . . . .

There have been about twenty descriptions of Mme Chiang and the surroundings in which people interview her, so I won't bother about it. She was used to writers and she put me at ease very quickly; we were chattering along like old friends when her husband suddenly entered the room. He hadn't been warned that she was not alone, and he was embarrassed at being in his slippers. I leaped to my feet. Even in his slippers the Generalissimo always had that effect on me; I found myself standing at attention whenever he appeared. His wife introduced us and he bowed and started to back out of the room.

'Hao hao,' he said, as she explained me rapidly in Chinese. 'Hao, hao, hao.' The door closed on another bow. What he had said was just, 'Good, good, good,' and it means anything polite that you like to put into it. Madame smiled and said, 'He didn't have his teeth in. Sit down, Miss Hahn.'

Emily Hahn, China to Me, 1944

Chongqing's natural defences, which proved so impregnable to the Japanese, probably encouraged the kingdom of Ba (see page 10), some 2,500 years ago, to locate its capital at a site near the present city. After Ba was absorbed by the Qin in the third century BC, the settlement was successively named Jiangzhou, Yuzhou and Gongzhou. 'Chongqing', meaning Double Celebration, was adopted in 1188. It was then that a denizen of the city, Zhaodun, having first been ennobled and then enthroned as emperor, renamed it to commemorate his dazzling rise up the political ladder.

As the gateway to the southwest, Chongqing impressed early foreigners in China as rather more important than the provincial capital, Chengdu. A British consular agent was at his post here by 1871; the consulate-general in Chengdu was not established until 1902. By the 1890 amendment to the Qifu (Cheefoo) Convention of 1876, Chongqing became a port open to foreign trade.

G E Morrison (1862–1930), the Australian who became *The Times'* correspondent in China, came to Chongqing in 1894. Approaching the city, he walked through fields of sugarcane and poppy. Opium was extensively grown in Sichuan (2,250 tons of it were exported from the province in 1893). Morrison was told that some 40 to 50 per cent of the men in Chongqing indulged in it. Edgar Snow, the American journalist, travelling from Chongqing to Xi'an in 1939, noted that opium was sold in the roadside inns. Perhaps it helped the guests to overlook the lice and rats, he speculated. The huge rat population of Chongqing was exterminated only when improvements to sanitation and public hygiene were made in the 1940s. Until then Chongqing was, as one British administrator described it in 1905, 'a dripping, mouldy, crass ant-heap'. And quite apart from the depressing conditions of the filthy and crowded streets, the damp winter and scorching summer, there was the difficulty of access over the rapids of the Yangzi.

Traditionally, junks and sampans plied the Yangzi, their progress over the rapids made possible by the labours of hundreds of trackers. It was an English merchant, Archibald Little (see page 179), who pioneered steam navigation on the upper reaches of the river as far as Chongqing. His scheme was initially opposed by the Chinese authorities, but when on 9 March 1898 his Shanghai-built launch *Lee-chuan* chugged triumphantly into Chongqing harbour from Yichang, the hair-raising moments of being pulled over the worst rapids by trackers were forgotten, and flags, cheers and firecrackers greeted its arrival at Chaotianmen.

The Yangzi, its flow steadier now that all the obstructing rocks along its navigable course have been blasted away, no longer poses any danger to shipping, yet a cruise through its corridor of towering gorges can still evoke all the excitement of earlier times.

(preceding page) *Pontoon bridge at Chaotianmen, Chongqing*

Sights in Chongqing

CITY CENTRE

Chongqing is best explored by car, but the downtown area on the rocky peninsula is compact enough to cover on foot. **Chaotianmen docks**, at the point where the peninsula thrusts itself into the mingled waters of the Yangzi and its tributary, should not be missed. Flanked by clothes and noodle stalls, narrow streets thread their way down to the harbour. Numbered wharfs line both banks of Chaotianmen, the first to ninth clustering at the tip from one side to the other. Down at the harbour, a throbbing panorama unrolls—steamers, tugboats, rows of pontoons, even a cable tramway to ease the ascent from shore to street. The river swirls past in a pale coffee-coloured arc. In winter, when the water level falls, wide stretches of mudflats lie exposed, and the only cargo transport to the ships is on the shoulders of porters. In the old days those mudflats were regularly colonized by itinerants who would put up temporary matshed shelters, so that a village would spring up overnight, until the summer flood drove them to seek a perch on higher ground.

Not that some of the huddled dwellings still to be found in the dark **stairway lanes** between Chaotianmen and the downtown area look any less temporary. Some of these alleys have traditional names: Fire Spark Lane, Beating Gong Lane; others are simply numbered. All of them have defied post-war town-planning and remain congested centres of life, most of it carried on in full sight of neighbours and passers-by. Baskets piled at the entrances bring the market to the inhabitants' doorstep; here they shop for their green peppers and pickled garlic, and have chicken pieces and tripe weighed out on steelyard scales. Communal taps, public latrines and bamboo poles hung with washing punctuate the length of the stairway. There is constant pedestrian traffic, but the children, sitting on wooden stools with their homework on their laps, seem impervious to it all.

Past the Chungking Hotel on Xinhua Lu, in a cul-de-sac running off Minzu Lu, is the **Luohan Temple**. This 19th-century foundation, all yellow and red paint, is glimpsed through an ornate passage whose walls are encrusted with rock carvings in the manner of Buddhist grottoes. *Luohan* are Buddhist saints; traditionally they number 500, although in this temple the pantheon, represented by individual painted statues, is 524 strong. They are of recent vintage, the last of the original Qing sculptures having been destroyed in the Cultural Revolution (1966–76). The ones you now see were moulded by the Sichuan Fine Arts Institute in 1985.

Northwest of the temple, the **Jialing cable car** starts its journey from Cangbai Lu to Jinsha Jie on the north bank (Jiangbei). The five-minute ride is fun on a clear day. Another cable car, at **Wanglongmen**, spans the Yangzi to the south.

Gathering round pet parakeets in a side street

Afternoon tea, Sichuan-style

The dreary, utilitarian **Liberation Monument** (Jiefang Bei) at the junction of Zourong Lu and Minquan Lu demarcates the city centre. In its vicinity are found the Chongqing Department Store (Baihuo Dalou), the Foreign Languages Bookstore (Waiwen Shudian), sidewalk vendors and Chongqing's most dedicated consumers.

WARTIME RELICS

Japanese bombardment and rapid population growth transformed Chongqing from the dank river town of its pre-war days to a large modern city. Superficially it no longer shows its battle scars. To be sure, every Sichuan-bound flight from Hong Kong has its complement of bewildered Taiwanese exiles, eager to revisit old haunts, but Chongqing's wartime experience survives more in the nostalgia of these Kuomintang veterans than in any physical aspect of the city. A few sites, though, are preserved for their propaganda value.

Two museums to wartime Chongqing are found northwest of the **Renmin Guesthouse** complex (itself worth a look for the sheer *folie de grandeur* of the **Chongqing People's Assembly Hall**—a replica of Beijing's Temple of Heaven—sandwiched between two wings of the hotel). There are many 'Mao-Zedong-slept-here'-type of museums in China, and **Osmanthus Garden** (Guiyuan) on Zhongshan Si Lu is one of them. In this gaunt, black brick house, with an ivy-covered porch and a walled yard to its rear, the 'Double Tenth Accord' was signed in 1945. KMT general Zhang Zhizhong, whose home Guiyuan was, vacated his house for Mao Zedong's brief stay in Chongqing. The accord was one of several Communist–Nationalist attempts to hammer out a joint government for post-war China. It proved to be a merely temporary truce.

Zhou Enlai, later premier of the People's Republic of China, stayed in Chongqing rather longer (1938–45). As Secretary of the South China Bureau of the Central Committee of the Communist Party, he lived and worked at **50 Zengjiayan**, close to Guiyuan. It was the time of the united front, although the spirit of cooperation must have worn thin at times, for Zhou's residence was overlooked on one side by a police station, and on the other by the house of Dai Li, head of the KMT secret service. A Japanese bomb wrecked part of the complex in 1940, but what is intact still evokes something of the personality of its famous inhabitant. A handsome statue stands at the entrance. Inside, the man is recalled in the simple quarters he shared with his wife, Deng Yingchao. An engaging caption in a kitchen crudely furnished with wood-burning stove, stacks of bamboo steamers, wooden ladle and stone water jar, reads (in Chinese): 'Here Zhou Enlai personally prepared his specialities, such as Red-cooked Lion Head Meatballs, for his friends and colleagues'. A bizarre touch in the common room is provided by a ping-pong table, which apparently doubled as a bed for visiting Party workers.

Fortress Chongqing
Wartime Capital

In 1937–8, during the Sino-Japanese War, a massive evacuation from enemy-occupied territory to *neidi* (the interior) rumbled across China. A textile mill in a central province was dismantled and conveyed a thousand miles to Sichuan; 380 junks heaved its 8,000 tons of machinery through the gorges. In Canton (Guangzhou) the library collection of Sun Yat-sen University was spirited out of the city by boat, only slightly ahead of the Japanese army. Countless refugees beat a path to Kuomintang-controlled provinces in the southwest. Once in Chongqing, Chengdu or Kunming, they reassembled their plants and campuses, found lodgings and work, and proceeded to wait out the war.

Chongqing behind its bastion of mountains was Chiang Kai-shek's last stand against the Japanese. The enemy had already taken Shanghai, Nanjing, Hankou and Yichang. Hankou proved a convenient base for launching bomb attacks on Chongqing, and for three hot summers the temporary capital endured the blitz, sometimes every few days, sometimes every few hours. The first alert of an impending attack was signalled by the raising of red lanterns on poles planted along the ridge line of the hills; shortly afterwards, at the sound of alarms, the wet and fetid tunnels under the Chongqing hills would fill with men, women and children—everyone had a designated shelter. As time went on, these raids came to be regarded as part of the routine of daily life, disturbing but not convulsive in their impact on a people already inured to hardship. Spilling out of the shelters as the all-clear sounded, the people of Chongqing went back to daubing black paint on their houses, or salvaging possessions out of the ashes of burnt-out homes, knowing that by winter, when thick clouds blotted out everything, the bombardment would cease.

Still, it was a feverish sort of existence. Flowing through the narrow muddy streets, jostling with rickshaws, sedan chairs, motor cars, water-carriers and pedlars, the citizenry was a motley lot. Bureaucrats and KMT bigwigs, profiteers and patriots swarmed around a ruined city too small to hold them all. Officers in uniform, accompanied by their silk-clad wives or concubines, mingled with beggars in rags. Many of the newcomers spoke in dialects incomprehensible to Sichuanese ears. The exiles themselves felt like an alien people, so backward and uncouth did the natives seem in comparison. From time to time, Generalissimo Chiang Kai-shek would issue forth from his Huangshan villa to lead some morale-boosting rally. There was a flickering revival of his New Life Movement, a campaign of moral regeneration launched before the war, so that life in Chongqing was made even more cheerless by the banning of such decadent practices as mahjong, permanent waves and dancing parties. Madame Chiang set an example by her patronage of orphanages, but for much of the time she was out of Chongqing altogether, wooing the Americans and raising funds for China's war. Meanwhile scarcity, hoarding and the increasing amounts of worthless currency churned out by the government took inflation to new heights. Corruption was rife.

In those days a foreign community of sorts, mostly minor diplomats and correspondents, still resided in the crumbling Western-style mansions on the south bank. Its members congregated at the Press Hostel or the Chung-king Club, spreading the latest rumours, processing the propaganda pumped out by the Ministry of Information, playing poker and eking out a dwindling supply of whisky and gin. At the beginning of the war, there was an air link over Japanese lines to the British colony of Hong Kong before that fell, but otherwise they were cut off from the outside world.

All this changed with Pearl Harbor and the United States' entry into the widening war. In the later stage of World War II Chongqing found itself host to generals and politicians and thousands of American servicemen. 'Vinegar Joe' Stilwell, sent by Washington to bolster Chiang's ill-trained and disorganized army, came and went. He was replaced by General Wedemeyer. Finally, despite differences between Chiang and the Allies on the conduct of the war, the Japanese were defeated. Chiang moved his capital back to Nanjing. But the conclusion of the Sino-Japanese conflict did not lead China to peace; instead, it removed the need for a united front and thus the last obstacle to civil war.

Red Crag Village (Hongyan Cun), the Chongqing base of the South China Bureau of the Central Committee of the Chinese Communist Party (CCP) and the Eighth Route Army office between 1939 and 1946, is on the south bank of the Jialing, further upstream to the west. Its grim exterior seems entirely in keeping with the secret work conducted here. Remnants of the Red Army, restyled as the Eighth Route Army by agreement with the KMT, were operating in the united front against the Japanese. But underneath the veneer of mutual cooperation, the CCP, though constantly under surveillance by the KMT, was laying the foundations for ultimate control of China. There is little in the museum here to interest the visitor, apart from a printing press, moved from Hankou in 1938, on which the Party newspaper—the *Xinhua Daily*—was produced.

On past the Sichuan Institute of Foreign Languages, the northwest road out of the city centre winds through a suburban district called Shapingba and up Gele Hill. Chiang Kai-shek lived in a mansion at the top in 1944–5. (His official residence, endowed with its own air raid shelter, was on Huangshan on the south bank; it now serves as a sanatorium for cadres.) **Gele Hill** is the site of the revolutionary **Martyrs' Memorial**, marked by a curiously bland collection of life-size statues scattered about in a park. The hill was a security zone during the war of resistance, the headquarters for China–US military intelligence (1943–6) known as the **Sino-American Cooperation Organization**. It was headed by General Dai Li, chief of the KMT secret service, a man feared throughout China and nicknamed 'the Generalissimo's Number One Hatchet Man'. The notorious complex of prisons and torture chambers, **Baigong Guan** and **Zhazi Dong**, was also located there. These are all now given over to propaganda purposes. Three hundred CCP members and communist sympathizers, as well as children and newborn babies, were put to death here before the KMT decamped in November 1949. Looking down on the chains, manacles and torture instruments at Zhazi Dong, the man who ordered the massacre gazes out from his photograph in the 'inquisition room'. The Generalissimo is shown dressed in full military regalia. It is not clear whether irony is intended by the display, on either side of the portrait, of two lines of precepts commending 'Loyalty, Filial Piety and Benevolence' and 'Good Faith and Peace'. The other exhibits consist of photographs of prisoners, cells and blood-stained corpses. Yet, for all the sensationalism of the captions, the barbed wire and the outrage expressed in the very name of the US-Chiang Kai-shek Criminal Acts Hall (a name no longer used by the Chinese), the events recorded on Gele Hill already appear blurred and shadowy, an effect enhanced by the air of neglect pervading the site.

Art and Culture

The earthenware figurines and brick reliefs exhibited in the **Chongqing City**

Museum (Pipa Hill, open daily 9 am–12 noon, 2.30–6 pm) are from the Eastern Han period (AD 25–220). They came from tombs, most likely of wealthy and important men. As was the custom, the deceased were buried with objects recalling the preoccupations and high points of everyday life—farming, hunting and entertainment. Look for the effigy of a slyly grinning actor, his head cocked between muscular hunched shoulders, or the bas-relief panels decorated with rows of galloping calvary—both are fine examples of tomb sculpture. While Han tombs were elaborate affairs, the people of Ba, who roamed the plains of eastern Sichuan two thousand years ago, disposed of their dead in an even more singular fashion, encasing corpses in canoe-shaped wooden coffins. Two of these boat-coffins, found near Chongqing, are exhibited in this museum.

At the **Chongqing Natural History Museum** in Beipei district north of the city, pride of place is given to skeletons of the Tuojiang stegosaur and the *Omeisaurus zigongensis* dinosaur, both dating from the Jurassic period (see page 209).

Often on tour group itineraries, the **Sichuan Fine Arts Institute** (Sichuan Meishu Xueyuan) in Huangjiaoping and **Painters Village** (Huajia Zhi Cun) in Hualongqiao are some way out of the city and difficult to reach by public transport. Both establishments have galleries and pieces for sale. Of the two, the Painters Village is more interesting, particularly if you can arrange to be admitted into some of the individual studios and meet the artists at work. Located in the western suburbs, the Painters Village was established in the 1950s to nurture artists who would create paintings and lithographs to glorify the revolution. These state-sponsored artists, who come from all over China, include members of minority nationalities whose paintings, perhaps because of their exotic subject matter, appear more arresting to the eye than the examples of *guohua* (landscapes and brush-and-ink compositions of birds and flowers) executed in traditional Chinese style. Since China embarked on economic reforms, the painters here have had to become commercial because the government no longer buys all their work.

Sights around Chongqing

Chongqing residents flock to the city's two hot springs when the weather turns warm enough for outings. Neither of them holds much interest for the Western visitor. The **Southern Hot Springs** (Nan Wenquan), 26 kilometres (16 miles) from Chongqing, is closer. You can rent a towel for a small charge and either take a dip in the outdoor swimming pool or have a bath indoors. Beside a small dirty creek punts can be hired for Rmb 2 an hour.

Southern Hills Park (Nanshan Gongyuan) is an arboreal enclave on the south bank in an area once colonized by the US consular office, the KMT and rich businessmen. Rather dilapidated Western-style villas, now used by jaded cadres sent on rest-cures by their work units, are still dotted among the trees. Nobody seems to mind visitors taking a look around. Huangshan, commanding the top of one of the hillocks here, was where Chiang Kai-shek had his villa and personal air-raid shelter. One of the other hills, Yushan, is associated with emperor Yu's wife, who reputedly lived here in around 2000 BC (see pages 101 and 184). Yu, the legendary regulator of the flood that submerged the main river valleys of China, laboured for 13 years without once returning home, even though thrice he passed the door of his house and heard the cries of his wife and children.

Dazu: Buddhist Grottoes

To see monumental religious sculpture is the reason one comes to Dazu. This unassuming county town 165 kilometres (102 miles) northwest of Chongqing has something like 40 Buddhist grottoes secreted among its terraced hillsides. None of them was carved before the last two decades of the Tang Dynasty (618–907), when the more famous cave temples in northern China—at Dunhuang, Yungang and Longmen—were long since completed. By that relatively late date, Buddhist sculpture had broken away completely from the Indo-Hellenistic influences so evident in the earlier Buddhist caves, and evolved a distinctly Chinese style. This development is amply illustrated in the grottoes at Beishan and Baodingshan, the two most stunning petroglyphic sites at Dazu.

The County Town

Local legend has it that 'Dazu'—literally Big Foot—commemorates an outsize footprint left on the bed of a Baodingshan pond by Sakyamuni (the historical Buddha). 'Dazu' also means Great Sufficiency, and the county town, set amidst lush furrowed fields, palpably justifies its name in the less fanciful sense of amplitude or prosperity.

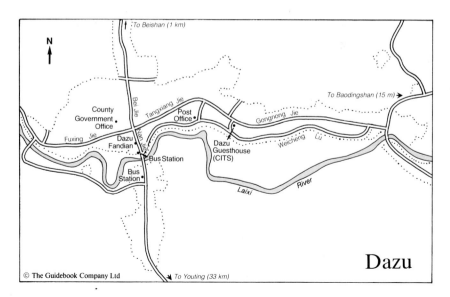

Serving from bamboo steamers at a food stall

Rock sculptures at Baodingshan, Dazu:
(clockwise) *a drunk behaves improperly to his mother; a disciple of the Buddha; Sakyamuni*
bearing the coffin of his father; the Revolving Wheel; the keeper of hens

BUDDHISM IN CHINA
From the Eastern Han to the Tang

Chinese lore attributes the introduction of Buddhism to an imperial inspiration. An emperor of the Eastern Han (AD 25–220) had a dream that a
golden deity was to be found in the west. He promptly sent envoys to India,
and they returned with the *Sutra in Forty-two Articles*, the first Indian Buddhist work to be translated into Chinese.

Actually the faith first spread from India through central Asia along the
fabled Silk Road, probably around AD 65. No other foreign import had such
profound influence on Chinese life until the 19th century. A highly developed creed in India by the time it reached China, Buddhism had already
been wracked by sectarian schisms from which had sprung two opposing
schools, Hinayana (Lesser Vehicle) and Mahayana (Greater Vehicle). It was
the Mahayana version which won converts in China, but the brand of
religion that ultimately triumphed there was, in the end, to bear little resemblance to its Indian roots.

The final goal of traditional Buddhists is 'Nirvana', when the believer is
released from the cycle of birth, death and reincarnation and enters the state
of the Buddha. Gautama, the religion's founder and the 'historical' Buddha,
taught that all men possessed the propensity for achieving Nirvana, but
diverse schools have debated on the means of salvation, with one branch
stressing metaphysics, another professing the efficacy of meditation, a third
glorifying benevolence and so on. Within the Hinayana tradition the ideal
Buddhist is represented by the *arhat*. In practice an arhat is usually a monk
and ascetic who, through several rebirths, achieves salvation by his own
efforts. Mahayana Buddhism, by contrast, reveals a much less arduous way
to salvation, for followers may look to saints for help. These saints or *bodhisattvas* can be monks or laymen. Out of compassion for living beings,
they have postponed their own entry to Nirvana in order to remain in the
world to help suffering humanity towards that blessed state. By praying to
these bodhisattvas, by making offerings and performing good works, a
believer could aspire to eternal bliss as well as any monk. And since any
human being may attain buddhahood, Gautama becomes only one reincarnation in an infinite multitude of buddhas stretching back to the past and
into the future.

The egalitarian element in Buddhism, not to mention its promise of rewards in the next life to compensate for suffering in the present existence, found favour with the Chinese. But they welcomed the alien faith as much for the resemblances it seemingly bore to indigenous traditions of religion and morality as for its metaphysics. The popular Chinese mentality, ever pragmatic, had no trouble reconciling the apparent contradictions between Buddhist doctrine and existing folk beliefs, such as Taoism. It embraced Buddhist saints, merely grafting them on to the plethora of deities that were already worshipped; it delighted in the mysticism, with its overtones of magic, which might just as well be a form of Taoist trance; it even, at one time, recruited the Buddha into the Taoist pantheon of immortals; and it somehow squared the celibacy of the Buddhist priesthood with the Confucian cult of the family. Such muddle could hardly be wondered at, since the first translations of Sanskrit texts borrowed Taoist expressions to elucidate unfamiliar Buddhist concepts.

Progress in translating Sanskrit texts by monks and laymen, especially the indomitable pilgrims who spent years travelling to India in search of original scriptures, gave such impetus to the diffusion of Buddhism in Chinese society that by AD 400 it had become a mass religion, at least in the northern part of the empire. By the sixth century Buddhism was widespread in the south as well. It enjoyed royal patronage, notably of Liang Wudi, an emperor of the Southern Dynasties who tried in AD 527 and 529 to renounce his throne and withdraw to a monastery in his capital, Nanjing. Under the Sui Dynasty (581–618), which accomplished the reunification of the northern and southern empires, and the first two hundred years or so of the Tang (618–907), which gave rise to a splendid efflorescence of art and literature, Chinese Buddhism entered a golden age of influence and prestige. Religious fervour was to manifest itself in generous endowments to monasteries, in building temples and in casting colossal statues. Its most ecstatic expression was one borrowed from India and central Asia: cave shrines hollowed out of rock.

Grain, fruit, fish and pigs are farmed in the surrounding countryside. Half the rolling, verdant landscape is water, ribbons of irrigated terraces broken by spindly trees. In the foreground of this timeless landscape there might be a water buffalo squelching its ponderous way through mud.

In the town life eddies around the main street market and teahouses. Any of the open-fronted restaurants along Zhongshan Dong Jie near Dazu Guesthouse will be eager to serve a fizzy drink or a meal, with each dish cooked in the all-purpose wok set on a coal-burning stove. You can ask for simple combinations of the raw ingredients laid out on the counter: these may be seasonal vegetables, potatoes, peppers and a little pork. Potatoes are grated into slivers and fried, the result tasting rather like greasy, underdone chips. In the early morning, hot fist-size stuffed dumplings sold direct from kerbside steamers make a satisfying breakfast.

Beishan

The Beishan (North Hill) sculptures owe their existence to a rebellion in AD 881. When the rebel leader, Huang Chao, reached the then imperial capital, Chang'an (Xi'an), Emperor Xizong fled to Chengdu. Loyalist generals and their armies followed, and this so outraged local sentiments that one of the provincial commanders, Wei Junjing, despatched his own troops to Beishan to forestall further encroachment. Perhaps to make sure that his actions would be blessed, he later had Buddha images carved on the sandstone cliff-faces around his military base. Begun in 892, this meritorious exercise was to be continued by others for a quarter of a century afterwards.

The iconography consists of statues and high reliefs set in caves and grottoes or cut into the facades of a crescent-shaped cliff known as Buddha Bend (Fowan). Each grotto or shrine has a painted number, but there are no explanatory labels (the shrines are identified by the same numbers in the descriptions below). The southern section, containing work from the Tang (618–907) and Five Dynasties period (907–960), should be seen first. Considering the severe persecution of Buddhism in AD 843–5, when foreign religions were proscribed by imperial decree, it is remarkable that the faith remained sufficiently tenacious for piety to be flaunted on such an unbridled scale, as it was in these shrines. One reason for this was undoubtedly Sichuan's remoteness from the imperial capital.

Even so, the northern sculptural style persisted, as can be seen in the rendering of the disciples and saints that flank the Buddha (Sakyamuni) in **shrine 10**. In this relic from the later Tang, the modelling of the figures is sensual and imposing, but the plump, bland faces suggest absence of emotions. There is little emphasis on drapery: garments fall in folds delineated unfussily by intaglio lines. On the right, Bodhisattva Mahasthama with his golden crown and lotus bud is an incomparably fine representation of serenity and detachment.

'Western Paradise' or 'Pure Land' is illustrated in **shrine 245**, the pride of the small Tang collection. Diverse schools of doctrine held sway in China at various times. The Pure Land school arose during the sixth century and became immensely popular. Although based on interpretations of an Indian sutra (scripture), it dispensed with the more obscure teachings of the original religion and believers were encouraged to strive not for Nirvana, but for Pure Land, a happy paradise. Presiding in paradise is Amitabha Buddha (Amituofo in Chinese). In a previous existence he was a monk named Dharmakara who had spent millions of years practising meditation and performing acts of charity. As it is only by the grace of Amitabha Buddha that men will be led to salvation, constant recitation of his name is an essential element in the Pure Land form of worship. It is said that Emei Shan, Sichuan's holy mountain (see page 63), was named from the first two syllables of this invocation.

Here, then, is Amitabha Buddha in his Western Paradise, the centrepiece of the ensemble. Seated under a lotus, he is flanked by the bodhisattvas Guanyin (see below) and Mahasthama. Altogether, though, there are more than 500 figures in this intricately wrought work. It is also full of surprising detail. The top third of the shrine is a rollicking composition of cranes and parrots wheeling between canopies of clouds, of bodhisattvas and urchins, and of many-storeyed pavilions and lotus ponds. A veritable celestial orchestra is suggested by depictions of Chinese zither, *pipa*, conch and cymbals. The use of colour, particularly aquamarine blue and gilt, heightens the richness of effect. Below Amitabha Buddha, running across the base and along the sides of the shrine, are narrative bands of bas-reliefs which recount how Vaidehi, the mother of a prince, is led through renunciation to the way of truth.

About a third of Beishan was carved in the Five Dynasties, a transitional period between the decline of Buddhism and a brief revival of influence in the Song Dynasty (960–1279). Note the androgynous representation of Avalokitesvara (**shrine 273**), whom Chinese Buddhists later transformed into Guanyin, the Goddess of Mercy and bestower of sons. At this point the feminization of the bodhisattva was clearly still incomplete. By the Song Dynasty, as we shall see, this bodhisattva had become—at least as far as the plastic arts were concerned—an unequivocally female deity inspiring enthusiastic devotion and her sculptors' most ardent energies.

Song-dynasty sculptures cluster in the northern section of Buddha Bend. If Tang sculpture was vigorous and unadorned, that of the Song Dynasty reflected a tendency towards refinement and a greater concern with decoration. By the 11th century, although certain sects still had their adherents among the populace, Buddhism had lost its prominence. This decline in spiritual conviction is manifestly reflected in religious iconography, where the concern with expressing otherworldliness was overtaken by an urge to portray deities naturalistically. Certainly the figures carved here appear rather more human than divine. Some of them are elaborately clothed; several representations of Guanyin, for example, are richly draped, bejewelled and crowned with ornate head-dresses (see **shrines 136** and **180**). This bodhisattva's transformation from Avalokitesvara into the Goddess of Mercy is now complete: there is no mistaking the femininity of this matronly, double-chinned figure, who resembles, as one Chinese writer put it, 'a lady of noble birth'.

As a whole, shrine 136 is known as 'The Revolving Wheel'. It is the largest cave in the complex and took four years to carve (1142–6). The Wheel of Law, balanced on eight carved columns, is sculpted in the round. This solid piece in turn supports the roof of the cave. On the wall behind and to the sides of this centrepiece are ranged a statue of Sakyamuni Buddha and more than 20 bodhisattvas, guardians and donors in various poses. Two seated and two standing images of Guanyin apart, there is Puxian (Samantabhadra) mounted on an elephant (Puxian, the Bodhisattva of Universal Benevolence, is particularly associated with Emei Shan, see page 68). Like Guanyin, Puxian is here portrayed in female form, with a gentle expression, downcast eyes and the merest hint of a beatific smile. In a parallel composition to the left of the wheel, the Bodhisattva of Wisdom (Manjusri) rides crosslegged on a lion.

There is nothing matronly about the Guanyin with a Rosary (**shrine 125**). Here she cuts an altogether more delicate figure, trailing ribbons and framed by an elliptical aureole. There is movement and grace in the twist of her body and the tilt of her head—a refreshing contrast to the stillness of other Guanyin figures at Beishan and an astonishing departure from the restraint traditionally exercised in religious sculpture. It is an unashamedly romantic image. Sadly, it has not weathered the centuries without some damage, although the lissom young goddess has come through with her enigmatic smile intact.

A similar absence of solemnity characterizes Guanyin Gazing at the Reflection of the Moon (**shrine 113**). Although the lower part of this piece has crumbled away, it is nonetheless possible to discern in Guanyin's relaxed pose an almost playful mood, as if she is splashing a foot in water. The same cannot be said of the rigidly seated goddess in **shrine 133**; she, too, is gazing at the reflection of the moon, but she does so in a posture which somehow exudes disapproval and severity.

Shrine 155 exemplifies the thousand-buddha cave, a favourite motif in Buddhist iconography whereby countless tiny figures are chipped out in niches over an entire wall. A surprising number of the ones here have been preserved. They wrap round the gorgeous figure of the Peacock King (Mayurasana-raja) on his blue and russet-coloured throne.

Baodingshan

Echoing an earlier tradition of Buddhist iconography, the rock sculptures at Baodingshan (Precious Summit Hill) form a series of narratives based on Buddhist scriptures. This stupendous project was launched by a monk, Zhao Zhifeng, an adherent of Tantric Buddhism, in the Southern Song Dynasty (1127–1279). By the time Zhao was preaching in Sichuan, Buddhism was in retreat in northern China. Nevertheless he was able to collect enough donations to have more than 10,000 icons chiselled out of the hillsides here. They are most concentrated at Great Buddha Bend (Dafowan), a U-shaped valley reached by a stone staircase from the south. Along the sweep of the craggy surfaces sacred and secular images erupt out of the ochreous background like some phantasmagoric vision of heaven and hell. They were the last of their kind, for no known cave sculpture on such a huge scale was carved anywhere in China after 1249, when Dafowan was completed. The scale, nevertheless, is rather less daunting than that of the cave temples in the north of the empire, where the harshness of the terrain itself lent awesomeness to the sculptures wrested out of it. Nor, in comparison, do these sculptures have the polish and spiritual force of great art, but their very coarseness does give them a certain rough-hewn grandeur.

Zhao Zhifeng's creation was a brilliant stroke of proselytization: the message of some of the stories-in-stone, whether it is retribution for unfilial acts or the evils of drink, would have been quite explicit to all manner of believers. When the whole spectacle is plonked down in the open countryside so that it is easily accessible (unlike, for example, the caves in the high cliffs of Yungang), the crowds of pilgrims gathered here every spring, to burn incense at the **Sacred Longevity Temple** (Shengshou Si) and to take in the sideshows, would have been numerous indeed.

Visiting the temple today, you are more likely to be greeted by souvenir and bottled drinks hawkers than by any vendor of incense. A path leading from the temple winds its way to the entrance to Dafowan. Thirty tableaux, each numbered, unravel as you proceed round the amphitheatre of rock. The nine demonic Guardians of the Law (**shrine 2**), some brandishing swords, all of them snarling, prepare one for contemplating the Revolving Wheel (**shrine 3**) in a suitably subdued frame of mind. The wheel symbolizes the Six States of Transmigration through which all living beings pass. Depending on their moral actions, living beings may be reborn into any of these states: as gods in paradise, as men in a world of prosperity, as gods

Revolutionary Love

Thus in 1964, I met in the Old People's Home at Chingkangshan, Well Ridge Mountain, where Mao Tsetung had established his first base in 1927, a very old peasant who for years had kept buried in the mud floor under his bed a jar full of salt. He was waiting for the Red Army to return, having been one of those who supplied it with salt, of which the base was being deprived by the Chiang blockade. For twenty-two years this old peasant had waited with the jar under his bed . . .

In Szechuan, most feudal province of all, when the Red Army passed through villages and made propaganda, it was the women, the downtrodden women of Szechuan, who were the first to revolt, to organize women militias, to raid the landlords' houses and their hoards of grain.

Many of the women walked miles to collect food and bring it to the armies on the Long March. And when the soldiers left, the women would give them shoes; not only those straw shoes used for padding about the mud roads, but also the more precious cloth shoes, made of slabs of cotton cloth felted together layer by layer with glue for the sole, and stitched evenly, through and through; and which they would embroider with the name of the soldier stitched on the inner sole:

> *Using my needle, as a pen*
> *To write clearly, in stitches*
> *Your name and my thoughts . . .*

they sang, and this was not romance, but revolutionary love, greater than romance.

And the soldiers would carry these shoes, fastened round their necks, and never wear them, but keep them clean, in memory of the peasant women who had stitched them, asking the names of the soldiers and painfully copying down the characters, for they knew not how to read them . . . In the reprisals which followed, the landlords and warlords killed both men and women. Here, too, in the so quiet-seeming countryside of Szechuan, people waited for the Red Army to return.

Han Suyin, Birdless Summer, 1968

and 'hungry ghosts' (tormented spirits) joined in battle, as animals, as hungry ghosts, or in hell. As the wheel is ever revolving, so the cycle of rebirths is infinite, and only the attainment of Nirvana through the practice of Buddhism brings it to an end.

Next comes the rock sculpture's creator, the monk Zhao Zhifeng, in youth, mid-life and old age (**shrine 4**). The three characters for 'Baodingshan' are in the calligraphy of an official in the Southern Song. Also commemorated is Vairocana Buddha, believed to be the founder of Tantric Buddhism (**shrine 5**). He is flanked by the Bodhisattva of Universal Benevolence (Samantabhadra) and the Bodhisattva of Wisdom (Manjusri), and together they are known as the Three Saints of the Avatamsaka School (Huayan to Chinese Buddhists). This lowering triad, seven metres (23 feet) high and inclined slightly forwards, is plainly designed to be viewed from below.

Just before the curve of the valley doubles back upon itself there is a pavilion (**shrine 8**) whose precious occupant is an amazing seated **statue of Guanyin**, the Goddess of Mercy, characteristically endowed with a thousand arms (actually 1,007, according to a monk who counted them by pasting a numbered gold leaf on each hand). It is a magnificent object, a gleam of burnished gold, blue and turquoise in the opaque half-light of its modest shelter. Arms flare out behind the seated goddess and give way to a coiling tangle of hands, some clutching a rosary, others balancing a miniature pagoda. Each upturned empty palm is carved with an all-seeing eye.

A reclining Buddha (**shrine 11**) marks the eastern end of Dafowan. So massive are the head and torso that they fill the entire surface; thus chopped off at the knee, the Buddha lies on his right side in the position of final deliverance, at the moment of entering Nirvana. With his enormous head and foreshortened body, he is a mildly grotesque figure. The Birth of the Buddha is the theme of the relief (**12**) on the corner. As recounted in scriptures and legends, the Buddha was born to the king and queen of Sakyas, a state at the northern edge of the Ganges plain, in around 563 BC. He was named Siddhartha. His birth was foretold in a dream that his mother had, in which a white elephant entered her womb through her side; Brahmins summoned by her to interpret the dream took it to be a sign that the child, when born, would become either a universal monarch or a Buddha. This extraordinary boy grew up in luxury, was eventually married to a cousin and fathered a son. But he was to renounce all this out of compassion for the suffering in the world. Adopting the life of an ascetic, the prince (now known as Gautama) wandered from place to place in quest of the truth. After years of intense study and many struggles, the truth was revealed to him as he meditated one evening under a tree in a place which has come to be called Bodhgaya. As night turned into dawn, Gautama's '. . . mind was emancipated . . . Ignorance was dispelled, knowledge arose . . . darkness was dispelled, light arose.' This account of Gautama's life, amplified by the legends and myths that have developed around the man, is retold in countless works of sculpture and painting. Here, at Baodingshan, the legend invoked in the corner grotto has a distinctly Chinese flavour. It relates how nine dragons appeared out of the sky at the moment of Siddhartha's birth, their mouths spewing warm and cold water for the baby's bath. The choice of subject was probably dictated by the existence of a natural spring nearby; by channelling the water through the dragons' heads to flow over the bust of the infant prince the ancient craftsmen neatly devised a means of drainage.

Past the images of the Peacock King, Vairocana, bodhisattvas, devotees and flying *apsaras* or angels (**shrines 13–14**), you come upon a touching illustration of how traditional Confucian thought was fused with Buddhist beliefs. Filial piety is the virtue advocated in Parental Kindness (**shrine 15**): lest undutiful children forget, the pains of childbirth, the suckling of an offspring, a mother's care and other scenes of parental tenderness which are vividly depicted in 11 panels should induce a proper sense of gratitude.

So serious is the sin of filial ingratitude to the Chinese mind that yet another huge relief (**17**) is devoted to condemning it. Perhaps the awful warning represented by the deities of the wind, thunder, lightning, clouds and rain (**shrine 16**) is designed to put the pilgrim in a suitably chastened mood; at any rate, the next tableau will reassure him that the wrath of gods is not visited upon the world of men if human relationships are conducted with propriety, particularly relationships between children and parents. The Buddha himself (the bust in the centre of this relief) has convincingly demonstrated his filial piety, even in his previous births—as related in the Jataka stories—for all that the Six Heretics (bottom row) may jeer and point the finger. There is no clearer refutation of their slander than the vignette (bottom left) in which the Buddha is shown bearing the coffin of his father. Any contradiction between Siddhartha's renunciation of his family and the Confucian ideal of the dutiful son (as exemplified by the figure, lower right, dangling his aged parents from a shoulder pole) appears to have been resolved. The whole ensemble provides an interesting gloss on the intellectual temper of the times, for by the 12th century, various earlier attempts to syncretize indigenous cults with Buddhism had given way to a resurgence of the influence of Confucianism. From reinterpretations of the Sage's teachings, which actually drew on Buddhist and Taoist ideas, an ethical and metaphysical system emerged to supplant Buddhism as the prevailing orthodoxy.

Before moving on, take a look at the girl playing a flute in a niche just above the heretics. This lovely figure seems an aberration, as irrelevant to a sermon on filial piety as the girl feeding chickens is to the punishments of hell (shrine 20). We can only imagine her as a flight of fancy on the sculptor's part, a whimsical re-creation of a farmer's pretty daughter once glimpsed briefly in the countryside.

What distinguishes **shrine 18**, the story of Amitabha and his Pure Land, is not so much its scale, nor the configurations of its many elements, but its groups of some

60 cherubic children straddling balustrades, playing music and lolling in lotus blooms. They symbolize the happiness promised by rebirth in the Western Paradise (see page 167).

All the same, the halls of heaven look very much like a scene on earth. Not so the lower depths of hell (**shrine 20**). Here one sinner is portrayed on the point of dismemberment; there another lost soul, hair and haunch gripped by a demon with a horse's head, is seconds away from being boiled in a cauldron of oil. Repugnant ghosts writhe and grimace in torment, ravaged by hunger, fire and cold. Above and to the right, cautionary tales signal dire warnings against the iniquity of drink: a drunk kills his father and rapes his mother; a wife, a brother and a sister are spurned by their unrepentant boozy relative; shifty-looking characters tempt with bowl and pitcher of wine; an inebriated father fails to recognize his son.

It is with some relief that one turns to the keeper of hens, whose sin is the taking of life but who looks, for all that, entirely undeserving of terrible retribution, so lovingly has she been rendered in her wholesome comeliness.

The western end on the same side of the valley is dominated by the shrine (**21**) dedicated to Master Liu, Zhao Zhifeng's teacher. Master Liu's asceticism took the form of self-mutilations including gouging out an eye and severing his left arm. If the disciple was inspired by reverence for his mentor, though, he failed to give it expression in this clumsily executed and rather static ensemble. Besides the details of Master Liu's austerities, the shrine is studded with secular figures from scholars to warriors. Strung out below the gilded figure of the master are the Ten Great Vidyarajas—manifestations of the Buddha and bodhisattvas in their combat with evil; they are unfinished pieces.

Across the bridge, look in on the Cave of Complete Enlightenment (**29**). In a classic composition three images of the Buddha are ranged against the back wall while a dozen bodhisattvas line the walls on either side. The disciple kneeling in front is carved in the round. The artisans responsible for this cave have thoughtfully improved the natural lighting of the vault by cutting an opening above the entrance. To stall erosion by seeping moisture, they carved a dragon on the left wall to trap the water that trickles in and to conduct it, drip by drip, into a bowl held aloft by the figure of a monk. The water then flows through the monk and out of the cave.

Finally, a parable with a rustic touch (**30**). The tale unfolded in this relief suggests that, just as cattle are gradually tamed into quiescence, so the clamours of earthly desires may be eventually overcome through the practice of Buddhism. First the recalcitrant buffalo tries to run away. A few lashes of the whip later, it submits to being led to a stream for a drink. The herdsmen relax as the cattle feed. A flute is produced for a spot of music. The last scenario showing man and beast at rest hints at the blessed state in which all cravings are extinguished.

Getting to Dazu

By Air An airline service has been established between Chengdu and Dazu by the Sichuan Provincial Airline Company. The 40-minute flight operates on Tuesday and Friday between the two destinations: from Chengdu departure time is 9.30 am, and from Dazu 10.50 am. There is also a weekly flight (Tuesday) from Xi'an via Chengdu. The Chengdu ticket office for these flights is at 16 Renmin Dong Lu (tel 672083); in Dazu travel arrangements should be made through CITS at Dazu Guesthouse.

By Rail Dazu's nearest railhead is **Youtingpu**, 36 kilometres (22 miles) away. Youtingpu is on the Chengdu–Chongqing line; convenient trains to take are the number 307 from Chengdu (departing 7.20 am and arriving 2.40 pm) or the number 308 from Chongqing (departing 7.45 am and arriving 12.17 pm). Buses leave the railway station every hour or so for Dazu.

By Road A long and bumpy ride from Chengdu on a bus starting from the Xinnanmen Bus Station at 6.30 am will cover the 280-kilometre (174-mile) distance in seven hours. From Chongqing, Sichuan Provincial Transportation Company buses leave from Jianxin Bei Lu passenger bus terminal every day starting at 8 am, taking about five hours to reach Dazu. A rather more comfortable way to get there from Chongqing is by the air-conditioned buses run daily by Kangfulai (KFL) Company. A one-way ticket, obtainable in advance, guarantees a seat. Board the bus at 7.40 am from the depot at 223 Renmin Lu (ten minutes' walk west of the Renmin Guesthouse). There is a catch, though: as a touch of luxury a video unit mounted at the front of the bus plays two or three B-feature movies, at full volume, every minute of the way. The bus arrives in Dazu some time after midday.

Beishan, only two kilometres (1.2 miles) north of Dazu, is within walking distance of the town centre. To get there from Dazu Guesthouse turn right at the second crossroads. Past the sports ground, you ascend to the grottoes by a long flight of stone steps. Baodingshan is 15 kilometres (ten miles) to the northeast of Dazu, and involves a journey by car along a winding road. Either hire your own transport and driver from CITS or CTS, or fight your way on to a bus from the main depot across the river, a 15-minute hike from Dazu Guesthouse. The service begins at 7 am and runs every hour or so until mid-afternoon, with the last bus from Baodingshan leaving at 4 pm. Crowded at the best of times, the bus virtually overflows on its last service of the day, so avoid this if possible. Despite the short distance the ride still takes around 35–40 minutes. You can ask to be dropped near Dazu Guesthouse on the return journey.

The Yangzi: Long River

Rising at an elevation of 5,490 metres (18,000 feet) in the mountain ranges along the Qinghai-Tibetan border, the Yangzi flows for 6,400 kilometres (3,900 miles) down to the East China Sea, the third longest river in the world. Here are some more, equally impressive, statistics: the Yangzi admits more than 700 tributaries and drains a fifth of China's land area in which a third of the population live; the river basin is the country's granary, contributing as much as 70 per cent of the gross production of rice; huge cities have been founded on its banks—Chongqing, Wuhan and Nanjing among them, and Shanghai south of its estuary; it carries a tremendous flow of water, the average volume at its mouth more than 28,300 cubic metres (a million cubic feet) per second; annually six million tons of silt accompany this flow, causing its delta to creep into the sea by an average of 25 metres (82 feet) a year.

THE UPPER COURSE

The mental picture most of us have of the Yangzi is the wide, junk-thronged yellow-brown channel of its middle and lower basin. In fact, by the time the river reaches the plains, it has already covered half its length.

It was in 1976 that its glacier-fed source streams were traced to the cold grassy steppes of the Qinghai-Tibetan Plateau. First merging into the **Tongtian River**, then spilling over the plateau edge in a tremendous drop, the source streams discharge their waters into the **Jinsha Jiang** (River of Golden Sand), as the river is called from the point it leaves Qinghai Province and enters Sichuan. This stretch, cleaving a southward passage through narrow, perpendicular canyons, runs parallel for more than 320 kilometres (200 miles) with two other great Asian rivers, the Mekong and the Salween. For much of this tempestuous course, it also demarcates the boundary between China and Tibet (see page 118). In the summer of 1990 a British Hovercraft Expedition led by Squadron Leader Mike Cole travelled to within 24 kilometres (15 miles) of the Yangzi's glacier source by hovercraft four months after setting off. Carrying vaccines to remote settlements, the team was part of a United Nations (UNICEF) campaign to eradicate such diseases as tuberculosis, polio and whooping cough.

Besides 'Jinsha Jiang', the river is known by several other names. The Chinese never refer to the entire river as the Yangzi; that name (spelt Yangtze) was adopted by Europeans and strictly speaking applies only to the lower stretch from Wuhu, in Anhui Province, as far as the estuary. To some people it is occasionally the Dajiang (Great River); to locals it is often just the Jiang, looming as it does too importantly in their lives to be mistaken for any other river; but to most Chinese it is never less than the **Changjiang** (Long River). For the purposes of this guide, however, the European tradition will be observed and the whole river referred to as the Yangzi.

This long river describes two huge hairpin bends before entering its basin. In doing so it crosses and recrosses the provincial border between Sichuan and Yunnan to the south, capturing on its meandering way the waters of another great tributary, the **Yalong**, before a final, abrupt turn to the northeast. Here it once again serves as the provincial boundary with Yunnan until it returns to Sichuan just above **Yibin**. By now the river has dropped more than 5,200 metres (17,000 feet).

A short distance above Yibin the Yangzi becomes navigable by regular craft, although passengers will find themselves in for a choppy ride as their boats lurch over rapids and a brisk current—visible signs that the river is still falling. Now the river sheds its upstream name, thus endowing Yibin with the distinction of being the 'First City on the Changjiang'. Located astride a rocky peninsula at the union of the Changjiang and its tributary, Minjiang, the city is a lively entrepôt for Sichuan and its southern provincial neighbour, Yunnan. A neat, eight-tiered pagoda high above the city overlooks the point where the rivers collide and mix, the one turbid with silt, the other clear and green in comparison.

Yibin is also renowned throughout Sichuan for its Wuliangye, a liquor made from five grains which has flowed from the city's distilleries for 400 years or more. Still further back in time, an aboriginal people, the mysterious Bo, lived in the forests

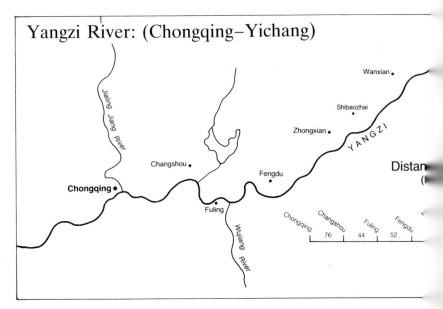

Yangzi River: (Chongqing–Yichang)

hereabouts. They grew powerful but suddenly vanished in the late Ming Dynasty (1368–1644), possibly annihilated by imperial armies despatched to suppress threatening 'barbarians' in China's frontier regions. The curious **Bo hanging coffins**, either projecting from cliffs on wooden props or inserted in deep caves bored into rock, have tantalized Chinese archaeologists ever since they were discovered. They can be seen in the southern outskirts of **Gongxian**, a town accessible from Yibin by train. Another site worth a detour is the **Sea of Bamboo** (Zhuhai), which can be reached from **Changning**, a county town southeast of Yibin. As its name suggests, it is a huge green forest of bamboo—around 40 square kilometres (9,980 acres)—stretching over hundreds of small hills.

THE MIDDLE COURSE

For 1,010 kilometres (630 miles) the Yangzi slices through the hills and plains of Sichuan and crosses into Hubei Province until halted by the gigantic Gezhouba Dam at Yichang. As it surges across the Red Basin, the river falls another 250 metres (820 feet). More tributaries flow into it: notably the **Tuojiang** and the **Jialing Jiang** from the north, and the **Wujiang** from the south.

All this water, swollen by summer rains, has to pour through the deep constricted throat of Sichuan's eastern mountain barrier before easing into the flatlands of its lower course. In the **Three Gorges** the enormous pressure of the torrent is palpable,

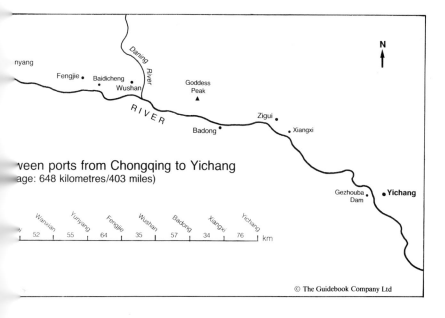

© The Guidebook Company Ltd

A Barbarian's Diet

I had been making friends with the cook. This was easy. I simply told him the truth—that his food was good.

In the very first days of the trip, I had understood my status on the junk from the nature of the food that had been given me. The cook served me no meat or chicken at all, and only certain vegetables, and certain measures of rice, and I saw that the grade of my diet was far below that of the owner and his wife, below that of the head tracker, the bow steersman, the cook himself, the drummer, and other specialists, and just above that of the common trackers. Perhaps this was one reason I had fallen sick; not, I mean, of undernourishment, but of dismay at seeing such a mediocre value put upon my person. I was an American, and I had received an advanced education in the great science of engineering—and I was ranked just a few leeks' worth above these paupered, ignorant men.

Gradually, however, the cook relented and morsel by morsel upgraded me. As I have said, he had made me various broths during my illness. He and the owner's wife seemed to reach some kind of understanding about me, for they nodded, winked, and laughed over me, as if I were some rare and comical taxidermist's specimen. The cook was by turns amused and horrified by my, to him, uncouth and barbarous habits. When he saw me one day deposit two blasts of nasal phlegm in a square of cloth and treasure these excreta in one of my pockets, he actually went to the owner and complained, requesting that I be put ashore at the next port on the river. But evidently his curiosity transcended his disgust. My diet improved, and I did not lie to the cook about the goodness of his food.

John Hersey, A Single Pebble, 1914

and it would not be entirely fanciful to imagine the riverbed littered with wrecks. Since the building of the Gezhouba Dam in the early 1980s, some of this hydraulic power has been harnessed and unleashed as billions of kilowatt hours of electricity. A controversial project, to build the Three Gorges Dam, has been on the drawing board for some 40 years. It was finally given the go-ahead by the Chinese government in early 1992. Besides a massive hydro-electric power station, the project encompasses a huge reservoir. The rising waters will displace an estimated one million people (the majority of them in Sichuan), and change the landscape and ecology of the river forever.

This middle section also swarms with cargo and passenger traffic: steamers, tugs, ferries and—in recent years—the odd hovercraft plying between Yibin and **Chongqing** (see page 148). The Yangzi may not be the longest or the broadest river, but it is unquestionably the busiest inland waterway in the world. There is no getting away from its crucial transportation role; many river towns, yet to be linked by highways, are still dependent on it for communicating with each other and with the coast. In past centuries no effort or ingenuity was spared in taming the obstacles to navigation. These were formidable, for not only did the water level fluctuate at different seasons by as much as 30 metres (100 feet) in places, but reefs and rapids lay in wait to snare even the most carefully piloted craft. And the variation in depth could be far greater in the gorges. It was problems such as these that gave rise to the trackers, the gangs of junkmen always seen along the shoreline, bent double as they towed boats upstream or over rapids, usually for no greater reward than three square meals and perhaps a pipe of opium a day. Their backbreaking work, condemned by Isabella Bird (see page 192) as 'inhuman', is the most poignant image to have come down to us from the age of sail on the Yangzi.

It was an Englishman who sounded the death knell of the trackers by introducing the steamer to the Yangzi. **Archibald Little** (1838–1908) first travelled on the river in 1883; his voyage from Shanghai to Chongqing took nearly two months. Little thought he could do better with 'a powerful steamer, easily handled, of a draught of water not exceeding that of the present junks.' In any case, he must have found the challenge thrown down by the Qifu (Cheefoo) Convention of 1876 well nigh irresistible. This treaty, while opening the door to foreign trade in the interior, specifically forbade officers of the British government from residing in Chongqing or opening warehouses there so long as no steamers had access to the port. 'When steamers have succeeded in ascending the river, so far, further arrangements can be taken into consideration,' the relevant treaty article read.

Some 15 years after that first river trip, Little at last brought his project to fruition. Even so, not only did his seven-ton steam launch *Leechuan* still require trackers to help it breast the rapids, but it had limited commercial use, not being designed as a cargo carrier. All the same, Little had proved that steamers could be put into service on the Yangzi. In 1890 the terms of the Qifu Convention were augmented by an article declaring Chongqing a Treaty Port with all the special concessions to foreigners which that status entailed.

Little's heir in revolutionizing shipping on the Yangzi was S **Cornell Plant**. Brought to China by Little, Plant later became the first man to run a regular steamship service on the Yangzi. Having persuaded a consortium of Chinese merchants to set up the Sichuan Steam Navigation Company, he launched a tug-cum-barge vessel, the *Shutung*, in 1909. Designed by Plant, built in sections in Britain and assembled in Shanghai, the *Shutung* made a maiden voyage with 50 tons of cargo and 60 passengers from Yichang to Chongqing in eight days. Thereafter she averaged two round trips a month during the navigation season.

Chongqing waterfront, photographed by Cecil Beaton in 1944, in the course of several months'
travelling in China as official photographer to the British Ministry of Information

Plant is best remembered for his very useful *Handbook for the Guidance of Ship-masters on the Ichang–Chungking Section of the Yangtsze River*, written shortly after his appointment as River Inspector in 1915. On his retirement, the Chinese government installed him and his wife in a house on the river, above the notorious rapid, Xintan, where many boats had previously come to grief. In time it became the custom for passing ships to salute him with a whistle blast, to which Plant, watching from a window, would acknowledge with a wave of his handkerchief.

With the introduction of the first full diesel motor vessel in 1925 Yangzi shipping's last links with the lumbering but strangely elegant high-sterned, square-sail junk were all but severed. Today the junk makes only an occasional appearance, rambling in some backwater, for it was not adapted to sail in the churning wash of a high-powered vessel, and the few to have survived are now relegated to the minor channels.

THE LOWER COURSE

Below Yichang the Yangzi loops via Dongting Lake to Wuhan, an industrial metropolis and important inland port. Flowing onwards between embankments built up as barricades to floods, the river becomes a complex system irrigating the most agriculturally developed region of China. It is now in the land of rice, silk and tea. From here to the delta it traverses a landscape characterized at different seasons by flooded paddy in expanses of pearly grey, fields golden with ripening grain, or hill slopes green with mulberry and tea. Here and there are barelegged men and women stooping to hoe, to transplant, to reap—the eternal picture of China. Past Nanjing, one-time capital of Republican China, then Zhenjiang, the southern terminus of the Grand Canal, the Yangzi approaches its labyrinthine outlet to the sea. It finally debouches its waters and sediment just north of Shanghai.

The Three Gorges cruise makes different stops for shore excursions, depending on whether it goes upstream or downstream, and passengers should note that not all of the towns described below will be visited on any one trip. As scheduled passenger ships call only briefly at some of the ports, stopping to sightsee may involve disembarking altogether and picking up the next available vessel for the onward journey.

Chongqing: Inland Port

Chongqing is 2,250 kilometres (1,400 miles) from the sea. Down at the harbour, the river falls 30 metres (100 feet) in winter, laying bare a wide foreshore and the lower steps of its worn staircase streets. None of this has deterred the Sichuanese from

forging a link with the mercantile activities of the eastern seaboard, and the conduit for Sichuan's trade has been the Yangzi. Without this waterway Chongqing could hardly have burgeoned into the teeming transportation hub it is. The energies of the port have never ceased to infect life in this city.

Away on the south bank, **Southern Hills Park** spreading across wooded slopes is a cool retreat from the incessant bustle of ships, downtown traffic and pedestrians thronging the city's streets. According to early classical references the wife of **Yu the Great** lived among these hills. Few people today are impressed by this possibility, but the story is interesting for its symbolic value, revealing as it does Sichuan's link with one of China's mythical heroes and foreshadowing one of the principal themes of Chinese history—that of water control. The maintenance of irrigation canals and the prevention of floods was to become so paramount a task that emperors would later be held responsible for it; indeed, the ebb and flow of dynastic fortunes came to be dependent upon successful centralized control of water resources, particularly that of the Yellow River basin, the fount of Chinese civilization.

Yu was heir to China's prehistorical tradition of philosopher kings and founder of the legendary Xia Dynasty, an era dated at around 2000 BC, but it is for his work in hydraulic engineering that he is revered. Parts of central and southwest China originally lay under an inland sea. Yu's great feat consisted in draining this sea by cutting a network of channels according to a pattern delineated in the markings of a tortoise shell. In the process he diverted and tidied up the courses of nine rivers, one of them being the Minjiang (see page 102). Yu's legacy to Sichuan was thus a superbly well-irrigated land in which agriculture could thrive. Chinese veneration for the pioneers of water conservancy is also demonstrated in the shrine raised to Li Bing and his son at Guanxian (see page 57).

For an account of Chongqing's history and sights see pages 148–160.

Fengdu: City of Ghosts

In traditional China, folk belief held that no departed soul, whether noble or lowly in life, could expect to evade a final judgement before the King of Hell. Horrendous punishments awaited sinners, the worst being perpetual exile in the boundless sea of hunger and want. However, redemptive religious services might be arranged in temples to mitigate spiritual suffering in the 18 levels of hell and to escort the deceased out of them. A 'passport to heaven' expedited this journey. And while temples up and down the length of China were able to offer such services, Fengdu had something of an edge, having early on gained the monopoly as the '**City of Ghosts**', a

(preceding pages) *Logs are floated on the Minjiang,*
a major tributary of the Yangzi, down to saw mills near Chongqing

station for all departed souls in their transition from mortal life to heaven or hell.

No-one is quite sure how Fengdu acquired this reputation, but two celestial beings are supposed to be responsible for it. In the Eastern Han period (AD 25–220) there was one Yin Changsheng who, disillusioned with life as an official, repaired to a mountain in Fengdu to become a Taoist ascetic. Eventually he ascended heaven as an immortal. Sometime later, another scholar-official, equally learned and an expert in divination besides, came to the same mountain. This Wang Fangping also cultivated Taoism. In the year 233, a rainbow was seen stretching skywards from the mountain top, signifying that Wang, too, had joined the band of immortals. Accounts of these wondrous events spread; by the seventh century, the names of these two immortals had been abbreviated to 'Yin-Wang', which happened to mean, literally, 'King of the Nether World'.

In 704 the first of many temples was erected on the hallowed Taoist mountain, nowadays known as **Ming Hill** (Mingshan). At the end of the 19th century there were 27 temples here, and on feast days Fengdu saw an unending stream of worshippers, all laden with incense, candles and offerings to their various deities, including Lord Tianzi, the King of Hell.

'The mighty King of Hell is hereby respectfully requested by the applicant, a devotee of the Buddha, to issue a pass.' Thus began all pleas for a 'passport to heaven' which, once issued to bereaved relatives, was sent by them through the celestial post in a burnt offering along with paper garments, paper houses and boats, paper money and even paper sedan chairs. The ceremonies which attended death were as elaborate as family wealth permitted. When a Yangzi tracker died, there was usually little money for a lavish send-off; still, his colleagues would see to it that a pass, signed by Fengdu's incumbent abbot and the local governor and bearing the seal of the King of Hell, was sent on its way with a modest amount of smoke and incense.

Fengdu will appeal to anyone with a taste for the outlandish. A visit offers a thoroughly delightful half-day distraction on a Yangzi River journey, and also provides a chance to stretch one's legs by climbing the 700 steps of Ming Hill to reach the gates of hell. Visitors can also take a turn on the suspension bridge which links Ming Hill to a 'heavenly peak' on the other side of town.

Ming Hill is entered through a triple-roofed gate surmounting two side walls on which the emblazoned character for 'Longevity' strikes a mocking note, as if it were a last futile appeal by the dying to stay the inexorable march of time. The gate leads to a small park centred on a charming 'chair' bridge, a favourite rendezvous, it appears, for the town's senior citizens and the infant grandchildren in their charge.

The ticket booth is found some way up the hill, in a courtyard formed by several pavilions. Here is the entrance to the 'Nether World', as announced by four characters above a pavilion: *Youming Shijie*. Visitors can buy a drink here, and take a look

In the Temple to the Son of Heaven, Fengdu

at the rice-paper paintings framed in glass that have been set into the lattice windows on the right.

Two gods rejoicing in the onomatopoeic names 'Heng' and 'Ha' guard the nether world against intruders. They glower from their own temple, **Heng Ha Ci**, one with his mouth shut, the other with his mouth open. Their special weapon is a poisonous gas; assailed by a snort of white fumes from Heng, or an exhalation of yellow breath from Ha, any trespasser who dares to encroach would be asphyxiated.

Halls and pavilions multiply near the summit, each with its own history intermingled with folklore. Over the triple-arched **Naihe Bridge** (which should be crossed in three strides to ensure reincarnation as a human being), the Hall of the Heroes stands between shrines dedicated to the King of Heaven on the right and the King of Earth on the left. Various side pavilions were being refurbished at the time of writing. One of them, on the left-hand side, has the curious **Star Block** (Xingchen Dun); this consists of a ground-level pointed stump of stone and, just balanced on it, a solid hemispherical iron block said to weigh more than 100 kilos (220 pounds). The iron block can be easily removed but is extremely difficult to replace on the tip of its stump. Only the righteous and the truly faithful can do it, the local guides say.

Behind the complex, the **Hundred-children Temple** (Baizi Dian) is a fairly conventional shrine to Guanyin (the Bodhisattva of Mercy), Wenshu (the Bodhisattva of Wisdom) and Puxian (the Bodhisattva of Universal Benevolence). Pregnant women used to come here to pray for a safe and easy delivery. The temple halls are wrapped round a plain but serenely quiet courtyard dominated by a beautifully luxuriant ilex growing out of a planter in the centre.

Through **Ghost Gate** (Guimenguan), at which a 'passport' was traditionally inspected, the **Temple to the Son of Heaven** (Tianzi Dian) stands to the left. This largest of the temples on Ming Hill has a history of 1,600 years. Note that the walls are painted blue, a colour associated with death.

We are now in the realm of the bizarre. Tianzi, for all that his name means the Son of Heaven, is here the King of Hell, whose plaster statue is housed in the main hall of the four-pavilioned temple. He is supported by the Four Great Judges and the Ten Great Commanders of the Nether World, stern and vengeful figures giving a foretaste of the horrors to come. A short step away, the two galleries flanking a lower hall unfold gruesome scenes of crime and punishment. In these torture chambers clay models grouped into tableaux demonstrate the torments of the 18 levels of hell. Sinners are shown floundering in a fiery abyss, being lacerated until the skin is torn and the flesh gapes open, eviscerated or frozen by cold and ice, tossed in cauldrons of boiling oil, mashed beneath a grindstone, impaled on spikes. Here a malefactor is cloven in two; there a nun, negligent in life, is condemned to reciting her scriptures to eternity. They are all represented in hideous detail.

Fengdu was inundated by the river in 1870, but a new town erected higher up on a nearby hill proved unpopular and the city was rebuilt on its original site.

Shibaozhai: Precious Stone Fortress

The 12-tiered pavilion of Shibaozhai is an unexpected splash of colour above the leached grey banks of the Yangzi. It is painted a bright red, with a line of blue defining the eaves of its swooping roofs. Round windows rimmed in yellow appear as gaping portholes in the wooden facade. Piled on the vertical wall of a north-bank cliff, this extraordinary pyramid of a structure tapers to two free-standing storeys projecting above the summit. Inside, a staircase spirals to the monastery at the top, easing an ascent which previously could only be made with the aid of an iron chain. The first nine storeys were built in 1819; three more tiers were added in the 1950s. They rest on a white brick and stone foundation pierced by an ornately decorated yellow gate.

It is said that once upon a time the monks of Shibaozhai were supplied with a miraculous flow of rice. (The hole from which the rice issued is there still, at the back of the monastery.) While this happy state of affairs lasted, no boat was wrecked along the part of the river guarded by the monastery. But one abbot, wishing to enrich the monastery, sought to make the hole bigger. The enraged gods stopped the flow of rice and withdrew their protection of passing boats, and wrecks were once again seen below Shibaozhai for generations afterwards.

The site of Shibaozhai, little more than a huge rectangular sandstone rock with an uneven covering of scrub, is said to resemble a jade seal, hence the name Jade Seal Hill (Yuyin Shan). To visit the temple and the village at its foot, Yangzi passengers disembark at **Xituozhen** on the south bank and transfer to local ferries for the crossing.

Wanxian: Gateway to Eastern Sichuan

In the old days the profusion of cypresses growing around Wanxian made it a famous junk-building centre. It was also the headquarters of the boatmen's guild. With the establishment of trade relations between Britain and China's interior, Wanxian was opened to foreign shipping in 1902. For its part Wanxian enjoyed the right to levy duties on imports. People called the port 'Gateway to Eastern Sichuan' in deference to its importance as a station for riverine traffic. Since then the junk industry has died, but the city now supports some light manufacturing—silk, textiles, and bamboo ware. It holds a market every night on the first street reached from the jetty; besides the inevitable snacks, which no Chinese market is without, every permutation on the theme of bamboo is available for sale, from mats and baskets to furniture wrought in wickerwork and cane.

Yunyang: Zhang Fei Temple

Yunyang, on the north bank of the Yangzi and some 55 kilometres (34 miles) downstream from Wanxian, boasts one tourist site, the **Zhang Fei Temple**, although this fine-looking structure, nestled under the lee of a wooded hill, is actually situated on the opposite shore. It consists of several buildings roofed with slates in a smudgy shade of green. The main hall is a three-storeyed pavilion painted white; even from the river, the four characters inscribed on a tablet over its entrance are clearly legible: *Jiangshang Fengqing* ('On the River, the Breeze is Refreshing'). In the great flood of 1870, which swept away Fengdu (see above), the river rose as high as this tablet.

Zhang Fei was a general of Shu Han, one of the three independent states which ruled China in AD 220–265. He met an untimely end at the hands of two disloyal officers in his army, who, having murdered their general, took fright and disposed of his severed head in the Yangzi. Retrieved by an old fisherman, the head was buried at Yunyang. A commemorative shrine was raised here during the Northern Song Dynasty (960–1127). Most of the pavilions that we now see are later reconstructions, though, as the 1870 flood wreaked considerable damage to the originals. Two of the pavilions, Deyue Lou and Dujuan Ting, are dedicated to the poet **Du Fu** (712–770). Du Fu lived in Chengdu for six years (see page 52); after leaving the city in 765, he travelled on the Yangzi, reaching Yunyang a very ill man. During his long convalescence he wrote more than 30 poems, some of which are wonderfully evocative of the sights of the river, like this one:

> By grassy banks in a gentle wind
> Under a straight mast, a lone boat sails in the night.
>
> Stars hang above the broad, flat plain,
> And up rides the moon as the Great River flows on.
>
> How stands my name among poets?
> Still, old and ill, I should retire from office.
>
> Floating, drifting, what am I
> But a single gull between earth and sky?

Fengjie and Baidicheng: Monument to the Three Kingdoms

Fengjie and Baidicheng are within a half-hour ferry ride of each other. Located 26 kilometres (16 miles) below Yunyang, Fengjie basks in the reflected glory of its more famous neighbour, Baidicheng, although it is a far from uninteresting town itself, boasting a history of 2,000 years and displaying several old gate towers and part of its battlemented Ming city wall.

Like many riverine towns, **Fengjie** is approached by a long, broad stone stairway leading from the river bank. In days gone by, the first sight of Fengjie from the river might be of cauldrons bubbling on its shingly shore, for as soon as the waters subsided in winter, salt boilers would be set up on the exposed strand, right alongside the places where brine pits were dug. The town was formerly named Kuifu, and made a rich living from the perks attached to its function as a customs house. Fleets of junks would be tied up here for days at a time while their cargo was inspected and a transit tax levied on any dutiable merchandise. However, the opening of Chongqing as a Treaty Port deprived Kuifu of its most lucrative collections, these being then siphoned off by the imperial Chinese Maritime Customs instead of swelling the coffers of the local authorities.

Baidicheng, as the Chinese are first to admit, is really a shrine. The whole place is given over to celebrating the romantic saga of the Three Kingdoms, that blend of fact and fiction which is popularly accepted as history. Featuring in the repertoire of every wandering storyteller in the past and chronicled in a 240-chapter novel during the 14th century, the episodes of the Three Kingdoms period have as familiar a ring to the Chinese as, say, the story of King Arthur and his Round Table knights would to an English audience. Obscure and confusing though the era will seem to the Westerner, it is really impossible to travel on the Yangzi without encountering references to Zhuge Liang, Liu Bei, Cao Cao, Zhang Fei and Sun Quan, so a brief outline of this period may be useful for disentangling the *dramatis personae*.

Towards the end of the second century, when an uprising by peasant rebels known as the Yellow Turbans was pushing the Han Dynasty (AD 25–220) to the brink of collapse, three strong warlords emerged to wrest power from an increasingly feeble emperor. They had progressively built up their private armies in the course of suppressing the revolt, and were now poised to fight it out among themselves for control of China. Cao Cao, Prime Minister of the Han government, arrogated to himself the Yellow River basin, the territory which took the name 'Wei'. He was depicted in later literature as a merciless and ferocious man, the villain of the piece. Liu Bei, an otherwise inconsequential figure, made his claim to the throne on the basis of a distant blood relationship with the Han emperor. His good fortune was to have enlisted supporters like Zhang Fei (see page 188) and Zhuge Liang. In due course he was to hold the southwest and establish the state of Shu Han (Sichuan). A third clan ruled the lower Yangzi plain: the Sun family's writ ran large around this rich and fertile region, and one of its members, Sun Quan, was to found the kingdom of Wu.

Against this backgound of dynastic decline, the three commanders played out a political and military drama filled with such resounding themes as courage, honour, loyalty and betrayal. It was said that Liu Bei had to go three times to Zhuge Liang's mountain home to entreat that reclusive genius to join his cause. Zhuge Liang's wise counsels helped Liu Bei to win many a battle against the stronger forces of Wei. There are numerous stories of how Zhuge Liang tricked the enemy. One incident was as brilliant a piece of subterfuge as the stratagem of the Trojan Horse: once he was staying in an undefended city when Cao Cao's army unexpectedly arrived. Zhuge Liang immediately ordered the city gate to be opened, and took himself and one young servant to the wall above it. The invaders, as they approached the gate, saw Zhuge Liang calmly playing a harp and, suspecting a trap, promptly withdrew.

Daning River, site of the Three Lesser Gorges

Isabella Bird
Lady Traveller in Sichuan

Isabella Bird (1831–1904), daughter of a clergyman, seemed destined to become one of those Victorian invalids whose mysteriously debilitating illnesses kept them confined at home to a life of sickly spinsterhood and occasional good works. Yet she was to turn into one of the most adventurous and celebrated travellers of the 19th century.

She was born in the north of England and grew up in Cheshire. Wracked by a chronic spinal disease, she took to travelling to improve her health. Wandering in remote places and writing about them became a lifelong preoccupation. Her last great journey was to China (started in January 1896 and concluded in the summer of the following year), and her account of it, *The Yangtze Valley and Beyond*, was published in 1899.

When Isabella Bird Bishop set off for China, she was a 64-year old widow (she had married an Edinburgh doctor, John Bishop, in 1881). Starting in Shanghai, she steamed up the Yangzi as far as Yichang. There she transferred to a 'native boat' and continued to Wanxian. In her passage through the gorges, she observed the trackers closely and later described their 'inhuman work' with vividness. They were a rough lot, she thought, but as the journey went on their courage, endurance, and good nature won her sympathy and admiration. She regretted their addiction to opium but showed remarkable tolerance of it. Although her river voyage was free of accidents, it was not without excitement, and she would have been fully alive to the dangers that lurked when she saw on two occasions down-bound junks being tossed in rapids, hit rocks and vanish in smithereens of timber.

Some of the Three Kingdoms' most stirring encounters took place in the middle Yangzi basin. Zhuge Liang had succeeded in persuading the Sun faction into an alliance with Liu Bei, and it was their combined forces which routed the army of Cao Cao in the critical battle of Red Cliff, at a site upriver from modern Wuhan. This battle decided the geopolitical form of China for the next half-century: it led to a tripartite balance of power between the three kingdoms from AD 220, when the Han Dynasty fell, to AD 265.

Baidicheng (White Emperor City) got its name from the self-styled White Emperor, a first-century king based in this area who allegedly saw a wreath of vapour issuing from a well in the courtyard of his palace, pronounced it as the apparition of

The towns along the Yangzi captivated her, especially those with fine temples roofed in glazed green and yellow tiles. She thought the Zhang Fei Temple magnificent, and was only sorry that the crowds of curious locals who surrounded her camera, trying to peer through its lens and shaking its focusing cloth, prevented her from taking a photograph of the pavilions. The countryside of the river valley was, to her eye, alternately grand and picturesque. Above Wind Box Gorge, she gazed upon distant forest-covered or snow-crowned mountains, and, below, clusters of villages with 'white-washed, black-beamed, several-gabled, many-roofed, orange-embowered farmhouses', around which every slope and level was 'cultivated to perfection, the bright yellow of the rapeseed blossom adding a charm to greenery which was never monotonous.'

From Wanxian Isabella Bird went upcountry, venturing into towns in the Jialing valley, across to Wenchuan and out towards the fringes of Manzi (barbarian) territory—a land journey on foot and by sedan chair of nearly 2,000 kilometres (1,200 miles). This foray took her to Chengdu; then she floated down the Minjiang to Suifu (today's Yibin), where she rejoined the Yangzi. It was, even by today's standards, a formidable voyage. Throughout, her fascination with every detail of alien customs and surroundings never flagged. There was always a bounciness in her approach to new experiences. She never whined about the discomforts or dangers encountered, and continually displayed an immense resourcefulness that is the mark of all great travellers.

a dragon and took it as a favourable omen for his reign. Since then his fame has been eclipsed by the heroes of Shu Han. It is Liu Bei and his followers, not the White Emperor, who command the limelight at **Baidi Temple**. They are represented by modern life-size statues in the main hall; apart from Liu Bei, Zhuge Liang and Zhang Fei, there is Guan Yu, a general and sworn brother of Liu Bei, who was beheaded after the victory at Red Cliff by an ungrateful and traitorous Sun Quan.

To avenge Guan Yu, a grief-stricken Liu Bei launched what turned out to be a disastrous campaign against Sun Quan. Before battle was joined, treachery struck again: this time Zhang Fei was murdered by two perfidious officers (a group of statues tells the story). In despair over his defeat by the army of Wu, Liu Bei retreated to

Baidicheng. There, on his deathbed, he committed his two sons to Zhuge Liang's charge. This scene is also portrayed in a tableau.

Qutang Xia: Wind Box Gorge

A 40-metre (131-foot) tall rock with the deceptively innocuous name of Wild Goose Feather Crag used to guard the upper mouth of Qutang Gorge just below Baidicheng. Until it was blown up in the 1950s, boatmen used it as a navigability gauge: in summer it was totally submerged by the swelling waters, a signal for river traffic to be stopped until it was visible again.

Though the rock has vanished, **Kui Men** (Kui Gate) still presents a dramatic entrance to Qutang Gorge. Viewed from upstream, two lunging mountains on the banks momentarily block the river from sight. Closer to the mouth a passage is revealed to the right. The river is only 107 metres (350 feet) wide here, a rushing torrent which, in a record year, rose to nearly 86 metres (275 feet). On the north bank, the cliff face is scarred by a horizontal ledge. This shallow concavity, the trackers' towpath, was scooped out by hand a hundred years ago. Trackers could proceed along it only by stooping low beneath the overhang. One false step, and a man would plummet into the swirling river below.

Several Western observers on the Yangzi wrote about the trackers and their precarious livelihood, which was generally pursued, they thought, with stoic resignation and even good humour. Tracking has become an integral part of the lore of the Yangzi, yet another example of Chinese improvisation in the ageless struggle against the intractable forces of nature, in which the only weapon is backbreaking human exertion.

An up-bound junk usually carried a gang of trackers as part of its crew. More men would be hired to haul it through the most difficult stretches, such as the races and rapids in the gorges. Qutang, or Wind Box Gorge as it was known to foreigners, was notoriously dangerous. There a couple of hundred trackers might be engaged. First the junk would be lightened by disembarking its cargo; passengers went round the rapids on foot, leaving only the essential crew on board, including the skipper, the pilot and the drummer, whose job it was to co-ordinate the action of the trackers on shore. The rest of the crew was distributed fore and aft: one lot to steer the bow oar according to the pilot's instructions, the other to work the rudder and pole off rocks.

Much time was spent laying out the tow-line. The tracker attached himself to it by a simple halter looped round one shoulder and across his body. Thus hitched, the

Hanging coffins

Cool Depths

Stars and Moon on the Yangtse

After sudden rain, a clear autumn night.
On golden waves the sparkle of the Jewelled Cord.
The River of Heaven white from eternity,
The Yangtse's shallows limpid since just now.
Reflections, pearls from a snapped string:
High in the sky one mirror rises.
Afterlight which fades as the clock drips,
Still fainter as the dewdrops settle on the flowers.

Du Fu (712–770),
translated by A C Graham

Sadness of the Gorges

Above the gorges, one thread of sky:
Cascades in the gorges twine a thousand cords.
High up, the slant of splintered sunlight, moonlight:
Beneath, curbs to the wild heave of the waves.
The shock of a gleam, and then another,
In depths of shadow frozen for centuries:
The rays between the gorges do not halt at noon;
Where the straits are perilous, more hungry spittle.
Trees lock their roots in rotted coffins
And the twisted skeletons hang tilted upright:
Branches weep as the frost perches
Mournful cadences, remote and clear.
A spurned exile's shrivelled guts
Scald and seethe in the water and fire he walks through.
A lifetime's like a fine-spun thread,
The road goes up by the rope at the edge.
When he pours his libation of tears to the ghosts in the stream
The ghosts gather, a shimmer on the waves.

Meng Jiao (751–814),
translated by A C Graham

trackers pulled in perfect tandem, making just under five kilometres (three miles) an hour under favourable conditions. The drummer maintained the rhythmic team-work by keeping up an incessant roll, slowing or quickening as guided by the pilot. A short sharp beat alerted trackers to stop. The head tracker at the front end of the tow-line might also mark time with a ditty or a chant while his team, bent over the tow-line almost on all fours, heaved their shuddering, tossing junk over the powerful current. At particularly arduous moments, such as when hauling a junk through Qutang Gorge, the din would be deafening: the drum changed its beat in rapid suc-cession as reefs and whirlpools loomed; the head tracker would shout and gesticu-late, and swing his stick over the men as if about to hit; the trackers gave out some-thing between a gasp and a cry as they planted each painful footstep along their narrow path. All too often, the tow-line would snag on a rock, requiring some track-ers to slip off their halters and plunge into the watery depths to extricate it; or it would break, jerking the men off balance and throwing them, face down, onto slip-pery mud or sharp, cutting rocks.

Although Qutang is the shortest of the three gorges, spanning only 7.2 kilome-tres (4.5 miles), it is the most spectacular, inspiring down the centuries a host of legends and superstitions to explain its most peculiar aspects. There is a zigzag pat-tern of holes, for instance, on a cliff to the south, known as **Meng Liang's Stairway**, which marks the way by which a whole army escaped. The ships of Meng Liang, a general of the Song Dynasty (960–1279), were trapped in Qutang Gorge by iron chains strung across the river. An enemy force laying siege on the north bank cut off their retreat on one side, so Meng Liang's soldiers chiselled out a ladder on the other, inserting wooden pegs up the cliff as they ascended. The flaw in this story, though, is shown by the abrupt cessation of those holes well below the mountain top.

In former times, foreigners used to refer to the entire gorge as **Wind Box Gorge**. Actually the name refers to some rock formations on a precipice opposite Meng Liang's Stairway, which were reputed to be the petrified bellows of Lu Ban, the god of carpenters. The resemblance to bellows was very likely sustained by Bo coffins (see page 177), which once hung from this very cliff. The coffins that were placed inside caves survived into our time, being discovered in 1971.

Archaeological investigation also revealed evidence of a New Stone Age commu-nity at the eastern end of Qutang Gorge, in two digs during 1959 and 1975. Around the town of **Daxi**, 214 excavated burial sites yielded a multitude of implements made of bone, stone and jade, including fish hooks, spears and arrowheads.

Wushan: The Lesser Gorges

Wuxia in Wushan County is the archetypal river town, preoccupied with the seasonal ebb and flow of the Yangzi's flood, a market place for the villages in its neighbourhood where hillsides are etched in terraces planted with corn, potato and winter wheat. Rice is a luxury in this area. The most easterly town in the province of Sichuan, Wuxia stands above the downstream entrance to the second of the great gorges, at the junction of the **Daning River**, a small tributary, and the Yangzi.

Named after the 12 peaks of Wu Gorge, Wuxia's streets overflow with farmers, baskets strapped on their backs, who have come to do their shopping in the agricultural stores. The majority of tourists, though, disembark straight onto the bank of shingle and sand at the mouth of the Daning River, where covered motor boats are drawn up to take them to the Lesser Gorges.

These tourist boats were adapted from the traditional fan-tailed sampan which have plied the Daning River for a thousand years or more. Having a high stern with a splayed end, those sampans have been compared to gondolas but were designed specifically to negotiate the many rapids on this boulder-strewn river. Vessels still have to be poled or dragged across those rapids, their crews resorting to the age-old method of the Yangzi trackers, and indeed, when going upstream, it is not unusual to see a boat, as yet unmodernized by the installation of an engine, being thus propelled along the resisting current.

Here, as on the Yangzi, tow-lines are made of plaited bamboo skin. Bamboo ropes are stronger than hemp—especially when wet—and easily uncoiled. With hawser and pole, the Daning boatmen virtually recreate the heart-stopping ascent of the Yangzi Gorges in former times as, with its engine turned off, their vessel rides head-on into each foaming rapid and finally shoots clear of the jutting rocks. Going over **Silver Nest Shoal** (Yinwo Tan) is especially exciting: the water suddenly becomes a clear white froth, roaring as it tumbles swiftly round the grey and yellow sandbanks lying athwart the river, and up-bound sampans can make little headway against the current without a flurry of frenzied effort on their boatmen's part.

The Daning River is a beautifully unpolluted stream, and an excursion through its **Three Lesser Gorges** (Xiao Sanxia) is an enjoyable way to spend a day, with a break for lunch at **Shuanglong**, a riverine village where a restaurant has been opened for visitors. Two of the gorges—**Dragon Gate Gorge** (Longmen Xia) and **Misty Gorge** (Bawu Xia)—are passed before Shuanglong. Their western cliffs are riddled with two rows of holes. One traces the line of an ancient *zhandao* (see page 87) which stretched some 110 kilometres (68 miles) along the river. This hanging footbridge is no more; it was after all built long ago—in the Han Dynasty (206 BC–AD 220) according to the annals of Wushan County. The second row of holes are be-

Rivers in Sichuan are harnessed for transporting logs

lieved to have been sockets for the rivets of a long bamboo pipeline, whose purpose was to conduct brine. But historians are still perplexed by the hanging coffin in Bawu Gorge, also chillingly called Iron Coffin Gorge; although blackened with age, the wooden coffin has otherwise defied the ravages of time and is still perched on one of the crags there (it can be seen with binoculars).

All the way through **Vivid Green Gorge** (Dicui Xia), the sky is a strip of blue above the valley walls. The river is deep and quiet here, and very clear. Sometimes an eagle soars across the skyline, or you may see a pair of mandarin ducks floating serenely in the shallows. But the most talked-about inhabitants of these gorges are monkeys, whose incessant cry along the Yangzi, immortalized by Li Bo (701–762) in his poem *Leaving Baidicheng at Dawn* (see below), now echoes only around the gorges of the Daning. Past the third gorge, the boat turns round and returns to Wuxia.

The Daning River tours are arranged by the Foreign Affairs Office of Wushan County, located in Wuxia Guesthouse (see page 236), and included in the package for Yangzi River cruises.

Wuxia: Witches Gorge

This long gorge (40 kilometres or 25 miles) is flanked by 12 peaks, six on the north bank and six on the south, of which the most famous, **Goddess Peak** (Shennu Feng), is said to be the petrified form of a celestial being who helped Yu (see page 101) to drain China's flooded earth. Up above, pervasive mists add to the mystery of this dim, sunless chasm. No wonder it was named Witches Gorge.

Rising sheer from the water into craggy spires, the peaks are ramparts of limestone rock whose bases, weathered by the ever-flowing river, are gashed and corrugated like folded cardboard. Perhaps these were the 'myriad layered mountains' of Li Bo's poem:

> Leaving Baidi at dawn amidst rosy clouds,
> A thousand *li* to Jiangling* takes only a day.
> From both banks comes the incessant cry of monkeys;
> My light boat has passed a myriad layered mountains.

> (* Jiangling is downriver, in Hubei Province; *li* is a Chinese unit of length,
>   equivalent to about half a kilometre or a third of a mile.)

On **Congregated Immortals Peak** (Juxian Feng), the last of the six on the north side, there is a carved inscription known as **Kongming Bei**. 'Kongming', meaning 'Enlightened by Confucius', was Zhuge Liang's other name (see page 190). But the characters, though ascribed to him, were actually carved much later. A few kilometres on, before the terminus of Witches Gorge, the Yangzi flows out of Sichuan into Hubei Province.

Xiling Xia: Western Hills Gorge

Xiling is the longest of the three Yangzi gorges, funnelling the river for 76 kilometres (47 miles) between the seven minor gorges within its span. It has two terrible rapids, the scourge of many a junk before the days of steam. **New Rapid** (Xintan) was formed as a result of a landslide in the 16th century. It was above this turbulent shoal that Cornell Plant lived in his retirement (see page 180). Even more hazardous was **Kongling Rapid**; here is Plant's account of it: 'An immense mass of black rock, some 50 feet high at low level, sticks up right in mid-stream, which, surrounded by a number of smaller ones, during low level, renders the passage on the one hand impassable, leaving only the other which is studded with submerged rocks, the channel between them being very narrow, crooked and dangerous.'

Southern Sichuan

Southern Sichuan is not on the tourist map although several cities and county towns there have recently become 'open'. Most of them are industrial centres. The city of Panzhihua, for instance, situated in the province's southernmost tip close to the Yunnan border, is southwest China's largest iron and steel producer. Besides iron ore and associated metals, coal is also mined, for the region as a whole is rich in mineral resources, which is good news for the local economy but holds limited interest for the traveller. The relatively few tourists who penetrate southern Sichuan usually go no further than Xichang. One other city stands out from the rest. **Zigong**, famed capital of salt, is a gem of a place.

Southern Sichuan is also home to one of China's largest ethnic minorities, the **Yi**, who cluster around the foothills of **Daliang Shan** (Great Cool Mountains), a range of highlands to the south of Emei Shan. It is in the **Liangshan Yi Autonomous Prefecture**, where more than 1.3 million of them live, that their largest single community is found. The rest of the Yi, whose total population exceeds 5.5 million, are distributed among the provinces of Yunnan, Guizhou and Guangxi.

Formerly known to the Hans (ethnic Chinese) as Lolos, the Yi came from the eastern Tibetan highlands and had retreated southwards as Chinese colonization spread to the peripheral tribal territories. They were mentioned in Chinese historical records two millennia ago, in which their customs were described in some detail, including that of arranging their hair upright on their crowns in a horn-like protrusion supported by a sheath of black string. The Yi believed that their hair conducted spiritual impulses and forbade anyone to touch it.

Holed up in remote inaccessible mountain areas after giving up their original territory to the Chinese, the Yi resisted foreign control and kept their traditional society alive up until very recent times. Until 1958 they practised a caste system, with the nobility (known as the 'Black Bones') lording it over serfs (the 'White Bones'). Of Han Chinese and other tribal stock, the White Bones were most probably captured in raids and later enslaved. Since the aristocrats disdained menial work, agriculture and animal husbandry were undertaken by these slaves. They cultivated mainly corn, buckwheat and vegetables (although, like their Chinese neighbours, they also grew opium), and they raised cattle and ponies. The Black Bones inclined to more pugnacious pursuits, and one which particularly suited their independent spirit and bellicose temperament was banditry. Yi bandits accosted the first of the Long Marchers (see page 144) when they arrived in southern Sichuan in May 1935, demanding money and weapons and killing some of the men. The main force, however, were allowed to pass through unmolested as the result of a safe conduct agreement negotiated between commander Liu Bocheng and the Yi chieftain. There is another well-known story told of the Yi, about a US air force pilot who was captured and kept by one of the tribes as a slave for 12 years. The events were later dramatized in a Chinese-made film.

The Yi ethnic minority is divided into many sub-groups with differences of customs and dress, but they share a common Tibeto-Burman tongue and have their own script. In appearance the Yi are tall, dark-complexioned and distinguishable from the Han Chinese by their aquiline noses. While nowadays the pressures of modernization are prompting people everywhere to adopt functional Western-style clothes, Yi men have not yet abandoned their poncho-like woollen cloaks, nor Yi women their bits of embroidered accessories like colourful bags and belts. On festival days all their attractive jewellery is displayed. The women are adorned with silver collars and hooped and pendant earrings made of gold, silver or bone. Some men also wear earrings, often of a large lump of amber or coral, which dangles from just one ear. Quite complicated hairstyles are sometimes worn, including the horn mentioned in Chinese historical literature 2,000 years ago.

Xichang: Yi Capital

Although this city is officially the seat of Liangshan Yi Autonomous Prefecture, Xichang's 150,000 denizens are mostly Han Chinese. (**Zhaojue** to Xichang's northeast, which is still a closed area, is a predominantly Yi town.) A remaining section of the city wall encloses the old town to the north. Lying at a relatively high altitude, Xichang enjoys a pleasant climate, with frequent spells of clear skies and beautiful moonlit nights—hence its epithet, 'Moon City'. Every year, on the 24th of the sixth month by the lunar calendar, the Yi people celebrate their torch festival with a programme of horse-racing, dancing and general merry-making.

The few foreign travellers who come here are directed to **Qionghai Lake**, the city's scenic resort five kilometres (three miles) to the south. Here is the site of Xichang's fanciest hotel, here was once held a national waterskiing competition, and here is located a lakeside park under a lushly forested hill. Opposite the park is the fascinating **Liangshan Yi Slave Society Museum**. It has more than 2,000 exhibits which are unfortunately labelled in Chinese only. Among them are ancient books covered in the distinctive Yi script, murals, exquisite costumes, jewellery, weapons, saddles, household utensils and some gruesome photographs of slaves being tortured. Continuing up the hill from the museum, you find yourself among the ancient trees of **Lushan** (Mount Lu). There are cypresses planted in the Han (206 BC–AD

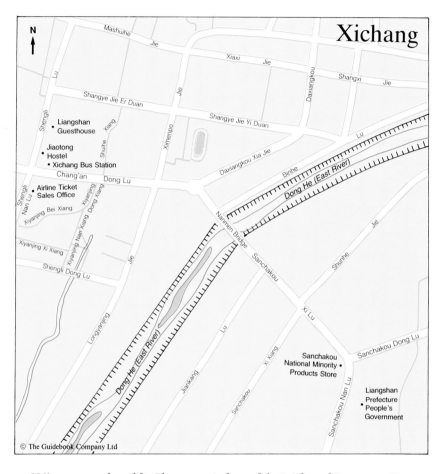

N

Mashuihe Jie

Xiaxi Jie

Shangxi Jie

Daxiangkou

Lu

Shangye Jie Er Duan

Jie

Shengli

Shangye Jie Yi Duan

Liangshan Guesthouse

Ximenpo

Xiang

Shuihe

Jiaotong Hostel

Daxiangkou Xia Jie

Lu

Xichang Bus Station

Chang'an Dong Lu

Daxiangkou

Binhe

Dong He (East River)

Shengli Nan Lu

Airline Ticket Sales Office

Xiyanjing Bei Xiang

Xiyanjing Dong Xiang

Jie

Nanmen Bridge

Sanchakou

Shunhe

Jie

Xiyanjing Xi Xiang

Xiyanjing Nan Xiang

Shengli Dong Lu

Jie

Xi Lu

Longyanjing

Dong He (East River)

Lu

Sanchakou Dong Lu

Jiankang

Xi Xiang

Sanchakou National Minority Products Store

Sanchakou Nan Lu

Sanchakou

Liangshan Prefecture People's Government

© The Guidebook Company Ltd

Xichang

220), crape myrtle and fir. The cypress in front of the **Bright and Prosperous Temple** (Guangfu Si), the biggest of the religious establishments on Lushan, is said to be more than 2,175 years old.

Xichang is one of the centres of China's space programme. Five Long March III rockets have been launched so far from the **Xichang Space Flight Centre**, the latest in April 1990, when a Sino-Hong Kong venture put a Western telecommunications satellite into orbit. A later attempt, made in the spring of 1992, proved unsuccessful when the Long March 2E rocket carrying Aussat 1 failed to get off the ground. The launch station, which may be visited, consists of a lift-off ramp and a computer-equipped control room in addition to various technical installations and assembly plants. Some 1,200 technical and support staff live and work at the base.

Noble Savages

The home of the Black Lolos is in the Taliangshan, which is a mountainous country five hundred miles long and roughly one hundred miles wide which separates the vast Chinese province of Szechuan from the newly created province of Sikang. The Black Lolo always means the Noble Lolo or, as they call themselves in Chinese, Hei Kuto (the Black Bone). Actually the word Lolo is derogatory and should never be used to their face. It is best to refer to them in conversation as Hei Yi (the Black Yi), for an unwary choice of the word may mean instant death. I prefer to call them the Noble Lolos because they were, as a whole tribe, the most noble-looking people I have seen in my life. They are very tall and are of regal bearing. Their complexion is in no wise black but, like certain mulattoes, of a chocolate and cream tint. Their eyes are large and liquid, with a fire always burning in them and their features are aquiline and almost Roman. Their hair is black, slightly wavy and very soft; and its arrangement is a distinctive feature of all Lolos. It is gathered through a hole at the top of their dark blue or black turbans and hangs as a limp tail or, more often, springs up like a miniature palm-tree, supported by a sheath of black strings.

Peter Goullart, Forgotten Kingdom, 1957

Yi script

Zigong: Salt and Dinosaurs

In the early days of the People's Republic there were only three centres in Sichuan large enough to be designated for administrative purposes as cities, and Zigong was one of them, sharing the honours with Chengdu and Chongqing.

Zigong's prominence goes back a long way. It used to be called **Ziliujing** (Self-flowing Wells), which just about sums up the cause of its prosperity. When early travellers approached the site of Self-flowing Wells, they never failed to note the array of tall wooden derricks, festooned with ropes, that lifted up from the ridges of surrounding hills. These contraptions enabled underground brine, of which Ziliujing had a seemingly inexhaustible supply, to be drawn to the surface. In the heyday of salt production around the late 18th century, there were as many as 3,000 salt wells in Sichuan, and a majority of them were concentrated in the Ziliujing area.

The southwestern hinterland, so distant from the sea, relied for the bulk of its salt on the brine wells of Ziliujing. Salt played a key role in China's economy in imperial and republican times. As an essential commodity, it was a reliable source of revenue and its distribution and sale had long been a favourite means by which the central government levied taxes. To this end various methods to control the trade were devised, spawning a considerable bureaucracy in the process. During the Qing Dynasty (1644–1911), the government simply took the whole industry under its wing and ran it as a state monopoly, dividing the country into salt-producing regions each with its own sales organization. On the production side, a fixed quota of output had to be delivered to the government, while marketing was placed in the hands of licensed wholesalers who in turn distributed the commodity to designated retail agents. This led to huge fortunes for many a salt merchant (including wily Shaanxi traders whose splendid guild hall graces Zigong still). Such a system also yielded quite a few opportunities for abuse: corrupt officials enriched themselves by indiscriminate granting of licences which, once secured, were passed on within a family as if it were some kind of hereditary right. Thus it was that the salt, when finally bought by the consumer, came to fetch very high prices and that production workers were harshly exploited to maximize profits for the middlemen involved.

The statue of a salt worker in the first exhibition hall of the **Zigong Salt History Museum** is an evocative representative of the innumerable labourers who spent their lives in the shadow of the looming derricks. On the walls around, murals record the myths which had grown up to explain the discovery of the wells. One tells of a shepherdess who, following her flock, found their favourite spring to be oozing water which tasted salty. Li Bing, the pioneer of irrigation in Sichuan (see page 57), is credited with sinking the first salt well in the third century BC. Systematic exploitation of

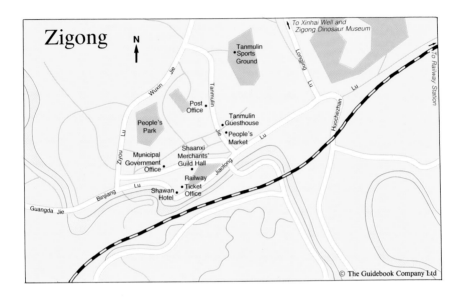

To Xinhai Well and
Zigong Dinosaur Museum

Zigong N↑

To Railway Station

Tanmulin
• Sports
Ground

Longling Lu

Lu

Wuxin Jie

Tanmulin Jie

Post
Office •

Tanmulin
• Guesthouse

Huochezhan

People's
Park

Ziyou Lu

• People's
Market Lu

Municipal
Government
Office •

Shaanxi
Merchants'
Guild Hall
•

Jiaolong

Binjiang Lu

Shawan
Hotel •

Railway
• Ticket
Office

Guangda Jie

© The Guidebook Company Ltd

brine wells began in the Eastern Han period (AD 25–220). Natural gas was discovered to issue from some of the borings as well as brine. These 'fire wells', when the
technology was eventually perfected to separate the gas, conveniently provided the
means by which brine could be boiled.

The West first learned about mechanical deep-well drilling techniques from
China, where 'percussion' drilling was developed at centres such as Ziliujing in the
11th century. It could take decades to drill a well but the tools, crude though they
were, bore through solid rock to depths of 1,000 metres (3,280 feet) and more. The
museum's comprehensive collection of drilling instruments, well repairing tools,
iron drill-heads and plummets conveys a fascinating picture of the ingenious if primitive technology employed.

Old photographs of Ziliujing show derricks with bamboo ropes dangling from
them. Ropes were passed through a pulley at the top and then coiled round an enormous windlass turned by oxen. The buckets of brine thus lifted were emptied into
vats and conducted along a maze of bamboo aqueducts, which either ran along the
ground or meandered on a framework of stilts like some flimsy roller-coaster, to
boiling factories where hundreds of pans would be bubbling away to evaporate the
salt. If there was gas in the well, another series of pipes was installed to tap it for use
as fuel.

A final section of the museum shows how modern technology was introduced to
the industry in the 1920s. The city acquired its present name in 1939, when Ziliujing

merged with neighbouring Gongjing. Today Zigong continues to benefit from its ancient industry, extracting natural gas and manufacturing a variety of chemical products from soda and ammonium chloride to monosodium glutamate. It produces 40 per cent of the nation's well and rock salt. At present rates of extraction, its salt reserves are expected to last 5,300 years.

Turning from past and present developments of Zigong's salt industry, spend some time looking at the museum itself. This is none other than the **Shaanxi merchants' guild hall**, known as Xiqin Huiguan. It seems entirely appropriate that this exuberantly ostentatious structure, located bang in the middle of Shawan—Zigong's commercial district—should now preserve the relics of an industry which had enriched its sponsors.

In the late imperial age (end of the 19th to early 20th centuries) Shaanxi natives were active in commerce; for whatever reason, they became particularly adept bankers and merchants, and like all successful businessmen before and since, they succumbed to the urge for acquiring status symbols. What they came up with was at once traditional, opulent and conducive to their own pleasure and comfort. They built a string of *huiguan* (literally meeting houses) in the cities in which they had business. These were lavish affairs, containing function rooms, shrines to patron saints and large courtyards in which to hold festive gatherings.

At Ziliujing, the salt merchants of Shaanxi excelled themselves. Their guild hall, 16 years in the building (1736–52), fully attested to their power and wealth. Its magnificent gate house, which rises on red pillars to layers of exaggeratedly upturned roofs, incorporates an architectural conceit: although it is a four-storeyed structure, the second floor (which is taken up by a stage) cannot be seen from the front, while at the back, as viewed from the courtyard inside, it is the fourth floor which is cleverly hidden.

Through the courtyard and an antechamber, a flight of steps leads to a raised reception hall. Panels of bas-reliefs illustrating the theme of filial piety have been let into the walls on either side of the staircase. The airy reception hall, open on all sides, straddles a fish pond. Behind this is a more formal hall; besides two rows of thick red pillars made of Shaanxi stone, its most prominent feature consists of wall tablets inscribed with the names of the building's sponsors. Both halls are decorated with intricate painted carvings of dragons and phoenixes on the beams and brackets.

Both the guild hall and the museum collection are beautifully maintained. Most of the buildings of **Wangye Temple**, though, have been pulled down. A short distance south of the guild hall, at a bend of the Fuxi River which swirls past the edge of the city, this late 18th-century temple was local residents' antidote to the outflow of wealth into Shaanxi pockets. Since salt left the city by river, a temple on its bank, it was thought, would guarantee that the city's revenues would remain where the money was made. Unfortunately the temple had to give way to a riverside thorough-fare—Binjiang Lu and Jiaotong Lu—when that was widened. All that is left is a two-storeyed pavilion topped by a splendid roof encrusted with carved figures. Like the Shaanxi guild hall, the upper floor contained a stage, which now serves as a dance hall. A couple of small rooms to the side display local crafts such as tie-dyed cloth. Below it is a traditional teahouse.

On the way to the Zigong Dinosaur Museum at Dashanpu, 11 kilometres (6.8 miles) northeast of the city centre, look in at the **Xinhai Well**. Da'an district, where it is located, was one of Zigong's most active salt-mining sites in earlier days. Rickety lath-and-plaster houses sagging under grey-tiled roofs still line the streets. Zigong's distinctive buses, run on natural gas which is carried in huge floppy bags on their roofs, weave along the main thoroughfares. Each bag holds enough fuel to drive a bus for 80 kilometres (50 miles).

The Xinhai Well was the first well in the world to exceed a depth of 1,000 metres (3,280 feet). It was drilled in 1835. There is not much to the site apart from a der-rick, a rough shed under which the well and windlass are sheltered, and a workshop for boiling brine, but in those humble exhibits the whole process of Zigong's back-bone industry is interestingly illustrated.

Dinosaur fossils and skeletons have been excavated in some 70 sites around Zigong since the 1920s. The richest finds were at **Dashanpu**. In fact more than a hundred skeletons of dinosaurs, mammal-like reptiles, turtles, amphibious animals and fishes were found piled together in a mass which scientists believe must have been washed down by a flood in the middle Jurassic period, 160 million years ago. Ten years after their discovery in 1972, construction of the **Zigong Dinosaur Muse-um** over the excavation site commenced. The museum opened in 1986. Its centre-piece is the Hall of Specimens where ten varieties of Jurassic fauna are displayed. They include several species of *Shunosaurus* and two skeletons of the huge *Omeisau-rus tantuensis*. These, according to an explanatory brochure, were herbivores. Not so the *Yandusaurus multidens*, a small dinosaur with needle-like teeth, which suggest that it was omnivorous, feeding on insects and small mammals. Excavations also yielded the skeleton of a flying bat-like creature, the *Angustinaripterus longicephalus*, as well as of *Sinopliosaurus*, the first of its kind to be unearthed in southern China.

A rear hall contains the spectacular Fossil Burial Site, two partially excavated pits in which the curved spines of several dinosaurs are clearly discernible.

Zigong Dinosaur Museum

An Auction

I had planned to go on to Tzeliutsing (Zigong) in the same bus, but early the next morning the conductor came up and told me that the bus was full and there would be no room for me. This meant, of course, that I should be stranded in the far interior of China for more than a week. Hardly had he said this when the driver came up to me and said, 'If you are interested in a seat in the bus, I will see that you get one for a consideration.' This I agreed to; but when we were due to start I noticed that the bus was quite empty. When I commented on this, the driver advised me not to ask too many questions, but to get in without delay. This I did, and the bus immediately started. We rounded a bend in the road, and there came into view a fighting crowd of expectant passengers. The driver then proceeded to auction the seats inside the bus; he then dealt with the roof, the wings and part of the bonnet; and, when these had been knocked down to the highest bidder, baulks of timber were inserted in the rear of the bus and planks spread thereon, and these were likewise auctioned.

We stopped at many check stations on the route, and each time an inspector signed the form presented by the driver certifying that the bus was empty. When finally we came to the last mile of our journey the bus stopped, and we were told to get out and walk, for, said the driver, 'the bus must arrive at its destination quite empty'. The quite considerable sum collected was the monthly perquisite of the driver and was what the cricketers of England would call 'a benefit'.

G R G Worcester, The Junkman Smiles, *1959*

Getting There

Xichang is on the Chengdu–Kunming rail line. The daily special express train number 93 leaves Chengdu at 4.15 pm, stops at Emei Shan at 6.46 pm and arrives at Xichang South at 3.12 am. Special express train number 94 leaves Xichang South at 10.20 pm and arrives Chengdu at 9.15 the next morning. Xichang is 562 kilometres (349 miles) from Chengdu and nearly equidistant to Kunming.

The fledgling airline, Sichuan Airline Company, has Xichang on its list of destinations from Chengdu twice a week. Inquiries should be directed to the ticket office, 16 Renmin Dong Lu, Chengdu (telephone 672083).

Zigong is 269 kilometres (167 miles) from Chengdu. The simplest way to get there is by express train from Chengdu's North Railway Station (Beizhan). The route is a branch line that stops at Neijiang and terminates in Yibin. Express train number 89 leaves Chengdu at 12.55 pm and arrives in Zigong at 6.30 pm; the return journey can be made on express train number 90, departing 9.39 am and arriving Chengdu 4.10 pm.

Practical Information

Chengdu

■ HOTELS

Jinjiang Hotel
36 Renmin Nan Lu Er Duan (Section Two). Tel. 582222, 581982; telex 60109; fax
582348
锦江宾馆　人民南路二段36号
Four-star. Standard double room with bath, US$43 plus 10% service charge. All
services including business centre, post office, shops, bakery, clinic and hairdressers.
Coffee shop and Western and Chinese restaurants.

Venerable 1960s building renovated in the early 1980s, this oldest of the modern
hotels in Chengdu is well positioned, friendly and bustling if a bit shabby. Has
branches of CITS, CTS, CYTS and several other travel agents in its main building, as
well as the US consulate in a rear annexe.

Minshan Hotel
17 Renmin Nan Lu Er Duan (Section Two). Tel. 551384, 583333; telex 60247; fax
582154
岷山饭店　人民南路二段17号
Four-star. Standard double with bath Rmb 250. Shops, business centre, disco, sauna,
beauty salon. Several restaurants. Shiny newish hotel opposite the Jinjiang. Pleasant
comfortable rooms.

Chengdu Hotel
Shudu Dadao Dong Yi Duan (Section One East). Tel. 444112, 448888; telex 60164;
fax 441603
成都饭店　蜀都大道东一段
Four-star. Standard double with bath, Rmb 215. Several restaurants including a
'Food Bazaar', gymnasium, executive centre, good shops on mezzanine and ninth
floors (range of goods from Sichuan handicrafts through imported liquors to clothes
and bicycles).

One of the latest to join the ranks of Chengdu's tourist hotels for foreign guests.
Location outside the city's ring road puts it at some distance from the downtown
area.

Sichuan Hotel

31 Zongfu Jie. Tel. 661115; telex 661115; fax 665263

四川宾馆　总府街31号

Three-star. Standard double with bath, Rmb 200. Facilities include good restaurants.
    Convenient location east of the Exhibition Hall. This was previously the
Dongfeng Hotel, now renovated. Pleasant atmosphere.

Jinhe Hotel

18 Jinhe Jie. Tel. 672888; fax 662037

金河饭店　金河街18号

Two-star. Standard double with bath, Rmb 195. Small business centre; a revolving
restaurant on the top floor. Opened in 1989.

Tibet Inn (Xizang Fandian)

10 Renmin Bei Lu. Tel. 334001; telex 60309; fax 333526

西藏饭店　人民北路10号

Two-star. Standard double with bath, Rmb 140. Built with investment from Tibet's
provincial government, this is a medium-priced hotel between the North Railway
Station and the downtown area. It has the usual facilities and helps guests with travel
arrangments to Lhasa. Rooms were being refurbished by floors at the time of writing.

Jiaotong Hotel (Traffic Hotel)

77 Linjiang Lu, Xinnanmen Bus Station. Tel. 552814, 553146, 554962, cable 5279

交通饭店　临江路77号新南门汽车站

Standard double with bath, Rmb 80; triple with bath, Rmb 90; triple without bath,
Rmb 22 per bed.

    A favourite with backpackers. Tianfu Travel Service International FIT Reception
office on the premises. Bicycles for rent through a side door in the lobby.

Zhufeng Hotel

107 Shangxi Shuncheng Jie. Tel. 662441; telex 600023

珠峰宾馆　上西顺城街107号

Standard double with bath, Rmb 85. Characterless high-rise hotel opened in 1988.
Close to city centre. Most services.

Jinrong Hotel

Erhuan Lu Bei Yi Duan (Section One North). Tel. 337878; telex 60310

金蓉宾馆　二环路北一段

Standard double with bath, Rmb 80; triple Rmb 20 per bed. Run by the Sichuan Provincial Tourism Bureau. Sited one kilometre from the North Railway Station.

Black Coffee (Hei Kafei) and **White Hibiscus Hotel (Bai Furong Fandian)**
Binjiang Lu Yi Duan. Tel. 664108. Beds from Rmb 5.
黑咖啡、白芙蓉饭店　滨江路一段

A new hotel—**Silver River Dynasty Hotel** (Yinhe Dynasty) 银河王朝大酒店
—was under construction at the time of writing. It is located opposite the People's Market on the corner of Xi Shuncheng Jie 西顺城街.

■ RESTAURANTS
Chen Mapo Beancurd Restaurant
33 Jiefang Bei Lu Er Duan. Tel. 331636
陈麻婆豆腐　解放北路二段33号
Possibly the most famous restaurant in Chengdu or even Sichuan (see page 39). Pockmarked Grandma Chen created Mapo *doufu*, a classic Sichuan dish. There are several branches of the restaurant, but this one is recognized as the original. Upstairs, you can order a meal (in which beancurd features prominently, of course) for a set price from Rmb 20 a head.

Shufeng Yuan
153 Dong Dajie. Tel. 24055, 27629
蜀风园　东大街153号
Nicely decorated in traditional style, this restaurant serving classic Sichuan dishes is highly recommended. It has seven or eight private and semi-private eating halls around a central courtyard.

Ziweige
Renmin Park. Tel. 671131
紫微阁餐厅　人民公园内
Set within the park grounds, this restaurant is experienced in catering for foreigners, offering an English-language menu. Recommended: camphor duck, rice crust with squid, Mapo beancurd. However, it was inexplicably but firmly closed at lunchtime on one visit.

Chengdu Restaurant
134 Shangdong Dajie. Tel. 25338
成都餐厅　上东大街134号

Furong

124 Renmin Nan Lu. Tel. 24004

芙蓉餐厅　人民南路124号

Sichuan restaurant with a solid reputation.

Yaohua

Chunxi Lu Xiduan (Western Section). Tel. 26665

耀华餐厅　春熙路西段

Another old established restaurant.

Quanjude

11 Shaocheng Lu (opposite the main gate of People's Park). Tel. 663735

全聚德烤鸭店　少城路11号（人民公园对面）

A newly opened branch of the famous Peking duck restaurant from the capital city. Crisp and attractive dining room upstairs.

Beijing Roast Duck Restaurant

20 Zongfu Jie. Tel. 665817

北京烤鸭酒楼　总府街20号

Jinjiang Hotel

36 Renmin Nan Lu Er Duan (Section Two). Tel. 582222

锦江宾馆　人民南路二段36号

Several restaurants including top-floor grill room.

Jinshui Yuan

Binjiang Xi Lu. Tel. 765314, 761393

锦水苑酒楼　滨江西路

Close to the Jinjiang Hotel. New restaurant complex with snacks served at the front and a Cantonese restaurant at the back.

Minshan Hotel

17 Renmin Nan Lu Er Duan (Section Two). Tel. 551384

岷山饭店　人民南路二段17号

Three fancy restaurants for Chinese cuisine (the third floor Anhua specializes in Cantonese dishes). Recommended: **China Showcase Restaurant** (Huaxia Zhi Chuang) on the ground floor, run by the China Sichuan Corporation for International Techno-Economic Cooperation to train young people in catering. Cold dishes, Sichuan snacks, eel or shrimps in rice crust, sliced beef and tripe in chilli sauce.

Caixuan Korean Barbecue Restaurant
Chengdu Hotel, Shudu Dadao Dong Yi Duan. Tel. 444112
彩轩餐厅南韩烧烤四季火锅　成都饭店
The first Korean restaurant in southwest China.

■ USEFUL ADDRESSES
Abazhou Travel Company
103 Jinyucun. Tel. 668757. Also at North Railway Station (Beizhan)
阿坝川旅游公司　金鱼村103号

Chengdu Shuangliu Airport
Information tel. 23991 ext. 401
成都双流机场

China International Travel Service (CITS)
FIT Reception Center, Room 129 (second floor), Jinjiang Hotel, 36 Renmin Nan Lu
Er Duan (Section Two). Tel. 582222; fax 663794
中国国际旅行社　锦江宾馆129房
Will handle ticket sales including air tickets on Dragonair to Hong Kong.

China Travel Service (CTS)
Room 257, Jinjiang Hotel. Tel. 582222
中国旅行社　锦江宾馆257房

China Youth Travel Service (CYTS)
Room 252, Jinjiang Hotel. Tel. 582222
中国青年旅行社　锦江宾馆252房

China Southwest Airlines (CSWA)
15 Renmin Nan Lu Er Duan (Section Two)
Ticket office tel. 665911, 23087
西南航空公司　人民南路二段15号

Dragonair
Room 219, Jinjiang Hotel. Tel. 582222; telex 60109; fax 581849
港龙航空有限公司　锦江饭店219房

Golden Bridge Travel Service
Room 269, Jinjiang Hotel. Tel. 582222; telex 60109, fax 664325
金桥旅游公司　锦江宾馆269房

Scripture Printing House in Dege

Specializes in off-the-beaten-track routes. This company can also arrange local tours, as well as itineraries to Jiuzhaigou, Hailuogou and Tibet.

Sichuan Provincial Airline Company Ticket Office
16 Renmin Dong Lu. Tel. 672083; telex 660070
四川省航空公司集票处　人民东路16号
Set up in 1987. Return flights to Chongqing, Dazu, Kunming, Guiyang, Xichang, Wanxian, Nanchong. Tickets may also be purchased from the Sichuan Provincial Tourism Administration building beside the Minshan Hotel.

Tianfu Travel Service
Xinnanmen Bus Station. Tel. 552109; fax 581285
天府旅行社　新南门汽车站
Also has 'FIT Reception' for non-group tourists in Room 102, Jiaotong Hotel.

Tray Lee
16 Yihuan Lu Nan San Duan (Section Three). Tel. 554250
崔力　一环路南三段16号
Ask also at the Flower Garden Snackbar and Jiaotong Hotel.

Travel agents also operate out of kiosks at the North Railway Station (Beizhan). They offer bus tours—Emei, Leshan, Jiuzhaigou, Huanglong, Grasslands, Hailuogou—run for domestic tourists. Although the travel companies are bound to charge foreigners more, these tours are generally reasonably priced—useful for getting to the more distant sites which would otherwise entail several changes of public buses, and they always deposit you at a *zhaodaisuo* or somewhere to get a meal at the appropriate times.

US Consulate General
Jinjiang Hotel. Tel. 583514; fax 583520
美国总领事馆　锦江饭店
Visa hours: 8.30-11 am.

■ SHOPPING
Arts and Crafts Service Centre (Gongyi Meishu Fuwubu)
10 Chunxi Lu. Tel. 665009
工艺美术社　春熙路10号
Antiques, jewellery, carved jade, bamboo ware.

Binjiang Riza Company
20 Renmin Nan Lu Er Duan (Section Two), close to Jinjiang Hotel
滨江日杂公司　人民南路二段20号
Porcelain, paintings ('ancestor' portraits), calligraphy, seals, jewellery in
semi-precious stones, Tibetan prayer wheels, knives, tinder boxes and jewellery.

There is a string of stores in the same block, starting with the Binjiang Riza Company, which offer seal-carving, antiques, crafts, scrolls and embroidery.

Chengdu Department Store
Dongyu Jie
成都百货大楼　东御街

Chengdu Hotel
Shudu Dadao Dong Yi Duan (Section One East)
成都饭店　蜀都大道东一段
Well-stocked arcade: handicrafts, clothing, imported liquors and cigarettes.

Chengdu Lacquerware Factory
81 Jinhe Jie. Tel. 26781
成都漆器厂　金河街81号
Boxes, decorative plates.

Chengdu Shu Brocade Factory
105 Caotang Dong Lu. Tel. 669040
成都蜀锦厂　草堂东路105号
Shu brocade is a rich silk fabric. Hangings, table-cloths etc for sale.

Chengdu Shu Embroidery Factory
Caotang Dong Lu. Tel. 669804
成都蜀绣厂　草堂东路
The factory can be visited with a guide. Shu (Sichuan) embroidery is renowned. The retail shop at the factory sells wall hangings embroidered with such motifs as flowers, landscapes and pandas; also silk scarves.

Chengdu Woven Bamboo Ware Factory
12 Jiefang Bei Lu Yi Duan. Tel. 332421
成都竹编厂　解放北路一段12号
Here you can buy bamboo covered porcelain pieces (tea sets, vases, jars) as well as mats.

Exhibition Hall
Renmin Nan Lu
成都展览馆百货大楼　人民南路
Department store for everyday shopping. Not very exciting.

Foreign Languages Bookstore (Waiwen Shudian)
Yanshikou
外文书店　盐市口

Friendship Store (Youyi Shangdian)
Shang Dong Dajie. Tel. 666542
友谊商店　上东大街
Limited selection of stock; some silk and handicrafts. Imported liquors and cigarettes.

Garden Arcade (Jinjiang Hotel Shopping Centre)
Renmin Nan Lu Er Duan (Section Two)
锦江宾馆花园商场　人民南路二段
Imported toiletries, cosmetics, disposable nappies (diapers), film, fashions.

People's Market (Renmin Shangchang)
Yanshikou
人民商场　盐市口
Newly completed department store selling products for daily use, fashions, electrical
goods and foodstuffs. You can buy Kodak and Fuji slide and print film here.

Sichuan Province Antique Store
6 Shaocheng Lu. Tel. 661828
四川省文物商店　少城路 6 号

Sichuan Tourist Souvenirs Arts and Crafts Store
8 Shaocheng Lu
四川省旅游品工艺品商店　少城路 8 号
'Provincial No Fake Shop'; second floor is for 'foreign guests'. Mother-of-pearl inlaid
boxes, papercuts, sandalwood and lacquer boxes, scrolls, embroidery. Forex counter.

State-run Gold Shop (Guoying Jin Dian)
9 Chunxi Lu
国营金店　春熙路 9 号
Good jewellery store.

Noodle makers at work, photographed by Cecil Beaton (1904–1980) in the countryside of Sichuan. The noodles were made by hand, then strung out on a rack to dry. The workers wear the white bandeau still seen in Sichuan today. In his record of wartime China in 1944, Cecil Beaton has left a collection of photographs which reveal the essential dignity of the ordinary Chinese— peasant, coolie, soldier, student and others—patiently carrying out their appointed tasks in the part of China still free from Japanese occupation.

Xinhua Bookstore
Intersection of Renmin Nan Lu and Xiyu Jie
新华书店　人民南路西御街

Emei Shan Area

Hongzhushan Guesthouse
Emei Shan. Tel. 2528, 2430
红珠山宾馆　峨眉山
Number One Building: standard double with bath, Rmb 136-180. Number Four Building: standard double with bath, Rmb 80. Number Seven Building: standard double with bath, Rmb 64–66; triple without bath, Rmb 39.

Accommodation of varying standards and prices offered by seven buildings spread over extensive grounds. Number One right inside the compound has the best rooms, but do not expect international-class fittings or service (individual rooms have no telephones, for example). Sichuan cuisine in its separate dining hall. A small shop at the guesthouse entrance sells maps, cigarettes, candy and liquor.

Emei Shan Guesthouse
Mingshan Lu Nan Duan (Southern Section). Tel. 2260
峨眉山宾馆　名山路南段
Number One and Number Two Buildings: standard double with bath, Rmb 15 per bed. At the edge of town, on the main Leshan-Baoguo Si road.

MEISHAN
Meishan Guesthouse
Xiaxi Jie. Tel. 255
眉山宾馆　下西街
Several classes of accommodation; top of the list is Wangsu Building: standard double with bath, Rmb 40. Restaurant.

LESHAN
Jiazhou Guesthouse
Baita Jie. Tel. 22419
嘉州宾馆　白塔街

Standard double with bath, Rmb 94–104. Good situation on a small knoll. Some rooms have a river view. Hairdresser, small shop.

Dongfeng Hotel
Jialemen. Tel. 24560
东风饭店　加乐门
Rmb 15 per bed in a triple room. Central location between the Jiazhou Guesthouse and the bus station. Rooms being renovated at the time of writing.

Nanlou Guesthouse
Dafo Si. Tel. 23811
南楼宾馆　大佛寺
Standard double with bath, Rmb 30.

China International Travel Service/China Travel Service
Number One Building, Leshan People's Government Offices. Tel. 22154
中国国际旅行社/中国旅行社　乐山人民政府大院一号楼

Northern Sichuan

ZITONG
Xishu Guesthouse and Travel Service (Xishu Binguan Luxingshe) Zitong.
Tel. 22243
西蜀宾馆、旅行社　梓潼
Double room with bath, Rmb 20.

GUANGYUAN
Lizhou Guesthouse
13 Zhengfu Jie. Tel. 23661
利州宾馆　政府街13号
Upgraded *zhaodaisuo*. Double room with bath, Rmb 26–30; triple without bath, Rmb 12. Air-conditioning, no heating in winter.

Empress Villa (Nuwang Shanzhuang)
Huangze Si
女皇山庄　皇泽寺
Double room with bath, Rmb 34. Restaurant.

Close-up of a Tibetan house at Batang, near the border with Tibet

China International Travel Service (Guangyuan Branch)
183 Bei Jie.
中国国际旅行社　北街183号

JIUZHAIGOU
Jiuzhaigou Baihe Guesthouse
Baihe Luyou Zhen, Nanping County
九寨沟白河宾馆　白河旅游镇
Standard double with bath, Rmb 90. Opened in 1989; building based on the Potala in Lhasa. The classiest hotel at Jiuzhaigou, but located outside the reserve some four or five kilometres along a road to the right of Goukou. A sign in English points the way. (Visitors can also take pot luck at the more modest inns on the same road.)

Nuorilang Zhaodaisuo
Nuorilang
诺日朗招待所

Double room with bath, Rmb 75; double without bath, Rmb 50; triple Rmb 50.
A guesthouse complex within the nature reserve; three restaurants.

Jiuzhaigou Administration Office Zhaodaisuo (Jiuzhaigou Guanliju Zhaodaisuo)
Goukou
九寨沟管理局招待所　沟口
Double room Rmb 20. Communal facilities.

Yangdong Zhaodaisuo
Goukou
羊峒招待所　沟口
Double room Rmb 5 per bed. Communal toilets. Not much more than a roof over
one's head. Run by the Jiuzhaigou Travel Company.

Minzufeng Hostel (Minzufeng Lushe)
Shuzheng Zhai
民族风旅社　树正寨
Double room Rmb 8 per bed; triple Rmb 5 per bed. Privately run by local Tibetans.
Minimal washing facilities.

Rhinoceros Lake Lodgings (Xiniu Hai Shishudian)
Xiniu Hai
犀牛海食宿店
Rmb 4 per bed. Basic board and lodging in dormitories. Privately run by Sino-
Tibetan partners.

Rize Zhaodaisuo
Rizegou
日则招待所
Triple Rmb 6 per bed. Nine kilometres (five and a half miles) from Nuorilang, the
farthest hostel from the reserve entrance.

HUANGLONG SI
Se'ercuo Guesthouse
Huanglong
瑟尔磋宾馆　黄龙

Double room Rmb 8 per bed; triple Rmb 6 per bed. Simple lodgings, not even a communal washroom (a separate barn contains the hot water source), but the restaurant is nice.

SONGPAN
Songpan County People's Government Zhaodaisuo (Songpan Xian Zhengfu Zhaodaisuo)
Songzhou, Songpan County
松潘县人民政府招待所
Double room with bath, Rmb 18; double without bath, Rmb 10. Triples and dormitories also available. Dining room.

Songzhou Zhaodaisuo
Songzhou, Songpan County
松州市招待所　松潘县
Double room Rmb 16. Communal facilities including showers (Rmb 1 for a shower). Hot water on tap in the evenings but not necessarily in low tourist season. Dining room.

MAOWEN
Renmin Guesthouse (Renmin Luguan)
Nanqiao Jie, Maowen
茂汶人民旅馆　茂汶南桥街
Double room with shower, Rmb 18. Basic board but at least it boasts private showers and toilets. Located at the main crossroads and more upmarket than the Posts and Communications Zhaodaisuo (Youdian Zhaodaisuo), just a stroll along.

WENCHUAN
Wenchuan County Government Zhaodaisuo
Wenchuan
汶川县委招待所
Triple at Rmb 15 per bed.

HONGYUAN
Hongyuan Zhaodaisuo
Hongyuan
红原招待所

Florist on wheels, Chengdu

A plain cement building to which all foreigners and tour groups are directed—spartan lodgings although the showers do work when there are enough guests. There is a restaurant in the complex, but the food is practically inedible. (Private restaurants in town offer slightly better food but it is hard to find anything beyond basic fare.)

MA'ERKANG

Abazhou Minshan Hotel
Ma'erkang
阿坝州岷山饭店　马尔康
Rooms with four beds in each, at Rmb 10 per bed.

Minority Handicrafts Shop (Minzu Yongpin Shangdian)
Ma'erkang
民族用品商店　马尔康
Tibetan handicrafts for sale here.

Western Sichuan

YINGXIUWAN

Yingxiuwan Electricity Generator Factory Zhaodaisuo (Yingxiuwan Fadianchang Zhaodaisuo)
映秀湾发电厂招待所
Double room Rmb 10. Communal toilets, no showers.

WOLONG PANDA RESERVE

Wolong Administration Office Zhaodaisuo (Wolong Guanliju Zhaodaisuo)
卧龙管理局招待所
Single room with bath, Rmb 30; double without bath, Rmb 15; triple without bath, Rmb 10. Comprises bungalows set in a pretty garden.

XIAOJIN

Xiaojin Government Zhaodaisuo (Xiaojin Xian Renmin Zhengfu Zhaodaisuo)
3 Zhengfu Jie
小金县人民政府招待所　政府街 3 号
Double room Rmb 6 per bed. Communal facilities.

KANGDING

Ganzi Tibetan Autonomous Prefecture Zhaodaisuo

Guangming Lu
甘孜藏族自治州招待所　康定光明路
Single room with bath (fitted with electric water heaters which may not dispense any
water at all), Rmb 26. Four-floor building overlooking the lamasery. None too clean.
Rear building has cheaper triple rooms, Rmb 11 per bed.

Ya'an
Yazhou Guesthouse
9 Wenhua Lu. Tel. 2988
雅州宾馆　文化路 9 号
Double room with bath, Rmb 60. Restaurant, hairdresser, post office.

Ya'an Government Zhaodaisuo (Ya'an Renmin Zhengfu Zhaodaisuo)
Xinmin Jie. Tel. 2610
雅安人民政府招待所　新民街
Double room with bath, Rmb 60; without bath, Rmb 30; dormitory bed, Rmb 10.
Seven-storey building much used for conferences.

Luding
Luding Guesthouse
Luding
泸定宾馆
Double room with bath, Rmb 30-60; triple room, Rmb 7 per bed. The hot water
comes on at 9 pm, but the cold water is then reduced to a drip.

Hailuogou
Hailuogou Glacier Park Campsites 1, 2 and 3
海螺沟冰川森林公园一、二、三号营地
Beds from Rmb 8 to Rmb 17 each, the price rising with the elevation of the camp.
Meals available. Hot springs at Campsites 1 and 2.

Chongqing

■ **HOTELS**
Holiday Inn Yangtze Chongqing
Dianzi Ping, Nanping Xiang, Nan'an District. Tel. 483380, telex 62220, fax. 483388
重庆杨子江假日饭店　南岸区南坪乡电子坪

Standard double with bath, US$75 plus 15% service charge. Coffee shop, bars, grill room/continental restaurant, Cantonese and Sichuan restaurant, disco. Outdoor pool, health club , business centre.

The only international hotel in Chongqing, with 383 guestrooms, located on the south bank of the Yangtze River, ten minutes' drive from the city centre. Worldwide reservation through Holiday Inn sales offices.

Chungking Hotel (Chongqing Fandian)
41–43 Xinhua Lu. Tel. 49301, telex 62193, fax 43085
重庆饭店　新华路41-43号
Standard double with bath, US$38 plus 10% service charge. Coffee shop, restaurant, games centre, shops.

Good location in downtown area. Run by Hong Kong management. Reservations can be made through Hong Kong sales office: Soredic Co., 3911 Hong Kong Plaza, 186–191 Connaught Road West, Hong Kong; tel. 5591021, telex 84248, fax. 5590197.

Renmin Guesthouse
175 Renmin Lu. Tel. 351421, telex 62127, fax 352076
人民宾馆　人民路175号
Standard double with bath, Rmb 240.

The two older wings of this hotel abut the Chongqing People's Assembly Hall, a fake Temple of Heaven built in the style of the original in Beijing. The annexe to the rear was added in the last two or three years. Service is less than alert. Dining rooms serve Sichuan fare.

Chongqing Guesthouse
235 Minsheng Lu. Tel. 45662, telex 62122
重庆宾馆　民生路235号
Standard double with bath, Rmb 160; single Rmb 99. Restaurant, shop, bar and other usual services. Medium-range hotel in the heart of the city; not to be confused with Chungking Hotel.

Shaping Grand Hotel
84 Xin Jie, Xiaolongkan. Tel. 663194, 664194, telex 62194, fax 663293
沙平大酒店　小龙坎新街84号
Standard double with bath, Rmb 120, triple Rmb 120. Standard facilities.
Located in Shapingba, a suburban district west of the city centre.

Bon monastery, near Songpan

Huixian Lou
186 Minzu Lu. Tel. 45101
会仙楼　民族路186号
Standard double with bath, Rmb 70. Dormitory beds available. Restaurant on ground level. Budget hotel in downtown area.

■ RESTAURANTS
Weiyuan
37 Zourong Lu. Tel. 43592, 41806
味苑餐厅　邹容路37号
Sichuan cuisine.

Yizhishi
110 Zourong Lu. Tel. 42680, 47089
颐之时　邹容路110号
Sichuan cuisine. Coffee shop in basement.

Xiaodongtian
109 Minquan Lu. Tel. 41394, 46675
小洞天　民权路109号
Chongqing hotpot and other Sichuan specialities.

■ USEFUL ADDRESSES

China International Travel Service/China Travel Service (Chongqing Branch)
96 Jianbei Yicun, Jianxin Bei Lu, Jiangbei. Tel. 752051
中国国际旅行社/中国旅行社（重庆分社） 江北区建新北路建北一村96号
Renmin Guesthouse, 175 Renmin Lu. Tel. 51449
人民宾馆 人民路175号

China International Travel Service/China Travel Service (Yangzi Chongqing Sub-branch)
4 Shaanxi Lu, Chaotianmen. Tel. 45942
中国国际旅行社/中国旅行社（长江重庆支社） 朝天门陕西路4号
Services include arranging passage on cruise ships—the *Goddess* (*Shennu*), the *Three Gorges* (*Sanxia*), the *Emei* etc.

Chongqing Municipal Taxi Service
Tel. 52888
重庆市出租汽车公司

Chongqing Railway Station
Caiyuanba. Tel. 52607
重庆火车站 菜园坝

Chongqing Taxi Service for Foreign Tourists
Tel. 350145
重庆外事旅游车队

Chongqing Yangzi Shipping Passenger Ticket Office
Chaotianmen. Tel. (enquiries) 41342
重庆长江轮船客运售票处 朝天门

Civil Administration of China (CAAC) Ticket Office
190 Zhongshan San Lu, Shangqingsi. Tel. 52643, 52970
中国民航售票处 上清寺中山三路190号

Long-distance Bus Station
Qingnian Lu, Liberation Monument
解放碑青年路长途汽车站
Buses to Dazu, Yibin and Zigong among other destinations.

Kangfulai (KFL) Passenger Transport Company
223 Renmin Lu. Tel. 55500, 55400
康福来客运公司　人民路223号
Air-conditioned, reserved-seat coaches to Chengdu, Dazu, Yibin, Zigong and other destinations.

Dazu

Dazu Guesthouse
47 Gongnong Jie, Longgang Zhen, Dazu County. Tel. 22461
大足宾馆　大足县龙岗镇工农街47号
Standard double, air-conditioned with bath, Rmb 69. Back of the guesthouse stands a hostel with cheaper rooms (double without bath, Rmb 20; bed in triple room, Rmb 8). Restaurant provides fixed menu meals which it would be best to order in advance.

Beishan Guesthouse
Beishan
北山宾馆
Standard double with bath, Rmb 80. New hotel opened in 1989. Tour groups stay here.

China International Travel Service/China Travel Service
Dazu Guesthouse, 47 Gongnong Jie, Longgang Zhen, Dazu County. Tel. 22245, 22473
中国国际旅行社/中国旅行社　工农街47号大足宾馆

Yangzi River

Most travellers on the Yangzi will sleep on their ships, but for those who do short hops hotel accommodation is available at the towns en route. Useful addresses in Chongqing, including hotels, are listed in a separate section.

YIBIN
Jiuxiang Guesthouse
Zhuanshu Jie. Tel. 5669
酒乡宾馆　宜宾专署街
Restaurant, shop, hairdresser.

Yibin Municipal Guesthouse
Renmin Lu.
宜宾市招待所（宾馆）　人民路
Rmb 10 per bed.

CHANGNING
Zhuhai Guesthouse
Changning County. Tel. 22882
竹海宾馆　长宁县
Double room, Rmb 40.

WANXIAN
Taibai Guesthouse
30 Baiyan Lu. Tel. 3976
太白宾馆　白岩路30号
Restaurant, post office, foreign exchange, hairdresser.

Changjiang Passenger Ticket Office
Intersection of Yangjia Jie and Shengli Lu
长江客运轮船售票处　万县市胜利路杨家街口

China International Travel Service/ China Travel Service
39 Taibai Lu. Tel. 2212
中国国际旅行社/中国旅行社　太白路39号

FENGDU
Fengdu County People's Government Zhaodaisuo
丰都县人民政府招待所
Double room Rmb 20. Communal washing facilities.

China International Travel Service
223 Zhongshan Lu. Tel. 039
中国国际旅行社　丰都县中山路223号

Qiang girl in Maowen

FENGJIE
Baidi Guesthouse
Baidicheng. Tel. 193
白帝宾馆　白帝城

Golden Dragon Restaurant (Jinlong Jiujia)
3 Yueya Jie
金龙酒家　月牙街 3 号

WUSHAN
Wuxia Guesthouse
72 Jixian Jie. Tel. 226
巫峡宾馆　巫山县集仙街72号
Standard double with bath, Rmb 70

Foreign Affairs Office
Wuxia Guesthouse, 72 Jixian Jie
巫山外事办公室　集仙街72号巫峡宾馆

Shuanglong Restaurant
Shuanglong Zhen, Wushan County
双龙餐厅　巫山县双龙镇

YICHANG (HUBEI PROVINCE)
Three Gorges Guesthouse (Sanxia Binguan)
Yanjiang Lu. Tel. 23438, 24911, telex 40253
三峡宾馆　宜昌沿江路

Taohualing Hotel (Taohualing Fandian)
29 Yunji Lu. Tel. 22515, 23812
桃花岭饭店　宜昌云集路29号

China International Travel Service (Three Gorges Branch)
Three Gorges Hotel, Yanjiang Lu. Tel. 23225, telex 40253
中国国际旅行社（长江三峡支社）沿江路三峡宾馆

For reservations on the Yangzi cruise ship 'Bashan' (see page 19) it is necessary to book in advance from Hong Kong at the following address:

Abercrombie and Kent (Hong Kong) Ltd

27th Floor, Tai Sang Commercial Building, 24–34 Hennessy Road, Hong Kong.
Tel. 865 7818, 865 7892, 527 6073, fax 866 0556
雅柏金碧（香港）有限公司　香港湾仔轩尼诗道24-34号大生商业大厦27楼

Southern Sichuan

XICHANG
Qionghai Guesthouse
Xincun. Tel. 23992
邛海宾馆　西昌市新村
Room rates range from Rmb 80 for a double to Rmb 140 to a suite with two bedrooms, bathroom and sitting room. Dining room, hairdresser.

Wumao Guesthouse
Chang'an Zhong Lu. Tel. 22186
物贸宾馆　长安中路
Standard double, Rmb 60.

Liangshan Guesthouse
Shengli Lu. Tel. 23242
凉山宾馆　胜利路
Double room, Rmb 60.

Transportation Company Jiaotong Hostel (Qiche Yunshu Gongsi Jiaotong Gongyu)
Xichang Bus Station
汽车运输公司交通公寓　西昌汽车站
Double room, Rmb 20.

Sanchakou National Minority Products Store
Sanchakou Xi Lu
三岔口民族贸易商场　三岔口西路
Good selection of Yi products.

ZIGONG
Tanmulin Guesthouse
2 Tangkan Shang Lu. Tel. 224121, 221679, cable 0182
檀木林宾馆　塘坎上路 2 号

Number Four Building: Standard double with bath, Rmb 60. Number Two Building: dormitory beds from Rmb 7. Usual services including foreign exchange, taxi booking and post office. Extensive gardens; dining hall in separate building.

Shawan Hotel
3 Binjiang Lu. Tel. 222617, 224524
沙湾饭店　滨江路 3 号
Standard double with bath, Rmb 40. Located in city centre, near Wangye Temple.

Liaison Section, Zigong Municipal Government Foreign Affairs Office
2 Tangkan Shang Lu (in the Tanmulin Guesthouse complex). Tel. 222236, 221154, cable 0057
自贡人民政府外事办公室外联科
塘坎上路 2 号檀木林宾馆

Panning for gold in the Dadu River

Recommended Reading

GENERAL BACKGROUND

A History of Chinese Civilization Jacques Gernet, translated by J R Foster (Cambridge University Press, Cambridge 1982)

An Outline of China's Physical Geography Ren Mei'e (Foreign Languages Press, Beijing 1985)

China: A Macro History Ray Huang (M E Sharpe, Inc, Armonk, New York 1988)

The Soong Dynasty Sterling Seagrave (Harper & Row, New York 1985)

Yangtze: Nature, History and the River Lyman P Van Slyke (Addison-Wesley Publishing Company, Inc, Reading, Massachusetts 1988)

TRAVEL

Behind the Wall: A Journey through China Colin Thubron (Heinemann, London 1987)

Riding the Iron Rooster: By Train through China Paul Theroux (Hamish Hamilton, London 1988)

The River of Golden Sand: The Narrative of a Journey through China and Eastern Tibet to Burmah William Gill (John Murray, London 1880)

The Yangtze Valley and Beyond Isabella Bird (John Murray, London 1899; Virago Press, London 1985)

Travels and Researches in Western China E Colborne Baber (John Murray, London 1882; Ch'eng Wen Publishing Co, Taipei, 1971)

China Diary & Album Cecil Beaton (Batsford, London 1945; Oxford University Press & John Nicholson Ltd, Hong Kong 1991)

To the Source of the Yangtze Dick Bell (Hodder & Stoughton, London 1991)

20TH-CENTURY HISTORY

Thunder Out of China Theodore H White & Annalee Jacoby (W Sloane Associates, New York 1946; reprinted with a new Introduction by Harrison E Salisbury, Da Capo Press, New York 1980)

The Chinese Black Chamber: An Adventure in Espionage Herbert O Yardley (Houghton Mifflin Company, Boston 1983)

The Long March Harrison E Salisbury (Harper & Row, New York 1985)

FLORA AND FAUNA

A Naturalist in Western China: With Vasculum, Camera and Gun E H Wilson (Methuen & Co, London 1913; Cadogan Books, London 1986)

China's Nature Reserves Li Wenhua and Zhao Xianying (Foreign Languages Press, Beijing 1989)

Plant-hunting in China E H M Cox (William Collins Sons & Co Ltd, London 1945; reprinted with the addition of an Introduction by Oxford University Press, Hong Kong 1986)

The Alpine Plants of China Edited by Zhang Jingwei (Science Press, Beijing 1982)

Pandas Chris Catton (Christopher Helm, London 1990)

LITERATURE, FICTION, AUTOBIOGRAPHY

A Single Pebble John Hersey (Alfred A Knopf, Inc, New York 1956; Vintage Books edition, Random House Inc, New York 1989)

Destination Chungking Han Suyin (Jonathan Cape, London 1942; Panther Books, London 1973)

Li Po and Tu Fu Selected and translated with an Introduction and Notes by Arthur Cooper (Penguin Books, Harmondsworth 1973)

100 Tang and Song Ci Poems Selected by Xu Yuanzhong (Commercial Press, Hong Kong 1986)

Poetry and Prose of the Tang and Song Translated by Yang Xianyi & Gladys Yang (Panda Books, Beijing 1984)

The Junkman Smiles G R G Worcester (Chatto and Windus, London 1959)

A Guide to Pronouncing Chinese Names

The official system of Romanization used in China, which the visitor will find on maps, road signs and city shopfronts, is known as Pinyin. It is now almost universally adopted by the Western media.

Some visitors may initially encounter difficulty in pronouncing Romanized Chinese words. In fact many of the sounds correspond to the usual pronunciation of the letters in English. The exceptions are:

Initials

c   is like the *ts* in 'its'
q   is like the *ch* in 'cheese'
x   has no English equivalent, and can best be described as a hissing consonant that lies somewhere between *sh* and *s*. The sound was rendered as *hs* under an earlier transcription system.
z   is like the *ds* in 'fads'
zh   is unaspirated, and sounds like the *j* in 'jug'.

Finals

a   sounds like 'ah'
e   is pronounced as in 'her'
ê   is pronounced as in 'get'
i   is pronounced as in 'ski' (written as *yi* when not preceded by an initial consonant). However, in *ci, chi, ri, shi, zi* and *zhi*, the sound represented by the *i* final is quite different and is similar to the *ir* in 'sir' but without much stressing of the *r* sound.
o   sounds like the *aw* in 'law'
u   sounds like the *oo* in 'ooze'
ü   is pronounced as the German *ü* (written as *yu* when not preceded by an initial consonant). The finals *ê* and *ü* are usually written simply as *e* and *u*.

Finals in Combination

When two or more finals are combined, such as in *hao, jiao* and *liu*, each letter retains its sound value as indicated in the list above, but note the following:

ai   is like the *ie* in 'tie'
ei   is like the *ay* in 'bay'
ian   is like the *ien* in 'Vienna'
ie   similar to *ye* in 'yet'
ou   is like the *o* in 'code'
uai   sounds like 'why'
uan   is like the *uan* in 'iguana' (except when proceeded by *j*, *q*, *x* and *y*;
       in these cases a *u* following any of these four consonants is in fact *ü* and
       uan is similar to *uen*).
ue   is like the *ue* in 'duet'
ui   sounds like 'way'

Examples

A few Chinese names are shown below with English phonetic spelling beside
them:

Beijing	Bay-jing (*jing* sounds like *ging* in pa*ging*)
Cixi	Tsi-shee
Guilin	Gway-lin
Hangzhou	Hahng-joe
Kangxi	Kahng-shee
Qianlong	Chien-loong
Tiantai	Tien-tie
Xi'an	Shee-ahn

An apostrophe is used to separate syllables in certain compound-character words
to preclude confusion. For example, *Changan* (which can be *chang-an* or *chan
gan*) is sometimes written as *Chang'an*.

Tones

A Chinese syllable consists of not only an initial and a final or finals, but also a
tone or pitch of the voice when the words are spoken. In Pinyin the four basic
tones are marked ‾, ´, ˇ and `. These marks are almost never shown in printed
form except in language texts.

A Chronology of Periods in Chinese History

Palaeolithic	c.600,000–7000BC
Neolithic	c.7000–1600 BC
Shang	c.1600–1027 BC
Western Zhou	1027–771 BC
Eastern Zhou	770–256 BC
Spring and Autumn Annals	770–476 BC
Warring States	475–221 BC
Qin	221–206 BC
Western (Former) Han	206BC–8 AD
Xin	9–24
Eastern (Later) Han	25–220
Three Kingdoms	220–265
Western Jin	265–316
Northern and Southern Dynasties	317–589
Sixteen Kingdoms	317–439
Former Zhao	304–329
Former Qin	351–383
Later Qin	384–417
Northern Wei	386–534
Western Wei	535–556
Northern Zhou	557–581
Sui	581–618
Tang	618–907
Five Dynasties	907–960
Northern Song	960–1127
Southern Song	1127–1279
Jin (Jurchen)	1115–1234
Yuan (Mongol)	1279–1368
Ming	1368–1644
Qing (Manchu)	1644–1911
Republic of China	1911–1949
People's Republic of China	1949–

Tibetan house, western Sichuan

Index of Places